THE DATA JOURNALIST

GETTING THE STORY

Fred Vallance-Jones and David McKie

With additional contributions by William Wolfe-Wylie
and Glen McGregor

OXFORD
UNIVERSITY PRESS

OXFORD

UNIVERSITY PRESS

Oxford University Press is a department of the University of Oxford.
It furthers the University's objective of excellence in research, scholarship,
and education by publishing worldwide. Oxford is a registered trade mark of
Oxford University Press in the UK and in certain other countries.

Published in Canada by
Oxford University Press
8 Sampson Mews, Suite 204,
Don Mills, Ontario M3C 0H5 Canada

www.oupcanada.com

Library and Archives Canada Cataloguing in Publication
Vallance-Jones, Fred, author
The data journalist : getting the story / Fred Vallance-Jones
and David McKie.

Includes bibliographical references and index.
ISBN 978-0-19-902006-5 (paperback)

1. Journalism–Data processing. 2. Journalism–Technological innovations.
3. Journalism–Methodology. 4. Data mining.
5. Information visualization. I. McKie, David, 1959-, author II. Title.

PN4784.E5V34 2016   070.4'30285   C2016-902891-7

Cover image: © iStock/BlackJack3D

Oxford University Press is committed to our environment.
Wherever possible, our books are printed on paper which comes from
responsible sources.

Printed and bound in Canada

1 2 3 4 — 20 19 18 17

Contents

Foreword

I dream of a day when the term "data journalist" will sound as silly and redundant as "interview journalist," "storytelling journalist," or "fact journalist." Data is—or at least should be—a standard part of the toolkit of every journalist, not something to be handled only by an elite corps of stats geeks and computer-assisted reporters. For too long, newsrooms have had their "data guy"—the person everyone goes to for help with deciphering a spreadsheet of figures from a source or creating a graphic to represent a trend. By treating data as an option that reporters tap only on special occasions, we have come to see it as a fancy aperitif that enhances special meals rather than a standard of a well-balanced diet.

Every reporter should have a command of data journalism methods. Only by understanding these techniques can reporters avoid common mistakes when looking at statistics, know when and where to look for information, and develop ways of presenting data that are meaningful to the public. Once these muscles start getting built, reporters are more likely to use them, and the more they use them, the stronger they will become.

My dream of a world without the "data journalist" label is getting closer—because of two of the best journalists I know. David McKie and Fred Vallance-Jones are actually not the newsroom "data guys"—they are the ideal reporters who happen to be adept at finding data, assessing its quality, analyzing it, mapping it, visualizing it, and finding the stories within the numbers. It is telling that another one of their books, *Digging Deeper: A Canadian Reporter's Research Guide*—which has become the standard for teaching investigative reporting—does not have the words "investigative reporting" in the title. The book, which they co-wrote with *Toronto Star* reporter Robert Cribb and former *Chronicle Herald* reporter Dean Jobb, is used by investigative reporters, but it is also a textbook of choice for journalism instructors throughout the country who have integrated techniques that were once the exclusive purview of the "I-team."

My dream is also being helped by the preponderance of data in our world. A couple of years ago a factoid emerged claiming that 90 per cent of the world's data had been produced in the previous two years. I don't doubt this statistic. Technology has allowed more and more data to be kept on our every move. Inexpensive storage devices allow governments and corporations to store petabytes of data for what it used to cost to store megabytes. Within these documents and statistics are stories that are often kept from the public, but that are increasingly leaking out because of whistleblowers who declare that "data should be free!"

The public have also grown to expect data, and they count on journalists to find it, vet it, and present it in compelling ways. Data visualizations are popular, particularly on social media, because they can covey the core of a story in an easily shared nugget. As the floodgates of data begin to be pried open, the public are getting a glimpse of the mountains of information concealed from them, and they are expecting journalists to find ways to get behind those gates.

Sometimes the story is hidden in the data right in front of our eyes, and it takes a journalist with data sophistication to find the truth concealed among the facts. I do an exercise with my students in which I ask them to analyze one of two data sets about carbon emissions that result from the extraction of bitumen in Alberta. I give half the class a data set that was provided to me by an oil company, and I give the other half a similar data set that I got from an environmental organization. I then ask the students to find how the emissions number they come up with compares to the carbon output of traditional oil drilling. Half the class comes up with 20 per cent higher. The other half comes up with only six per cent higher. And both are right. The larger number, from the environmental organization, looks only at the extraction process. The smaller number, from the oil industry, represents the so-called "wells-to-wheels" emissions, a measurement that also takes into account the carbon output of the vehicles that eventually consume the fuel, which is where most carbon emissions occur. Both sets of data are rigged by organizations pushing an agenda, and a journalist who lacks skepticism of statistics can easily be manipulated.

Throughout my 25 years as a reporter—at CBS News' *60 Minutes*, ABC News, and *The New York Times*—I have encountered so many good reporters who have said "data journalism's not for me." When I ask them why they feel this way, they say things like "I'm bad at math" or "the technology keeps changing." This book is for those good reporters—a handbook that will dispel the myth that data journalism is hard and out of reach for average journalists. Computer programs have made it easier to compile, analyze, and present data. And this book is one that teaches the concepts of data journalism as much as it teaches the techniques, so when new tools come along, the reader will know how to start using them.

Veteran journalists spend their weekends and hundreds of dollars out of their own pockets to attend conference workshops with David and Fred, to learn data journalism techniques. This book, with its online companion, is more than a weekend seminar. It's an in-depth course in data journalism, and it will equip the reader with a lifetime's worth of tools for utilizing data in reporting.

My hope is that, someday, the title of this book will seem quaint and antiquated, a vestige of an era when data journalism was not yet a standard part of every journalist's toolkit. *The Data Journalist* goes a long way toward achieving that goal.

Peter W. Klein

Director, Global Reporting Centre

Professor, University of British Columbia's Graduate School of Journalism

Acknowledgements

A work such as this is the product of a great many people's labours. Thanks to my co-author, and longtime friend David McKie, who took the lead on chapters 2 to 4, 8 and 11; to William Wolfe-Wylie who wrote most of chapter 10 and checked over coding sections of chapter 9, to Glen McGregor, who contributed to chapter 9, and to Peter Klein of the University of British Columbia Graduate School of Journalism, who wrote the foreword. Thank you also to James Boxall, director of the GIS Centre at Dalhousie University for his invaluable technical review of chapters 6 and 7; to the anonymous peer reviewers who helped shape the book and in the process made it better; to Darcey Pepper and Peter Chambers, our editors at Oxford University Press; and to everyone else at Oxford who has had a hand in this adventure. Thanks are also due to Heather Macdougall, whose careful copy editing improved the book immeasurably, to the production team at Oxford, and to my students at King's, who inspire me to do this work. Thanks to Investigative Reporters and Editors, the organization that made so much of what I have done possible. And finally, thanks to my wife Louise, and my daughters, Laura, Anna, Kathleen, and Caroline, who put up with long hours of writing and editing and whose love makes my world go round.

Fred Vallance-Jones

This book is the culmination of many years of learning the fine art of thinking about, gathering, analyzing data for the purposes of telling meaningful stories. Though some of the techniques have become more sophisticated and the data more plentiful, the premise is still the same: find patterns in data worth writing about. In many ways the chapters, as they are laid out, represent the path that I followed—and still continue to navigate—in learning everything from the beginnings of the open-data movement and why it should matter to journalists, to using database managers like MySQL and mapping programs like ArcGIS and QGIS, to online visualization tools including Google's Fusion Tables and Tableau Public.

Journeys can be made easier with a little help along the way. My learning has been facilitated by my co-author, Fred Vallance-Jones, a colleague, inspiration, and mentor. He is one of the finest journalists I know and even a more remarkable human being. This represents our third—and most challenging—book together.

Singling out more people who have been influential would take too much space. However, many of those individuals belong to organizations like the National Institute for Computer Assisted Reporting, Investigative Reporters and

Editors, the Canadian Association of Journalists, and the journalism schools at Carleton University, the University of King's College, and Algonquin College.

And finally, as I always do, I would like to thank the people who mean the most to me, my immediate family. My wife, Deirdre, is my strongest supporter and toughest critic, whose opinion is second to none. Our children, Hannah Rose, Jordan, and Leila, are a constant source of joy, as is our son-in-law, Scott. And I must also give thanks to the recent addition to the family, our granddaughter, Nylah Violet.

David McKie

Author Biographies

Fred Vallance-Jones

Fred Vallance-Jones is an award-winning journalist and an associate professor at the University of King's College in Halifax, Canada. He teaches journalism research, and data and investigative journalism at the graduate and undergraduate levels. He coordinates and teaches in the annual King's summer schools in data journalism and coding for journalists, which attract working journalists from across Canada, and has been teaching data journalism at journalism conferences for many years. As well as co-authoring *The Data Journalist*, he is co-author of *Computer Assisted Reporting: A Comprehensive Primer*, and *Digging Deeper: A Canadian Reporter's Research Guide*, both from Oxford. Find Fred on Twitter at @Fvjones and online at DataProf.ca.

David McKie

David McKie is an award-winning journalist, journalism professor, and author. He has been on staff with the CBC for more than 23 years, and teaches two courses in research methods and data journalism at Carleton University in Ottawa, Canada. He designed and teaches similar courses at the University of King's College in Halifax, Canada. Throughout his teaching career, David has been one of the country's leading advocates of the need to teach data journalism skills to students and incorporate the practice into newsrooms. He leads a data-journalism boot camp through Carleton University's FPA Professional Institute, and is also co-author of *Computer Assisted Reporting: A Comprehensive Primer*; *Digging Deeper 3rd edition: A Canadian Reporter's Research Guide*; *Your Right to Know: How to Use The Law to Get Government Secrets*; and *Your Right to Privacy: Minimize Your Digital Footprint*.

Chapter 1

Introduction

In the dying days of the 2015 Canadian election campaign, visitors to the website of Montreal's *Metro* newspaper logged on to discover an original piece of journalism no other media outlet had. The interactive feature entitled (in translation) "What the Political Parties Are (Really) Talking About" allowed visitors to select one of more than 130 key electioneering words, and see a colourful chart transform itself to show how often each of the five main parties had used the word. The interactive visualization was an immediate hit with readers who could explore how much emphasis different parties put on key concepts raised during the campaign.

While the feature was accompanied by 800 or so words of explanatory text, it was the interactive magic that kept the audience on the page. "The most satisfying part was the reaction from the public," said Naël Shiab, the young journalist who created the visualization. "Many readers wrote to us saying that the app really helped them to make their choice. And since voting is one of the most important duties of a citizen in our society, I couldn't be prouder."[1]

Shiab created the visualization using a web-scraping **script** to mine speeches, statements, and platforms on the party websites, and **JavaScript** to build the interactive graph. It was the kind of journalism that is only possible in a connected world.

Naël Shiab has not been a journalist for very long. Raised in Montreal, where he earned his undergraduate degree from the Université du Québec à Montréal, his first job was with Radio-Canada, the French arm of the CBC, in Sudbury, Ontario. Keen to do more meaningful work, he enrolled in the master's program in investigative and **data journalism** at the University of King's College in Halifax. Soon after graduating in the spring of 2015, Shiab secured his job with *Metro*: "They realized that, of the 100+ applicants for the job, I was the only one that knew how to code. So I got it!" In the fall of 2015, the Fédération professionnelle des journalistes du Québec recognized

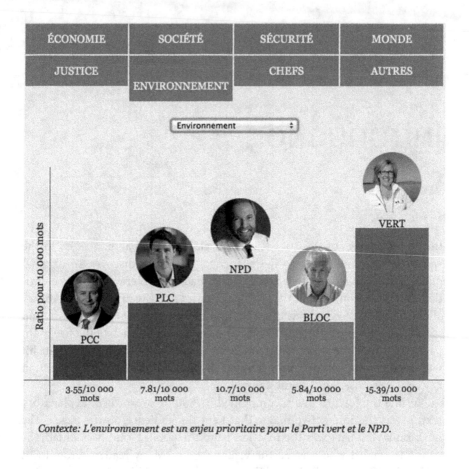

ÉCONOMIE	SOCIÉTÉ	SÉCURITÉ	MONDE
JUSTICE		CHEFS	AUTRES
	ENVIRONNEMENT		

Environnement ⬍

Ratio pour 10 000 mots

VERT

NPD

PLC

BLOC

PCC

| 3.55/10 000 mots | 7.81/10 000 mots | 10.7/10 000 mots | 5.84/10 000 mots | 15.39/10 000 mots |

Contexte: L'environnement est un enjeu prioritaire pour le Parti vert et le NPD.

In this interactive feature on *Metro*'s website, users could pick a word to see how often each party had used that word in its speeches and other election materials.
Source: Courtesy Journalmetro.com.

him as a top up-and-coming reporter, noting particularly his work with **data**. In 2016, Shiab was snapped up by *L'Actualité* magazine, again because of his data skills.

It's heady stuff, but his experience is not that unusual. All across North America, data journalists and coders have been in heavy demand, even while more conventional newsroom jobs have been under heavy pressure. It's a re-flection of a perfect storm in favour of data journalism: a very data-driven society combined with the means to present compelling data stories to the public via the web.

The trend was highlighted in April 2016 when one of the largest col-laborative investigative projects ever conducted launched online, in news-papers, and on the airwaves worldwide. Journalists from dozens of outlets spent a year combing through documents and data that revealed a secretive world of carefully cloaked companies, hidden financial transactions, and criminal activity. Dubbed the Panama Papers, the project was based on a massive leak of data from Mossack Fonseca, a firm few had heard of before that specializes in creating the shell companies that facilitate this secretive world.[2]

These days, just about everything you do involves data. From the moment you wake up in the morning to the moment you fall asleep, you will interact with it, unless perhaps you live in a small cabin in the deep woods, with no electricity, cellphone, or computer.

When you check your email or post to Facebook, you're making and using data. When you buy something at the grocery store, the checkout scanner is pulling data on how much each item costs. The street you cross on the way to work is described in a geographic **database** held by your city or town, and the counts of how many cars drive by that spot each day are recorded in another database. Your favourite lunch spot is likely inspected by health officials, and the inspections are recorded in a database. A quick tweet in the afternoon, more data. You buy an airline ticket for a trip in a couple of weeks; that too requires interacting with a database. The value of the place you live, that's in a database. Withdraw some money from the bank, ditto. And yes, if

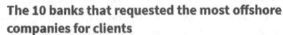

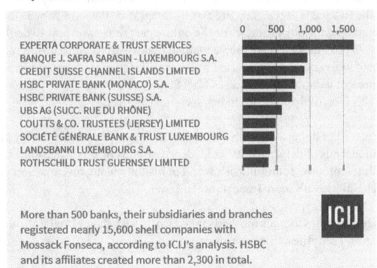

Data visualization from the Panama Papers
Source: Courtesy The International Consortium of Investigative Journalists

you aren't in the deep woods and you consume electricity, that's recorded in a database too.

The fact is, there is hardly an activity today that doesn't involve the creation, storage, or retrieval of data. Data, the computers that store it, and the **code** that manipulates it, is everywhere. We live in a sea of data, and journalists need to know how to swim. They need to understand what data is, where it is stored, how they can get and use it, and how data can drive incredible journalism. That's what this book is about.

This book has two components. The first component, which you are holding now or reading on a device, is an exploration of data journalism and its methods, perfect for independent study or a formal course in data journalism. Here, you'll learn about the what and why, read about inspiring work of leading data journalists, and work on exercises. We divided the book into four parts: getting data, analyzing data, an introduction to advanced techniques, and telling stories with data.

Just as important is the second, online part of this book. Whenever we have to tell you about a tool, technology, or procedure that is likely to change (and thus leave printed text outdated), we'll use an online tutorial that you can view on the web or download. If you are reading the e-book version of *Data Journalist*, the written tutorials are included in the book, though you should always check online for updates. As tools change, we'll update the tutorials. The companion website also has video tutorials on key subjects, and practice exercises based on prominent stories, with the actual data used by the journalists available for download. It's not just a book: it's a comprehensive learning package.

The two parts of the book are tightly integrated; the hard copy helps you understand data journalism while the online part shows you how to do it. The goal is to provide an indispensable manual that will guide you through a wide range of tools and techniques used by journalists today to obtain, understand, and present data-driven stories, as Naël Shiab does.

"It's incredibly powerful to bring context" he said.

Instead of doing a story about one car accident, you can do a story about thousands of car accidents, help identify trends or problems, and, sometimes, propose solutions. In a world of instantaneous coverage and news, I think that it's more important than ever.

He also notes that his most advanced work, with **data visualizations** and web apps, keeps the audience around.

Readers stay less than a minute on news web pages, if not less, on average. However, with data visualisations and web apps, it's still possible to attract readers with deep, researched work. And if it's interactive, they can stay for a long time on your web page. On some of my reports, readers stayed on average for more than five minutes.

In a world in which audience engagement with your stories can be measured precisely by web analytics, that's important.

The Origins of Data Journalism

There is no single definition of data journalism. In fact, there isn't even unanimous agreement on the term itself.

For many years, those who worked with data as a reporting tool called their corner of journalism "**computer-assisted reporting**," often abbreviated as CAR. While the earliest practitioners used large and costly mainframe computers, the growth of CAR was facilitated by the rapid development of personal computers in the 1980s and the emergence of powerful desktop software. Programs such as **Microsoft Excel**, and early desktop database programs such as FoxPro made it possible to explore and link government databases to find trends and patterns that pointed to stories reporters could not do before. Similarly, journalists began using **geographic information system** (GIS) applications such as ArcGIS to explore patterns and relationships in spatial (map) data.

In this first epoch of data journalism, the resulting journalism didn't differ much in form from that which surrounded it in the newspapers or on news broadcasts. The stories were often groundbreaking, but they were presented in the same ink-on-paper format, or alongside other conventional broadcast stories. Charts and maps were most often static, simply printed in the newspaper or displayed as images onscreen. Data work was particularly prominent as a feature of investigative journalism, as it was well suited for digging deeply into stories.

All this started to change in the latter years of the first decade of this century, as emerging web technologies made a whole new kind of presentation possible, one that was native to the web instead of simply being conventional content repackaged for online presentation. The scripting language JavaScript made it possible for content on web pages to change based on user interaction, and a technology called AJAX allowed new content to be sent to a **web browser** without having to re-serve the entire page. Now it was possible to create interactive experiences that made the content of a web page behave more like a standalone computer program than a standard page. Such technology is behind popular services such as Facebook and Twitter.

"The more data you get, the more you can personalize your information for each reader," Shiab said.

With data journalism, and some coding skills, you can create small web applications in which the readers, after answering a few questions for example, can get answers specifically for them. It's an effective way to give them answers, but also to make them realize that they are involved and part of the story. Data journalism can literally make the reader the main character of your story.

Journalists flocked to pre-packaged services such as Google **Fusion Tables** that allowed them to create interactive online content with little knowledge of how the applications actually worked. For those prepared to learn how web technologies created their magic, there were even more opportunities for storytelling. Most importantly, the data that had merely been the source material for stories in the early days of CAR could become part of the storytelling itself. The previously obscure term "visualization" became commonplace and news consumers could find their own stories by exploring maps or making choices in an interactive.

Today, all of these elements are present at the same time, so that data journalism now encompasses a range of activities, from traditional data-as-source CAR to quick visualizations using Fusion Tables and similar offerings to sophisticated web development using JavaScript and other programming languages to automation of social media content through the use of **application programming interfaces** (APIs).

At the heart of it, though, is data, and like data journalism, it can take many forms.

Traditionally, the data used by journalists came from governments. Governments collect vast amounts of data as they go about their business of overseeing us all. They keep track of who owns land and how much it's worth for taxation purposes; they inspect and regulate numerous sectors such as charities, food service outlets, and election finances; and they keep records about their own activities and their interactions with the public. Because the data is held by government bodies, it usually relates to activities in which the public has a genuine interest and which therefore are a legitimate basis for news reporting. Analyzing and understanding government data is also an important element in keeping public bodies accountable to the taxpayers who pay the bills. In earlier days, reporters often had to fight long and difficult battles to receive data through freedom-of-information requests, but there has been much change in this as well. A recent development has been the open-data movement, through which government bodies proactively make data available not only to journalists but to anyone who wants to use it, under liberal terms that place few or no restrictions on its use. While journalists often criticize open-data efforts for their reluctance to provide data on more contentious subject matter, there is no question that governments are far more open with data than they were a few years ago.

We'll discuss **open-data websites** in Chapter 2, and obtaining data through informal and formal requests in Chapter 3.

The problem for most data journalists is not finding data, but making sense of and sorting through the vast amounts of data available today.

"Governments and private companies use data all the time in their decision-making process," Shiab said.

Nowadays, almost every part of our lives is organized and analyzed by **computer programs**. Reporters need to be able to understand how all that works and how to recreate some of these processes . . . Otherwise, politicians and businesses will have an upper hand on us and reporters won't be able to monitor what they're really doing. Unfortunately, I suspect that it's already the case most of the time.

Technology: The Tools of Data and How Journalists Use Them

By its very definition, data journalism is technology-driven. The tools used by data journalists run the gamut from off-the-shelf **spreadsheet** software to programming languages such as JavaScript or PHP used for writing the code for complete websites. This means that the barriers to entry are low, but the opportunities to learn and grow are almost limitless.

The simplest data tool used by journalists is the spreadsheet. Programs such as Microsoft Excel and **OpenOffice Calc** allow you to view, sort and filter simple datasets ranging in size from just a few rows to a few hundred thousand. You can summarize information, do math, and focus your view to see just the details you want. Shiab uses spreadsheets heavily in his work: "I use Excel, Google Spreadsheet, and OpenOffice all the time. As soon as you know a little bit about formulas and some basic **functions**, spreadsheets are an incredible tool to see trends and anomalies."

Spreadsheets are also great tools for doing simple data preparation before using online tools such as Google Fusion Tables. This kind of program is capable of opening and manipulating a variety of file formats, including native spreadsheet files such as Excel and **delimited text files**. We introduce spreadsheets in Chapter 4.

The downside of spreadsheets is that they max out quite quickly in terms of how much data they can handle, and don't have any elegant ways of relating information contained in more than one data **table**. A table is a collection of structured information organized in **rows** and **columns**. As soon as the data analysis gets more demanding, you'll likely need to turn to a **relational database**. Like spreadsheets, these programs store data in tables made up of rows and columns, and they can sort and filter the information and do calculations on it. But the way a database manipulates information is different. Instead of constantly working with the actual data, with the ever-present possibility of corrupting or deleting it, you analyze information in a database program by writing queries in **Structured Query Language**, the short form of which is SQL. Relational databases allow you to **query** much larger amounts of data than is possible in a spreadsheet, in some cases limited only by the storage and processing capacity of your computer. "I really like to use MySQL . . . as soon as I have more than 20,000 rows, because it's faster and more efficient," Shiab said.

Databases and writing queries in SQL are covered in Chapter 5. The essential skills required to prepare data for analysis, including cleaning up "**dirty**" data with inconstancies and misspellings, is covered in the online Appendix A.

Web mapping services are another major tool of today's data journalist. There are a great many web map services, and all of them allow you to juxtapose your own geographic information, or information tied to geographic locations, on top of map layers that may show roads, a satellite view, terrain, or other similar backgrounds. The services vary in complexity, with such services as Google Fusion Tables, ArcGIS Online, and **CartoDB** allowing you to create sophisticated-looking maps without much experience, and others such as Leaflet, Mapbox, and the Google Maps API requiring a somewhat higher level of technical skill. All of them allow you to custom design elements such as the pop-up bubbles that appear when you click on a geographic **feature**, and the colours used on **choropleth maps** used to show variation from one district to another. "I . . . have to say that online mapping is getting incredibly good," Shiab said.

> CartoDB, for example, has a JavaScript library that allows you to customize almost everything, from visuals to interactions. There's also a very impressive API that lets you read and write your data (you need to know a bit of SQL to use it). With all these possibilities, you can make much more than just a regular map! And, for the moment, all of that is free.

You'll read about web-based mapping services in Chapter 6.

If you want to dig deeper into maps and use them as analytical tools, GIS programs allow that next step. If databases are the power tools of row-and-column data, geographic information systems fill the same role for geographic data. A GIS allows you to query geographic features based on their locations, revealing otherwise hidden geographic patterns. You can create new maps showing these relationships, which can then be uploaded to web-based mapping services.

Spreadsheets, databases, web maps, and GIS programs are at the heart of the data journalism toolkit. But more and more data journalists are turning to computer programming as an essential part of their work. **Coding** is a hugely complicated subject, and this book is not intended as a complete guide to learning to write code, but we cover some basics in Chapters 9 and 10.

Chapter 9 introduces you to **web scraping**. While government data is still central to the practice of data journalism, more and more data journalists would view the web itself as a vast repository of data. The data is not always in the form of structured rows and columns, but through scraping, journalists can extract elements from web pages and assemble them into a more structured form that can then be analyzed using spreadsheet, database, or mapping software. Vast social networks such as Facebook and Twitter accumulate almost unfathomable amounts of data, some of which can be accessed through APIs. Chapter 9 also touches on APIs and the legalities and ethics of scraping.

Chapter 10 introduces you to the work of newsroom developers, who work with code every day to produce the kinds of interactive visualizations we introduced to you at the start of this chapter. Quite deliberately, the chapter takes a 30,000-foot view, introducing you to the possibilities. Online tutorials on some of the key techniques will take you deeper.

Of course, data journalism is still journalism, even if the tools are computers and software instead of notebooks and pens, so we'll also explore how to tell stories with data and how to combine the results of data analysis with traditional reporting. "I think it's easy with data journalism to forget that we are not talking about data, but about human beings," Shiab said. "If you're doing a report about a database, you're making a mistake. Journalism should always be about something happening to someone because of another person's action."

Equally importantly, there is as much potential for mistakes by careless data journalists as there is by careless conventional journalists. "Data also gives the feeling that, because you have numbers, you are right," Shiab cautioned.

There's a risk that you simplify the reality because you have statistics. But all datasets have limits. In scientific fields, researchers always talk about the "limits" of their studies. Data reporters have to be aware of that too.

The way the data has been gathered and the way you analyze it always skew the reality.

Shiab takes a number of steps to preserve accuracy. He consults experts before publishing, always gives government agencies several days to respond to his findings, and triple- and quadruple-checks his work.

But, still, it's a very stressful job. When I was doing daily news, the stress was because of the deadlines. Now that I am a data reporter, the stress is because I am always afraid I made an error in my Python or JavaScript scripts, or in one Excel formula, or in any other calculation . . . So I check and recheck everything and I usually don't sleep well the night before publication.

That said, he says working with data and code has changed his life.

In a field where jobs are being cut, where the competition is getting tougher and tougher, where very few positions are created for young reporters, you can't be just good, you have to be exceptional, to be somehow unique. And that's what data journalism and coding skills gave me.

Through the next 10 chapters, we'll introduce you to many of the skills that can serve as the foundations of your career with data. We can't put everything in this book, so more advanced coding isn't covered. But what you learn here can form a basis for further independent study. There are many great resources available online, including the NICAR mailing list, maintained by Investigative Reporters and Editors (IRE.org), code-learning sites such as w3schools.com and CodeAcademy.com, and specialist websites maintained by data journalists. The authors of this book have their own sites, DataProf.ca and DavidMcKie.com. Shiab also maintains a bilingual (English and French) site that covers more advanced topics, at NaelShiab.com. In fact, there is no end of resources. The companion website has a comprehensive list.

For now, we'll start at the beginning, with getting data.

Notes

1. All of Naël Shiab's quotes are from an email interview with the authors on 6 December 2015.
2. *The Panama Papers: Politicians, Criminals, and the Rogue Industry That Hides Their Cash*, International Consortium of Investigative Journalists, http://panamapapers.icij.org/.

Part I
Getting Data

Chapter 2

Online and Open Data

What You Will Learn:

- The basics of data and data formats
- The origins of the open-data "movement"
- The kinds of downloadable data available
- Best practices for dealing with and testing any dataset

If we accept the proposition from the introduction that data is everywhere and involved with everything, the question of where journalists should get data ends up having a pretty simple answer: everywhere. But as with other kinds of information that journalists gather, there are places useful data is more likely to turn up, and we're going to spend the next couple of chapters exploring those. We'll start with data that you can easily download from so-called open-data sites and other online resources, then move on to how you can obtain public data from public officials, both formally and informally.

We'll start with one of the more widely read data stories in Canada in 2014:

It's the street equivalent of a desert mirage, an elusive piece of prime parking real estate that, for some strange reason, everyone else just happened to miss. Eventually, however, a telltale slip of paper tucked beneath a windshield wiper offers an explanation: you parked in front of a fire hydrant.

Maybe it was an honest mistake. Or maybe you thought you could slip in and out before your illegal parking job caught the attention of a passing bylaw officer. Either way, now you've been hit with a hefty fine.

And as it turns out, some hydrants seem to be more tempting—and more costly—than others.

Tutorials Included with the Companion Website

You will find these tutorials on the OUP Companion Website (www.oupcanada .com/Vallance-Jones):

· Getting Your Data out of **PDF**s and Other Difficult Formats

Since 2008, cars that parked too close to the hydrant at 393 University Ave. have been ticketed 2,962 times. Those fines add up to $289,620— more than any other hydrant in the city.[1]

So began Steve Rennie's story for the Canadian Press on parking infractions in Toronto. The story was published widely across the country in August 2014[2] and touched a nerve because there are hardly any drivers who haven't at some point got a parking ticket, or at least feared getting one.

There was a time when obtaining data like that, a dataset of every parking ticket in Canada's largest city, would have required long negotiations with civic officials and possibly a formal freedom-of-information request. It's sometimes still necessary to go the formal route, and we discuss that in Chapter 3. But the growth of open data, sometimes dubbed a movement by proponents,[3] has greatly simplified access to many datasets.

Now you can download easily digestible data on everything from animal control to zoning districts.

The idea has spread widely in recent years, notably in the United Kingdom, the United States, and Canada. There are a number of underlying principles of open data, but the most important is that the data is freely available, that it, is freely downloadable in a variety of formats that can be imported into spreadsheet or database software, and that there are few or no restrictions on reuse. Among other things, the principle that drives open data policies is intended to help make governments more accountable.

This has important implications for the practice of data journalism which, by definition, requires data. If data is available without having to clear high hurdles, practitioners can focus on creating content rather than on endless struggles to persuade government officials to part with data. Rennie learned this while working on his parking tickets story.

Having access to the Toronto parking data on an open-data website was incredibly valuable to me. For starters, it saved me from having to file a freedom-of-information request, which I had to do with the City of Ottawa [for its parking data]. The Toronto data was also much more specific than Ottawa's. It provided me with the exact location of each hydrant, whereas the Ottawa data only gave me the stretch of road (on which there could be multiple hydrants). It took seconds to download the Toronto data; I had to wait weeks for the Ottawa data. (The Toronto data) also cost me nothing.[4]

The word "data" is a Latin term, which in English means something given in an argument or taken for granted.[5] In Latin, "data" is the plural form of the singular "datum." However, in English the term functions as a plural or a collective singular, depending on the context. For instance, when referring to individual bits of data, we can say that "these data are reliable." Conversely, when referring to data in aggregate form, one can also say that "this data is reliable." We will use the latter form in the book, because of its wide usage in the data journalism community. On a more practical level, data for the purposes of our discussion means structured data, information organized into categories and arrayed into rows and columns to facilitate analysis.

By using tools such as spreadsheets, database programs, and geographic information systems (GIS) applications, journalists can drill down into this kind of data to find newsworthy examples such as a single serious crime, summarize it the way Rennie did to find the most-ticketed fire hydrant in Toronto, or put it on a map to find out how many toxic waste dumps are located near schools. The architecture of data is content agnostic. Data can be about almost anything. Once you understand how it is organized, you can analyze a great many datasets in similar ways. At times, data also refers to statistical data, data that is itself the result of some form of summarization. A city budget or census data are good examples of this.

While the architecture of structured data will be pretty much the same from dataset to dataset, there is no one standard for how the rows and columns should be stored. Just as word-processed documents can come in many different file formats, so it is with data. The two broad classes of data formats are **plain text files** and **binary files**. Plain text files store the data in ordinary text, not dissimilar to the basic text file you can create using a program such as TextEdit on a Mac or Notepad on a Windows computer. Within this broad category, files can be of different types. One is delimited text, in which column dividers are replaced by a character such as a comma or tab. Such files using commas as the separators—"delimiters" is the technical word—are so common they are often known as **comma separated values** (CSV) files. This is what a typical CSV file looks like:

```
Mark,Registration_sub_type_e,Registration_sub_type_f,Common_name,Model_name,Manu
" AAA","Continuing Registration","Immatriculation permanente","Dehavilland","DH6
" AAC","Continuing Registration","Immatriculation permanente","Piper","PA-28-235
" AAJ","Continuing Registration","Immatriculation permanente","Dehavilland","DH6
" AAM","Continuing Registration","Immatriculation permanente","Fokker","SUPER UN
" AAN","Continuing Registration","Immatriculation permanente","Bell","206B","127
" AAT","Continuing Registration","Immatriculation permanente","Fairchild","24 C8
" AAU","Continuing Registration","Immatriculation permanente","Dehavilland","DH6
" AAW","Continuing Registration","Immatriculation permanente","Waco","UIC","3771
" ABC","Continuing Registration","Immatriculation permanente","Stinson","108-3",
" ABD","Continuing Registration","Immatriculation permanente","Stits","STITS SKY
" ABK","Continuing Registration","Immatriculation permanente","Cessna","172K","1
" ABU","Continuing Registration","Immatriculation permanente","Corben","CORBEN B
" ABZ","Continuing Registration","Immatriculation permanente","Crusader","RP1 CR
" ADM","Continuing Registration","Immatriculation permanente","Cessna","180","32
" ADP","Continuing Registration","Immatriculation permanente","Bellanca","17-30"
" ADR","Continuing Registration","Immatriculation permanente","Cessna","A185E","
" AEK","Continuing Registration","Immatriculation permanente","Cessna","150K","1
```

Note the quotation marks around the various entries. Quotation marks are often used around text fields that may themselves contain commas. This ensures that the commas are not mistaken by the spreadsheet or data program as delimiters. Any commas within quotation marks will be ignored when the data is imported into a program such as Excel (see Chapter 4).

Another type of plain text file is the XML (**Extensible Markup Language**) file. In this type, individual elements of data are enclosed in tags. It is easily read by computers, making it a good format for files that will be read by automated programs, rather than by people. Here is part of an XML file:

```xml
<?xml version="1.0" ?>
<data xmlns="http://www.earthquakescanada.nrcan.gc.ca/api/earthquakes/">
    <metadata>
        <request>
            <licence>http://data.gc.ca/eng/open-government-licence-canada</licence>
            <name xml:lang="en">Available earthquake listings</name>
            <resultCount></resultCount>
            <dateCreated>2016-05-02T23:25:57-00:00</dateCreated>
            <dateModified>2016-05-02T05:10:07-00:00</dateModified>
        </request>
    </metadata>
    <link href="/api/earthquakes/latest/7d.xml" title="Latest 7 Days" type="application/xml" />
    <link href="/api/earthquakes/latest/30d.xml" title="Latest 30 Days" type="application/xml" />
    <link href="/api/earthquakes/latest/365d.xml" title="Latest 365 Days" type="application/xml" />
    <link href="/api/earthquakes/coordinates/35.xml" title="Latitude 35" type="application/xml" />
    <link href="/api/earthquakes/coordinates/36.xml" title="Latitude 36" type="application/xml" />
    <link href="/api/earthquakes/coordinates/37.xml" title="Latitude 37" type="application/xml" />
    <link href="/api/earthquakes/coordinates/38.xml" title="Latitude 38" type="application/xml" />
    <link href="/api/earthquakes/coordinates/39.xml" title="Latitude 39" type="application/xml" />
```

You can open an XML file as a spreadsheet, however you're better off downloading an Excel or CSV file.

JSON is another text format that is easily read by computers. It stands for **JavaScript Object Notation**. We won't get into the details here, but this format uses structures that come from the JavaScript programming language, widely used to create interactive features on web pages. Here is what JSON looks like:

```
{"gtf":{"total":16781796864.235,"ab":{"total":1692220072.120978,"2005-
2006":57229000,"2006-2007":57229000,"2007-2008":76305000,"2008-2009":95381000,"2009-
2010":190763000,"2010-2011":199503000,"2011-2012":199503000,"2012-2013":199503000,"2013-
2014":199503000,"2014-2015":208650536.060489,"2015-2016":208650536.060489},"bc":
{"total":2144940783.359482,"2005-2006":76272000,"2006-2007":76272000,"2007-
2008":101696000,"2008-2009":127120000,"2009-2010":254239000,"2010-2011":250697000,"2011-
2012":250697000,"2012-2013":250697000,"2013-2014":250697000,"2014-
2015":253276891.679741,"2015-2016":253276891.679741},"mb":
{"total":562819496.183309,"2005-2006":20070000,"2006-2007":20070000,"2007-
2008":26760000,"2008-2009":33450000,"2009-2010":66900000,"2010-2011":66157000,"2011-
2012":66157000,"2012-2013":66157000,"2013-2014":66157000,"2014-
2015":65470748.0916545,"2015-2016":65470748.0916545},"nb":
{"total":381236586.1056414,"2005-2006":13927000,"2006-2007":13927000,"2007-
2008":18570000,"2008-2009":23212000,"2009-2010":46424000,"2010-2011":44633000,"2011-
2012":44633000,"2012-2013":44633000,"2013-2014":44633000,"2014-
2015":43322293.0528207,"2015-2016":43322293.0528207},"nl":
{"total":266644117.2031204,"2005-2006":9870000,"2006-2007":9870000,"2007-
2008":13160000,"2008-2009":16450000,"2009-2010":32900000,"2010-2011":31166000,"2011-
2012":31166000,"2012-2013":31166000,"2013-2014":31166000,"2014-
2015":29865058.6015602,"2015-2016":29865058.6015602},"ns":
```

JSON is often used for data that is provided by an API, or application programming interface. We'll discuss APIs in Chapter 9.

There are also text-based map file formats, the most common of which is the KML (**Keyhole Markup Language**) file. KML is actually based on the XML specification, and also uses tags. We'll talk more about KML and other map formats in Chapter 6.

The other broad class of data file is the binary type. Binary files can't be opened properly in a text editor, and require specific software to be viewed. In fact, an easy way to check if a file is a binary one is to try to open it in a text editor; if it opens largely as unreadable gibberish, it's a binary file. Binary file types include all image formats, **Microsoft Access** database files, **portable document format** (PDF) **files**, and the ".shp" component of Esri **shapefiles**, a type of map file.

PDF files are worth breaking out on their own, because you will encounter them often. PDF files were developed to provide document publishers with a way to ensure their documents would look the same no matter what computer opened them. Along with whatever text they may contain, they also have information that dictates how everything should be presented on screen. Some PDFs contain the actual text, numbers, and so on of the original document, while others are **image files** that only contain a picture of the original content.

PDF files are popular with government agencies seeking to publish information for the public. And for reports and other formatted material, they have been a godsend for reporters and other researchers. But as a format for disseminating data, they cause more problems than they solve. They cannot be opened in **data analysis software** such as a spreadsheet, database, or mapping program, but must first be converted to extract the data. A variety of tools can be used to convert these files, some of them desktop-based and some cloud-based. The methods are constantly evolving. We've prepared a tutorial entitled "Getting Data out of PDF Files and Other Incompatible Formats," and you can find it on this book's companion website.

As we'll discuss in a moment, you may see any of these formats on an open-data site. In the case of the Toronto parking-ticket data used by Rennie, the data is made available in CSV format, with several sub-files for each year because there are so many parking tickets issued in the city, about 2.8 million every year.[6] In Rennie's case he used Excel to narrow down to tickets involving fire hydrants, and then used the Excel **pivot table** function (which we cover in Chapter 4) to find the most-ticketed locations. Having found the one hot spot, he took his camera and notepad to 393 University Avenue and interviewed people, many of whom had no idea a fire hydrant was even there because of its obscure location.

> We took a screen shot of the Google Street View image of the Toronto fire hydrant, which almost too perfectly had a car parked in front of it with a ticket on the windshield and a bylaw officer walking away.[7]

Later in the chapter, we'll discuss how open-data sites are structured, and how you can use them, but first we'll take a deeper dive into the theory behind them.

Principles

Open data has become a big activity for governments, and is often tied in with ideas of making government more open and transparent, what is often referred to as open government. The leaders of the G8 group of leading industrialized countries came up with a set of principles that they called the **Open Data Charter**. You can read the whole document at www.gov .uk/government/publications/open-data-charter/g8-open-data-charter-and-technical-annex. The five key principles are as follows:

- Data should be open by default. The G8 leaders agreed that "free access to, and subsequent reuse of, open data are of significant value to society and the economy." They agreed to "establish an expectation that all government data be published openly by default, as outlined in this

To avoid any possible confusion, we should point out that open data is not the same as "**big data**," another concept that has been widely discussed in recent years. Big data is data that is so large in volume or velocity (the speed with which it is collected and transmitted) that traditional desktop analytical techniques are not sufficient to make sense of it. An example of big data is the enormous volume of information collected daily by Google or Facebook. With specialized techniques, such as using many computers working together in what is called "distributed computing," important insights can be gained into people's behaviours and interests. This kind of data is typically beyond the capabilities of users such as journalists, and is decidedly not going to be found on open-data sites. Open datasets are generally more limited in size, from a few thousand to a few million rows of data. They can still be plenty big, but can normally be analyzed using the kind of software we discuss in this book.

Charter, while recognising that there are legitimate reasons why some data cannot be released." Those reasons include intellectual property rights and personal privacy.

- There should be both quality and quantity of data. This includes a commitment to release data from vast storehouses of government data as quickly as possible, and to make changes to ensure high quality. The charter also acknowledges that data may take time to prepare for release, and that it should be well documented and in plain language, to ease its use.
- The data should be useable by all, meaning it is released in open formats, in as great a volume as possible, "without bureaucratic or administrative barriers, such as registration requirements, which can deter people from accessing the data."
- Data should be released for improved governance. "We recognise that the release of open data strengthens our democratic institutions and encourages better policy-making to meets the needs of our citizens. This is true not only in our own countries but across the world."
- Data should be released for innovation. "The more people and organisations that use our data, the greater the social and economic benefits that will be generated. This is true for both commercial and non-commercial uses." The governments also agreed to work to increase data literacy.

One of the most important understandings is that data should be licensed in a way that encourages as wide use as possible, and released in **machine-readable formats**. It is worth noting that, for the most part, open data refers to datasets held by governments or quasi-government agencies. And this is where open government comes into play. Because this data is collected with taxpayers' dollars, there's a built-in assumption that the data should yield information that helps explain how governments operate, how they make decisions, spend money, recall vehicles or dangerous drugs, or inspect restaurants. Open data is supposed to increase transparency in that citizens can use the data to hold their governments to account, which could mean determining how well governments spend tax money. It is for this reason that "government" is sometimes used to qualify open data, as in "open government data." In this instance, "government" not only describes the origin of the data, but reinforces the notion that it is information to which citizens have a right.

All in all, it is a high-minded set of principles, but one that conflicts with the tendency of governments to control information, sometimes to achieve political ends. Canada for example is a signatory to the open-data charter, and has launched an ambitious open-data program, but at the same time a succession of Canadian federal governments, most recently the Conservatives under Stephen Harper, have been accused of being secretive and controlling access to information. Justin Trudeau's Liberal government has promised to "enhance the openness of government, including leading a review of the Access to Information Act," though the commitments are a work in progress as this book goes to print.[8] Similar statements have been made in the United States, which has endorsed open data even while the Obama administration has been accused of being extremely secretive in other areas.

The Newspapers Canada National Freedom of Information Audit, a study coordinated by one of the authors of this book, has repeatedly found that the altruistic principles of open data don't always hold true when formal requests are made for data not already made public on the open-data sites,[9] an area we cover in Chapter 3.

This kind of concern aside, there is no question that governments are far more open with data than they were even a decade ago when news organizations sometimes had to fight for years to free up one dataset.

The History of Open Government and Open Data

It is important to make a distinction between the availability of government data and the open-data movement. Some government agencies in the United States and Canada began making downloadable data available well before "open data" became the watchword. The Federal Aviation Administration had, for many years, made available key datasets such as service difficulty reports about aircraft in service, as well as accidents and incidents involving aircraft.

North of the border, Natural Resources Canada developed a large repository of geospatial data well before anyone had heard the term "open data." Election finance information was also widely available in both countries long before open data became trendy. In 2004, Paul Martin's Liberal government ordered federal departments to "proactively" disclose data on contracts and the hospitality expenses of ministers and senior public servants. There were many other examples. All in all, it is a high-minded set of principles, but one that conflicts with the tendency of governments to want to control information.

But open data moves us from a time when certain agencies made specific data available, to one in which all agencies are expected—though not legally required—to release data as part of their normal operation.

One of the first open-data sites was in Britain. The United Kingdom launched its data.gov.uk portal on 1 January 2009 to "provide opportunities for business, increase transparency and empower consumers."[10] Former British prime minister David Cameron issued two letters on open data, and in the second in July 2011, promised "the most ambitious open data agenda of any government in the world, [to] demonstrate our determination to make the public sector more transparent and accountable."[11]

A key impetus to open data came with directives issued by US president Barack Obama during his first year in office. Almost as soon as he assumed power, Obama indicated that under his administration, openness should be the default position of government. Then at the end of 2009, he issued an open government directive that not only required agencies to make information available online in open formats, but directed each agency to post at least three "high-value" datasets on Data.gov within 45 days.[12]

On 9 May 2014, the president issued the long-awaited open-data action plan that detailed a number of newly released datasets considered to be of high value, including adverse reactions to certain prescription drugs, Medicare reimbursements, and consumer product recalls.

Canada, meanwhile, was not to be left out of the action. The otherwise secretive government of former Conservative prime minister, Stephen Harper, extolled open data, with the president of the Treasury Board, Tony Clement, a vocal advocate. The Treasury Board published its own directive, stating that,

> The expectations of Canadians for increased access to, and the proactive release of, federal data and information will require government departments and agencies to make their information resources that are eligible for release to be more easily discoverable and reusable.[13]

On 1 March 2011 the Canadian government launched the open-data pilot project and that July introduced www.data.gc.ca, later folded into open.canada.ca. The provinces joined in, with British Columbia leading the pack in July 2011 by launching the first provincial open-data program in July 2011.[14] Ontario, Quebec, and Newfoundland and Labrador would follow in BC's footsteps.

Many municipalities in Canada and the United States also have portals, with Chicago's being perhaps the best known. In 2009, Vancouver formally endorsed the principles of open data, and on 1 June 2009 the city of Nanaimo unveiled the country's first municipal open-data site. Toronto, Edmonton, Ottawa, and Calgary were among other early adopters. All in all, open data has exploded from a standing start to hundreds of sites around the world. Journalists are among the lucky beneficiaries.

What Kind of Data Can You Get?

Each open-data site is a little different from the next, and some have dozens or hundreds of datasets, while others have just a few. Some of the earliest were geospatial, or mapping, datasets, such as the enormous collection from Natural Resources Canada that kick-started the Canadian open-data portal. These datasets, which might show the locations of streets, parks, and schools, for example, or boundaries such as those of electoral districts, are of great value to those working with mapping applications. They are also relatively non-controversial and do little to promote accountability.

Visitors to data.gov in the United States can find data on pipeline incidents and accidents, locations and inspections of nuclear reactors, climate change, how much businesses are investing in new buildings and equipment, and hourly, daily, monthly, and annual precipitation.

In the United Kingdom, Data.gov.uk similarly has a huge collection of datasets, on topics as diverse as four decades of highway accident casualties and the names, organizations, and addresses of individuals who can prescribe controlled drugs in England. The Canadian open-data site also has large numbers of datasets, including recalls of motor vehicles and the details of freedom-of-information requests that have received a response. Other open-data sites, including many that are maintained by municipalities, can be much more limited in scope, though not always. Even municipal sites can be impressively expansive, such as Chicago's open-data portal or those in Toronto or Vancouver.

The user experience differs from site to site, but typical features include a browsable alphabetical list, a search function, and explanatory information for each dataset, going over such details as the meaning of fields, codes used, and the frequency with which the data is updated. Sometimes there will be a preview feature that allows you to see a few rows of the data or a display of map data. Depending on the sophistication of the site, there may be the ability to visualize part or all of the data, which can be of great assistance to those without the skills to analyze the data themselves. Generally, you will be able to download the data in one or more of the formats discussed earlier in this chapter, typically delimited text, Excel, HTML, JSON, or XML for non-geographic data, and KML, **GeoJSON**, or shapefiles for map data. There are also sometimes links to APIs, allowing you to access data programmatically (see Chapter 9 for a more extensive discussion of APIs).

As time has gone on, however, more and more data has been published that sheds light on the operations of government and on subjects such as the locations of crimes. Let's take a deeper look at five datasets and what journalists might do with them.

Chicago's Crime Database

The Chicago open-data portal makes available files in several formats including CSV and xlsx of the location of every reported crime in the city since 2001 extracted from the police department's database.[15] Updated daily, the data excludes the most recent seven days of data and locations are identified by block only.

	Block	IUCR	Primary Type	Description	Location Description	
1	020XX W 68TH PL	0110	HOMICIDE	FIRST DEGREE MURDER	STREET	
2	076XX S PARNELL AVE	0486	BATTERY	DOMESTIC BATTERY SIMPLE	RESIDENCE	
3	091XX S COLFAX AVE	0460	BATTERY	SIMPLE	RESIDENCE PORCH/HALLWAY	
4	072XX S LANGLEY AVE	0486	BATTERY	DOMESTIC BATTERY SIMPLE	APARTMENT	
5	015XX N CENTRAL AVE	0486	BATTERY	DOMESTIC BATTERY SIMPLE	PARKING LOT/GARAGE(NON.RESID.)	
6	048XX W DRUMMOND PL	0560	ASSAULT	SIMPLE	STREET	
7	015XX W CHICAGO AVE	1320	CRIMINAL DAMAGE	TO VEHICLE	STREET	
8	020XX W SUPERIOR ST	0820	THEFT	$500 AND UNDER	STREET	
9	059XX W MADISON ST	0560	ASSAULT	SIMPLE	SIDEWALK	
10	078XX S CREGIER AVE	0486	BATTERY	DOMESTIC BATTERY SIMPLE	STREET	
11	041XX W EDDY ST	0810	THEFT	OVER $500	STREET	

What Journalists Can Do with It

This enormous resource can be used to identify the most common and the most serious crimes, where they occur, the times of day they occur, and trends over time in all of these areas, to name just a few applications. The data is also useful for analyzing enforcement patterns. This data was the impetus for ChicagoCrime.org, now folded into Chicago's EveryBlock site, seen here:

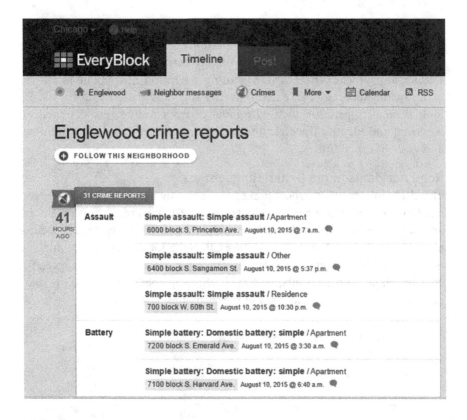

Toronto Payment Card Data

Some city of Toronto employees are issued credit cards for making purchases for the municipality. The city's open-data site provides monthly downloadable Excel files documenting the use of these cards going back to January 2011.

Division	Batch-Transaction ID	Transaction Date	Transaction Month	Card Posting Dt	Merchant Name	Transaction Amt.
ECONOMIC DEVELOPMENT & CULTURE	3275-1	2014-12-01	12	2014-12-03	METRO #720	34.09
ECONOMIC DEVELOPMENT & CULTURE	3302-1	2014-12-19	12	2014-12-22	LCBO/RAO #0217	75.00
PARKS, FORESTRY & RECREATION	3271-1	2014-11-27	11	2014-12-01	FOOD BASICS #692	116.60
PARKS, FORESTRY & RECREATION	3271-2	2014-11-27	11	2014-12-01	FOOD BASICS #692	61.72
PARKS, FORESTRY & RECREATION	3275-2	2014-12-01	12	2014-12-03	PAYPAL *PPGEAR	727.72
PARKS, FORESTRY & RECREATION	3294-1	2014-12-12	12	2014-12-16	BOSS STEEL	967.73
PARKS, FORESTRY & RECREATION	3294-2	2014-12-12	12	2014-12-16	CANADA POPCORN COMPANY	995.47
PARKS, FORESTRY & RECREATION	3300-1	2014-12-18	12	2014-12-19	SONSUH EDUCATIONAL SUP	489.42
PARKS, FORESTRY & RECREATION	3300-2	2014-12-18	12	2014-12-19	SONSUH EDUCATIONAL SUP	118.05
PARKS, FORESTRY & RECREATION	3302-2	2014-12-19	12	2014-12-22	AVRON FOODS	935.39
PARKS, FORESTRY & RECREATION	3302-3	2014-12-19	12	2014-12-22	GLOBALINDUSTRIALCANDA	320.99
ECONOMIC DEVELOPMENT & CULTURE	3285-1	2014-12-08	12	2014-12-10	JONG YOUNG MARKET	45.20
ECONOMIC DEVELOPMENT & CULTURE	3288-1	2014-12-10	12	2014-12-11	ROB'S NO FRILLS STORE	21.08
ECONOMIC DEVELOPMENT & CULTURE	3292-1	2014-12-12	12	2014-12-15	TAP PHONG TRADING CO.	47.12
ECONOMIC DEVELOPMENT & CULTURE	3292-2	2014-12-13	12	2014-12-15	LOBLAWS STORE #179	12.34
PARKS, FORESTRY & RECREATION	3280-1	2014-12-04	12	2014-12-05	STAPLES STORE #26	147.69
PARKS, FORESTRY & RECREATION	3294-3	2014-12-15	12	2014-12-16	PARKDALE HM HDW 1350-8	16.88
PARKS, FORESTRY & RECREATION	3302-4	2014-12-20	12	2014-12-22	PARKDALE HM HDW 1350-8	7.88
PARKS, FORESTRY & RECREATION	3302-5	2014-12-21	12	2014-12-22	MICHAELS #3990	32.75
ECONOMIC DEVELOPMENT & CULTURE	3271-3	2014-11-28	11	2014-12-01	METRO #720	22.29
ECONOMIC DEVELOPMENT & CULTURE	3276-1	2014-12-03	12	2014-12-04	BULK BARN	80.16
ECONOMIC DEVELOPMENT & CULTURE	3281-1	2014-12-05	12	2014-12-08	FRESHCO 9841	26.27
ECONOMIC DEVELOPMENT & CULTURE	3288-2	2014-12-09	12	2014-12-11	CDN TIRE STORE #00273	32.75
ECONOMIC DEVELOPMENT & CULTURE	3290-1	2014-12-11	12	2014-12-12	LOBLAWS 4.2	5.98
ECONOMIC DEVELOPMENT & CULTURE	3300-3	2014-12-17	12	2014-12-19	METRO #720	69.60
FIRE SERVICES	3290-2	2014-12-11	12	2014-12-12	IN *20/20 GENESYSTEMS	3,038.81

What Journalists Can Do with It

This is a key accountability dataset, permitting journalists and other researchers to mine deeply the spending patterns of civic officials using municipal payment cards, thereby shining a light on how public money is being spent. Reporters can explore overall spending patterns on the cards, look at smaller patterns such as purchases from online retailers such as Amazon, and identify the civic officials connected with the largest number and value of expenditures.

Road Accidents in the United Kingdom

The UK Ministry of Transport makes available downloadable data tables related to personal injury road accidents, from 1979 onward. Data is produced annually. There is data on the accidents, the vehicles, and the casualties, contained in a number of related tables (see Chapter 5 for a discussion of analyzing multi-table datasets). The data is extremely detailed, with geographic coordinates for the accidents, and fields showing road conditions, the date and time, speed limit, age and sex of the casualties, and so on.

Propulsion_Code	Age_of_Vehicle	Driver_IMD_Decl	Driver_Home_Area_Type	make	model
2	2	4	1	FORD	GALAXY ZETEC TDCI AUTO
2	2	-1	-1	MERCEDES	
1	12	-1	-1	BENTLEY	ARNAGE T AUTO
1	4	1	1	MINI	FIRST
1	2	7	1	HONDA	CBR 1000 RR-C
1	13	-1	-1	NISSAN	ALMERA TINO SE CVT
1	9	6	1	FORD	FOCUS ZETEC CLIMATE T
1	3	-1	-1	YAMAHA	YP 125 R-XMAX
2	9	3	1	CHRYSLER	GRAND VOYAGER LTD XS AUTO
1	13	4	1	HONDA	NES 125-Y
2	3	7	1	BMW	1200 SPORT
1	3	4	1	HONDA	WW 125 EX2-A
2	4	6	1	FORD	TRANSIT 85 T260S FWD
1	15	-1	-1	PIAGGIO	PX 125 (VESPA)
-1	-1	4	1	FORD	TRANSIT 115 T350L RWD
2	1	3	1	VOLKSWAGEN	SHARAN SE BLUEMOTION TDI S-
1	4	3	1	HONDA	XL 125 V-9
2	3	4	1	MERCEDES-BENZ	E220 EXEC-IVE SE CDI BLUE-C
1	1	5	1	SKODA	FABIA S 12V
1	2	7	1	MERCEDES-BENZ	SLK350 AMG SPORT BLUE-CIENC
-1	-1	4	1	PIAGGIO	MP3 300 YOURBAN LT
2	9	5	1	MERCEDES	VITO 111 CDI LONG
1	6	7	1	AUDI	A3 101 MPI
2	5	-1	-1	LONDON TAXIS INT	TX4 SILVER AUTO
1	1	4	1	PIAGGIO	FLY 125 3V
2	6	4	1	MERCEDES	E220 AVANTGARDE CDI A
2	12	6	1	VOLKSWAGEN	BORA TDI SE
1	1	1	1	HONDA	SH 125 AD-E
2	1	7	1	VOLKSWAGEN	TIGUAN MATCH TDI BMT AMOTN

What Journalists Can Do with It

Highway safety is a matter of great public interest, and reporting on it is in the public interest. This data allows for a fine-grained analysis of traffic accidents, and could be used for both a national analysis of road safety and for stories by local media outlets about the most accident-prone roadways.

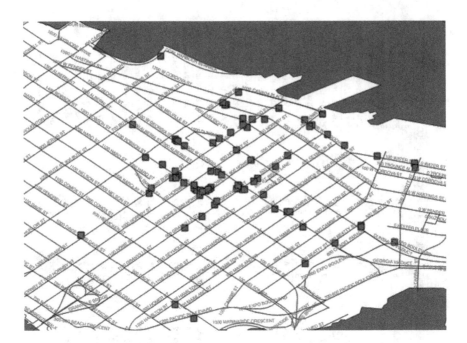

Vancouver Food Vendors

This dataset is also produced annually, and shows the locations of food vendors throughout the city of Vancouver, along with the business name and type of food sold.

What Journalists Can Do with It

This data, which is provided in both text and KML map formats (map seen above), isn't as serious in content as the datasets we've looked at so far. But there is room for fun in data journalism, and this data could be the basis for an interactive visualization of food vendors or a feature on the range of food options available on the city's streets.

Mine Accidents

The dataset on page 26 is supplied by the US Department of Labor via the Data.gov site, and the data goes back to 2000. It includes information on the mine where the accident occurred, whether the accident happened underground or in the millworks, the activity that preceded the accident, the number and nature of injuries, and work days lost due to injury, as well as the date and other fields. There is also a narrative column that provides a description of what happened. The data is updated regularly.

What Journalists Can Do with It

Mining is an important industry in parts of the United States and one of the most dangerous of all occupations. This data allows for detailed analysis of

ACCIDENT_TYPE	NO_INJURIES	TOT_EXPER	MINE_EXPER	JOB_EXPER	OCCUPATION_CD	OCCUPATION
Struck by falling object	1	7.62	7.62	7.62	374	Warehouseman, Bagg
Absorption of radiations, caustics, toxic and noxious substances	1	8.38	8.38	8.38	374	Warehouseman, Bagg
Caught in, under or between two or more moving objects	1	0.5	0.5	0.5	304	Maintenance man, Me
Fall to the walkway or working surface	1	0.4	0.4	0.4	116	Laborer, Bull gang, Pa
Fall from ladders	1	0.11	0.11	0.11	374	Warehouseman, Bagg
No Value Found	1				?	NO VALUE FOUND
Over-exertion in lifting objects	1	4.54	4.54	4.54	316	Laborer, Blacksmith, B
Struck by... NEC	1	7.62	7.62	7.62	302	Electrician, Lineman
Over-exertion NEC	1	20.54	20.54	10	414	Quality control technic
Over-exertion in lifting objects	1	3.23	3.23	3.23	304	Maintenance man, Me
Fall to the walkway or working surface	1	35.4	35.4	7	374	Warehouseman, Bagg
Contact with hot objects or substances	1	4.75	4.75	4.75	304	Maintenance man, Me
Accident type, without injuries	0				?	NO VALUE FOUND
Accident type, without injuries	0				?	NO VALUE FOUND
Struck by falling object	1	0.4	0.4	0.4	304	Maintenance man, Me
Over-exertion NEC	1	27	27	27	304	Maintenance man, Me
Fall onto or against objects	1	28.71	28.71	4	374	Warehouseman, Bagg
Over-exertion NEC	1	25.83	25.83	2.04	374	Warehouseman, Bagg
Struck against a moving object	1	14	14	2.5	4	Maintenance man, Me
Struck against stationary object	1	29.92	29.92	22	4	Maintenance man, Me
Accident type, without injuries	0				?	NO VALUE FOUND
Fall from machine	1	15.03	15.03	10.26	374	Warehouseman, Bagg
Over-exertion NEC	1	24.92	24.92	24.92	304	Maintenance man, Me
Contact with hot objects or substances	2	27.98	27.98	1.38	374	Warehouseman, Bagg
Caught in, under or between NEC	1	35.6	35.6	25.25	304	Maintenance man, Me
Struck by falling object	1		21.76	9.69	46	Roof bolter, Rock bolt
Struck by falling object	1	11.76	11.76	3.76	99	Miner, NEC
Over-exertion in lifting objects	1	5.34	5.34	5.26	16	Laborer, Bull gang, Fac
Struck by powered moving object	1	25.03	25.03	0.76	4	Maintenance man, Me
Struck by falling object	1		5.58	0.77	46	Roof bolter, Rock bolte
Struck against stationary object	1		5.12	5.04	104	Maintenance man, Me

trends and patterns of mining accidents, the companies and mines with the most accidents, the most common types of accidents and injuries, and total work time lost. Details on individual accidents would permit a reporter to find and talk to the people involved, as well as their families.

Data Quality Concerns

Even when open-data sites provide raw, row-level data, you shouldn't assume that it contains all of the data that a government body collects on a subject. Organizations exercise choices when they publish data, and one of the decisions is which data elements to make available.

Privacy is often a key concern. For example, the Chicago crime data we discussed earlier in this chapter doesn't reveal the exact location of a crime to protect the privacy of victims. In Canada, which has particularly strict privacy laws, anything that provides personal details about an identifiable person is likely to be removed from the dataset. Data may also be withheld for security reasons, to protect the integrity of ongoing investigations, and the like.

Sometimes datasets are scrubbed of detail not to protect such sensitive interests, but because officials do not wish to release certain columns of information. The Toronto parking-tickets data we referenced earlier doesn't include every field collected by the city. As an example, the city records the ID number of the officer who gave the ticket, but this is not included in the downloadable version. The data with the ID was released in response to a subsequent freedom-of-information request as the Ontario law (and many others) does not prohibit the naming of officials going about their duties.

Even though many **open-records laws** make it clear that electronic records are subject to release, Canada's information commissioner, Suzanne Legault, concluded that the government often ends up releasing information that it "wants" to disclose, rather than data that it "ought" to disclose. Consequently, she said that in order for the "Open by Default" policy to have any teeth, the government should "modernize" the Access to Information Act.[16] Still, open by default also means that citizens—including journalists—have the right to request the release of datasets and that they be released in more user-friendly formats. Open-data sites even provide online forms that can be filled out to make such requests. Unfortunately, the online process can take days, or even weeks. For quicker results, journalists may be better off phoning the keeper of the data, or attempting to make contact through the communications office.

Open-data principles indeed constitute a tall order for governments, and for the most part, the principles have not been given the force of law. In the absence of legally enforced standards, there is frustrating unevenness in the quantity, usefulness, and timeliness of data across government departments and agencies. In reality, open data is a perpetual work in progress that governments promise to regularly evaluate—in writing—with the help of third-party assessors. For journalists, this means that there will be weaknesses in datasets that must be taken into account.

In addition to dealing with incomplete datasets, open-data portals feature a lot of information that may be useful to app developers but of little use for journalists. On their own, the location of hockey arenas, parks, and playgrounds will not lead to news stories. Although institutions are uploading an increasing number of more robust and consequential datasets, many of the offerings inevitably fall into the useless or "so what" category. Some experts have dubbed this kind of information "zombie" data, that is politically neutral and of little practical use, especially for journalists.[17] That said, sometimes even this kind of data can be useful.

The location of parks and tennis courts may do little to explain what policies governments use to determine when and where to build these facilities. However, combined with other data, such as the locations of discarded hypodermic needles, even zombie data can suddenly spring to life and provide important context.[18]

Steps to Take When Working with Any Dataset

Great care needs to be taken when working with any external dataset, whether obtained from an open-data site or other online source, or through an informal or formal records request (see the next chapter). Before downloading an online dataset, be sure to open up or download the **ReadMe file**, **metadata** notes, or explanatory notes, which are files that explain what's in the data and what the information means. For example, the Canada Revenue Agency provides explanatory notes for its tax-free-savings-account data that contain the following: a note about the steps they've taken to ensure confidentiality ("data have been suppressed whenever a field is represented by fewer than 10 tax-filers"); the source of the data ("Income data were taken from income tax returns and related schedules filed by individuals for the 2013 tax year"); and a description of the six tables. Without these explanatory notes, you may miss important aspects of the data or misinterpret what columns contain or codes mean. The same advice applies when you have obtained data through a request, except that in that instance, it probably won't be online and you'll have to ask for it. More on that in the next chapter. Don't be afraid to call the public body to get more information if you need it.

For online datasets, there should also be a metadata file, explaining how the data was collected, defined, and aggregated, and what human decision processes contributed to its creation.[19]

In addition to reading explanatory notes or metadata files, it is also important to construct a checklist of questions that must be answered before going any further. The source agency may have already done a good job providing information, or it might not have. So here's a list of questions that represent a good starting point for obtaining the kind of context that you'll need.

- Who produced the data? This might not be as straightforward as it seems. In their attempts to become more efficient and spend less money, governments at all levels are streamlining their operations. At the federal level in Canada, for instance, the Shared Services department handles many of the information technology needs across government. So while a dataset may belong to a certain department, Shared Services is the arm of government often producing specific datasets.
- What was the department's intent in releasing the data? Earlier in this chapter, we saw descriptions of departments that released data for altruistic reasons such as increasing transparency and making it easier for citizens to make decisions. It's relatively easy to see why municipalities release restaurant-inspection data. Citizens can check out their favourite eateries. Restaurants are forced clean up their acts because being identified as a repeat offender is bad for business. Knowing the agency's intent makes it easier to tell the story. So if the intent is unclear, it is worth asking.
- When was the data collected? You need to know if you are dealing with the most recent information, or information that has become dated.
- Could there be errors? Are there extremely large or extremely small values in the data that could be mistakes? It's important to test the data in the real world. This may also involve consulting experts.
- Do the grand totals in the data match up with publicly known grand totals, for example in departmental annual reports? (You'll need skills from Chapters 5 to 8 to find this out.)
- Are there missing data (e.g. some columns not always populated), misspellings, or other inconsistencies? If so, you'll need to clean the dataset before you use it. This book's companion website has a detailed tutorial on **data cleaning**.
- Has any data been removed? As we've learned, open-data sites rarely provide totally raw data. The keepers of the datasets make decisions on what to provide, so determining what's not in the dataset is as important as what is included.
- Has the data been cropped and filtered, aggregated or transformed? It is important to explain how the data is assembled in order to protect privacy, for example. Such an explanation need not become a major part of the story, but can be explained in a sidebar, or a link that leads to a blog.
- How does the institution use the data? At the very least, many government institutions use databases to identify problems, or generate special

reports that contain important analysis. For instance, Health Canada will use its adverse drug reaction database as a "signal generator" or early warning system. A drug causing an unusual number of deaths should prompt officials to ask serious questions. However, departmental databases may receive limited use beyond detecting hotspots. Knowing this allows journalists to explain that a story or trend came about through an original analysis of the data. Such context adds greater heft to stories.

- Do the columns in the tables conform to the record layout (a listing of fields and data types)? Never assume this to be the case. Always check to make sure the table contains the columns indicated in the ReadMe file or other documentation.
- What time period does the dataset cover and how recent is the latest update? This should be evident from the dates in the table. If not, it is worth asking.

This list of best practices is important and highlights the need to think about your use of data, however you obtain it, before analyze it.

Study Questions and Exercises

1. Download one of the datasets discussed in this chapter or a new dataset that interests you. Explore the data, and look at it through the lens of the best practices enumerated at the end of this chapter. What do you find? What do you need to find out? Make a list, then try to answer your questions.
2. Visit an open-data site and explore the datasets there. Is this an open-data site that includes information that could hold governments accountable and increase transparency, or is it mostly "zombie" data? Explain your answers.
3. See the companion website for an in-depth study assignment based on live data that you can download.

Notes

1. Rennie, "This Fire Hydrant Costs Toronto Drivers the Most in Parking Tickets," *Toronto Star*, 11 August 2014, http://www.thestar.com/news/gta/2014/08/11/this_fire_hydrant_costs_toronto_drivers_the_most_in_parking_tickets.html.
2. Ibid.
3. Mary Francoli, interview with the authors, 20 May 2015. Fancoli's profile is available here: http://carleton.ca/communication/people/francoli-mary
4. Rennie, interview with the authors, July, 2014.

5. Daniel Rosenberg, "Data before the fact," in *Raw Data Is an Oxymoron*, ed. Lisa Gitelman (Cambridge MA: MIT press, 2013), 18–19.

6. "Parking Tickets," City of Toronto, "Open Data," http://www1.toronto.ca/wps/portal/contentonly?vgnextoid=ca20256c54ea4310VgnVCM1000003dd60f89RCRD&vgnextchannel=1a66e03bb8d1e310VgnVCM10000071d60f89RCRD

7. Rennie, in an email response to authors 3 June 2015.

8. President of the Treasury Board of Canada, Mandate Letter, 13 November 2016, http://pm.gc.ca/eng/president-treasury-board-canada-mandate-letter

9. Fred Vallance-Jones and Emily Kitagawa, *National Freedom of Information Audit 2015* (Toronto: Newspapers Canada, 2015) http://newspaperscanada.ca/sites/default/files/FOI-2015-FINAL.pdf.

10. Ellen Broad, Fiona Smith, Dawn Duhaney, and Liz Carolan, *Open Data in Government: How to Bring Change* (London: Open Data Institute, 2015), 14.

11. David Cameron, "Letter to Cabinet Ministers on Transparency and Open Data," 7 July 2001, https://www.gov.uk/government/news/letter-to-cabinet-ministers-on-transparency-and-open-data.

12. Peter R. Orszag, "Open Government Directive," 8 December 2009, http://www.whitehouse.gov/open/documents/open-government-directive.

13. Treasury Board of Canada, "Directive on Open Government," 9 October 2014, http://www.tbs-sct.gc.ca/pol/doc-eng.aspx?id=28108.

14. Province of British Columbia, "Open Data," DataBC, http://www.data.gov.bc.ca/dbc/about/open_data.page?.

15. City of Chicago Data Portal, "Crimes 2001 to Present," http://data.cityofchicago.org/Public-Safety/Crimes-2001-to-present/ijzp-q8t2.

16. Suzanne Legault, "Letter to the President of the Treasury Board on Action Plan 2.0," 5 November 2014, http://www.oic-ci.gc.ca/eng/lettre-plan-d-action-2.0_letter-action-plan-2.0.aspx.

17. Daniel Kaufmann, "The Development Challenge of the Decade: Natural Resource Governance," *Revenue Watch Institute*, 25 February 2013, 3, http://www.slideshare.net/EITI/oslo-roundtablee-itinorwayd-kaufmann.

18. Paul Jay, "More Discarded Needles Being Found in Ottawa's Suburbs," CBC *News*, 17 March 2014, http://www.cbc.ca/news/canada/ottawa/more-discarded-needles-being-found-in-ottawa-s-suburbs-1.2572573.

19. Alexander Howard, *The Art and Science of Data-Driven Journalism*, (New York: Tow Center for Digital Journalism, 2014), 4.

Chapter 3

When Data Is Not Conveniently Available

What You Will Learn:

- How to discover government datasets and where to look for them
- What to find out before you ask for data
- How to proceed from asking, to negotiating, to demanding data through open-records laws

Open-data sites and other government data repositories are becoming richer every day, and they can help journalists identify and tell important stories. But even the most open of open-data regimes has its limits, and most journalists working with data will eventually want to obtain a dataset that is not easily downloadable from the web. In this chapter, we'll discuss the kind of data that governments hold but may not publicize, how to identify and research data, then how to approach governments, first informally, and then if necessary, using open-records laws.

Public institutions use data to track public activities that have a direct bearing on public policy: police track crime; public health agencies chronicle the behaviour of diseases and inspect establishments serving food; federal agencies keep an eye on national security; local health departments keep tabs on nursing homes and restaurants; border agencies track contraband cigarettes, drugs, and many other commodities at ports of entry; the Coast Guard and the defence department document search-and-rescue operations; aviation authorities regulate airlines and certify aircraft; and the assessment bureau estimates the value of properties, so property taxes can be charged.

The list of activities that governments at different levels conduct, or oversee, is long, and a lot of the time, the resulting flood of information is kept in databases.

Governments also keep track of their own activities, how they spend money, and on what, grants to community organizations, property purchases, hiring and firing of public sector workers, and on and on it goes. Again, some of this data eventually makes its way to open-data sites, but more sensitive information, (perhaps requiring more privacy protections) or technically challenging information isn't easily available, and may never be. This means that you as a data journalist have to know how and where data may be kept, and have the necessary skills to work with public authorities to obtain access.

We advocate something we have come to call the **AND principle**, as a way of guiding our interactions with public agencies. AND stands for Ask, Negotiate, Demand.[1] First, you ask for the data you want; sometimes that's all it takes. If that fails, you negotiate, enter into a process of give-and-take, to persuade the agency to allow you to have it. Finally, if those avenues fail, you demand, by making a formal request under the appropriate open-records law. The AND principle is all about taking the easiest road possible, and only getting into the tough sledding if you have to. This is important because once you do resort to the formal, legal approach, it can become complicated and time-consuming. In this chapter we'll provide some tips on how to conduct yourself at each stage of the AND process, in hopes of getting data more quickly with less hassle.

Informing Yourself

The first step you need to take, before you approach a public official in any way, is to know as much as possible about the data you want to obtain. By doing the necessary homework, you can avoid directionless fishing expeditions that grind too many data quests to a halt.

Fortunately, public agencies tend to leave a lot of clues about the data they hold; you just have to look for them.

Perusing a government department's website can produce many leads. For instance, departmental annual reports will frequently contain references to databases or include tables containing summary data that obviously comes from larger datasets. For example, the Judge Advocate General (the legal advisor to the Canadian Department of National Defence) produces annual reports that summarize the occurrences of offences such as drug trafficking and sexual assault for which military personnel have been acquitted, charged, or convicted.

Similarly, municipal councils publish summaries of contracts and purchasing, most assuredly sourced from databases tracking these activities.

More obscure records such as official government gazettes can also be good places to look. They often contain notices of such things as name changes and corporation filings, information that is probably mirrored in a departmental database. Discovering how the department or agency exercises its legal authority can yield many insights. Checking the statutes and regulations, or municipal ordinances that apply to a sector, may reveal what information a government body is obliged to collect. Think of the discovery process this way: any time an institution performs a repetitive activity, it is probably tracked in a database. Those activities may include safety and health inspections, issuing of grants, levying of fines or penalties, receiving public complaints, and tracking campaign finances. A call to an agency official can help you understand how and where data is kept.

Another clue to the existence of a database is an online search tool. We discuss in Chapter 9 how to write computer programs to scrape online information, but for very large datasets, scraping may not be practical. Searchable databases normally name the data system, and give you a pretty good idea of the types of fields contained in the dataset. Do a trial search, and see what comes back.

Online listings of records holdings, often required under freedom-of-information laws, can be quite specific in their descriptions of data systems. Another place to look is online listings of completed open-records requests. If a dataset has been released before, you may be able to simply ask for it. Long before you approach an agency with a specific request, ask if it has ever done an inventory of its databases. You might be able to get a copy.

Open-data portals themselves can also be valuable in this regard; sometimes they include **summary statistics** that come from databases; other times, the open-data version of a database may not contain all of the fields, for a variety of reasons, but its very existence gives you clues about what else might be kept.

An old trick of computer-assisted-reporting veterans is to find a copy of the form used to gather information for a database. For databases that track regulatory activities, you may be able to get a copy from an organization or person who has to fill out the form. Being aware of what columns of data are kept in the dataset, and what they contain, can be extremely useful because if you are in a jurisdiction with strong privacy laws, you may decide to ask that fields containing personal information such as names and addresses be left out of the copy you obtain.

Other sources of intelligence about datasets include reports of auditors general, officers of Parliament, legislatures or Congress, and academic papers.

Another trick is to conduct a Google search for terms such as "database" or "information systems," or using the "site:" **operator** to limit a Google or Bing search to the web pages of the agency you are researching. For example, the search "database site:faa.gov" would look for references to databases on the Federal Aviation Administration website. Similarly, search using the "filetype:" operator to look for file types often used to store data, such as

.xls, .xlsx, .csv, .mdb, and so on, on a specific government website. Combine these more generic search terms with keywords related to a specific area of interest, and you may be surprised by what you find, perhaps databases to download, or excerpts from larger datasets that you can then ask for.

Don't forget human sources: they can be especially valuable in pointing you in the right direction. Interest and advocacy groups such as Greenpeace often research their sector deeply, and know a surprising amount about a government agency's information holdings, including data systems. They may have even requested the data themselves, and if you are lucky, have a copy of it.

Once you zero in on data of potential interest, you should try to find out as much about it as you can. Run Google searches to see what has been written about the database and the system that runs it. Find out who sold the system to the government, and search on that firm's website. Government agencies often buy off-the-shelf systems that have known capabilities that you can research. If you don't know who the vendor is, you can often find clues by looking at tenders and contract listings online; governments are often quite specific about the capabilities they seek in data systems. Following up with contract data to see who won a tender can point you toward the resources you need. As well, when governments purchase data systems, they're often mentioned in news stories, or in technical publications that cover the computer business.

Having some sense of the size of a dataset is also useful. For example, if you want the property assessment database kept by your city or county government, you know it will have from a few thousand to a million or more **records**, depending on the size of the municipality. Not only will this question be important technically in terms of choosing the appropriate software for analysis, but it will help you know if this is a dataset that could be emailed, or whether a thumb drive or other high-capacity storage device will be required. Typically, this is a real concern for the government bureaucrats responsible for providing the data, because larger databases may require more effort on their part to make you a copy.

Find out if a code book accompanies the database. I don't think we have explained it. Databases frequently use codes and identification numbers in place of plain-language entries. Without a code book, sometimes called a ReadMe file, or look-up tables that come with the database, such codes would be meaningless.[2] Also, find out how the database is structured. For example, is the data kept in a flat file, or are there multiple tables? Relational databases split it up in several tables you have to knit together using key fields, a topic we will discuss in Chapter 5.

Find out how frequently the database is updated: datasets can become stale in a hurry, especially if the negotiations have taken months to complete.

This means that by the time you get the data, months may have passed. So it is important to know how frequently officials update the database. If it is only once a year or four times a year, then you're in luck. If it is weekly, then you will be forced to update the dataset and run new queries shortly before publishing.

Your goal is to find out as much about the data and the system that it runs on before you ask for it. Officials, and especially government information technology officials, are skeptical of journalists and other members of the public, and you can gain a leg up by showing that you know something about what you are seeking. It's especially important to try to learn the name of the dataset you are seeking. Being able to name something explicitly shows you did your homework, makes it easier for officials to locate, and, perhaps more importantly, makes it even harder to deny the data exists.

Asking

Once you've learned as much as you can about the data, and the system on which it runs, you'll be in the best position to ask for it.

The first consideration is whom to ask. If you're a beat reporter, you may have good contacts. If you are a general assignment reporter, or unfamiliar with the subject matter in question, you'll have to dig up the right contact person.

A good early step can be to see if you can talk to the keepers of the data. If you have a way of using an off-the-record session to pick the brain of the database administrator, the input clerk, or the end-user, then solicit that individual's advice on the contents, how the material is gathered, what sections are the most sensitive, what fields are messy, and what a reporter has done with it or might do with it. You will then be empowered when you make your official request.[3]

In modern organizations, however, you may be forced to deal with the media or public-relations staff, which can be challenging because these people often have little knowledge of data systems and may even look askance at a request to obtain one. The job of many of these individuals is to control the flow of information, not willingly hand over material that could be used to put the agency in a negative light. So a conversation with the communications officer should simply be the first step in the search for someone more knowledgeable about the data. Although the more-knowledgeable official may ultimately need the official green light from the communications officer, he or she would at least be able to answer your questions produced by all the homework you have just completed.

The sooner you can connect with someone who actually runs the system or works with the data, the sooner you can put all of the knowledge you gained in your preparations to work.

When it finally comes to pitching your request, there are some basic things you should bring to the table. As mentioned, one of these is knowing the name of the system. Equally important is knowing what you want from the dataset: which fields, and if there are fields you can simply do without. With this kind of knowledge you can massage your request to make it as specific as possible. A well-focused request has far more likelihood of success than one that simply asks for a copy of the entire database. Here are some important things to include:

The format you would like. This may be dictated by the format in which the data is held (another reason to do your homework), but if the dataset is kept on a large system, it will have to be extracted or exported. Make sure you ask that it be given to you in a machine-readable format such as comma-delimited text or an Excel file. Specify that you don't want an image file or PDF file. These formats are popular for releasing information to the public because they have predictable formatting and are seen as more secure, but such files require the use of error-prone conversion techniques before they can be used in a database application.

The time period you would like. Begin with asking for a dataset that stretches back at least three to five years from the date of asking—or even farther if possible. This will give you enough data to spot trends and patterns. Depending on what is being tracked in the database, a single year of data could be misleading. This is why police forces combine crime data into multi-year groupings, which tend to eliminate spikes caused by random variation or special or unusual events. There is little difference technically between exporting 5 years' or 20 years' worth of data, though you may run into resistance for other reasons, if you ask for too much.

If you can, some sense of why you want the records. You don't have to give away the store, but something more than an opaque request can open doors. While it's true officials don't have a right to ask, they will perceive a difference between releasing documents and datasets. The former contains known and limited information. The latter are rich repositories of information that can be analyzed in ways beyond the institution's imagination and perhaps even your own. It is this seemingly unlimited potential that can create fears among officials about how you will use the data. To ease these fears, it does not hurt to explain—in general terms—why you want it. When asking for data, it's generally a good idea to avoid using the term "manipulate," as it carries a negative connotation; a phrase such as "analyze the data" is better and an accurate reflection of what you actually want to do. As Ziva Branstetter explains in his tip sheet for Investigative Reporters and Editors, "in electronic news-gathering, the reporter rarely has the upper hand. It helps to be able to describe goals that are a little more public spirited than a fishing expedition."[4]

As well, be prepared to put your request in writing: not a formal open-records request, but something that the person you are asking can take up the chain of command.

If all goes well, a well-crafted and enunciated request will result in speedy release of the data. If that works, you can start thinking about how you will analyze (there's that helpful term again) the data. Unfortunately, there are many instances where you will need to move to the second part of AND, negotiation.

Negotiating for Data

Think of negotiation as the follow-up to the initial ask. If you did your homework well, you should be in a good position to move to this phase.

The first rule of negotiating is to be polite. The approach you take and the attitude you convey could be the difference between success and being forced to move to the demand stage of AND. Your mindset and determination may be that of a tenacious watchdog, but your approach and manner must be anything but. Being courteous and polite doesn't mean dialing back your determination. It just means according officials with whom you're negotiating the same respect that you would expect them to give you. Once the negotiations progress, you want to convey the message that you are a force to be reckoned with: that is, someone who has done the legwork necessary to extract data from a potentially reluctant partner.

A key to successful negotiation is to know your legal rights. Research not only the provisions of the applicable open-records laws (you may need to cite these even during an informal process), but also any other statutes, regulations, rules, or policies that apply to access the records you want. So as not to show all your cards, you don't necessarily need to wear this knowledge on your sleeve, but it is important in case officials say you aren't entitled to something that you very obviously are.

Be prepared to compromise. This is as true in negotiating for data as it is in buying a car. In the showroom, you usually have a top line, a price you won't go over, and the dealership has a bottom line, a price it won't go below. The key to a successful compromise is finding middle ground. The same goes with data. The agency may well have certain data fields it simply isn't willing to give up voluntarily, and you may have certain fields you absolutely need. You have to figure out what is expendable, and what is not. In a jurisdiction with robust privacy laws, you may well start the negotiations knowing you will have to give up certain fields that could contain private information. You could also be ready to explore what Bob Warner calls a "computer-driven solution." He suggests that in a dispute over addresses, "you could design a simple program to change to '00' the last two digits of each number it encounters in an address field. This would generally allow you to identify blocks, but not specific homes."[5]

You also need to be ready for the kinds of standard excuses for withholding data. Here are some, with useful responses:

It will take too many hours to write a program that exports the data you want. Exporting data is a relatively simple process, or at least it should be. It often involves writing the same kind of straightforward SQL queries you will learn about in Chapter 5. Some agencies do struggle to modernize their information technology systems. Budget cutbacks can delay or compromise modernization. However, this is not your problem. You should not be on the hook for the agency's information technology shortcomings. Just as importantly, most of the time this is an argument that is predicated on you not knowing much about computer and data systems. If an agency has that much trouble extracting data, it's perfectly reasonable to ask why the system was purchased in the first place. The explanation may even produce a story.

It will cost hundreds of dollars in staff time to write a program to export the data you want. Challenge this argument. For instance, Transport Canada initially slapped the *Hamilton Spectator* with a fee of several thousand dollars for the release of a copy of its Civil Aviation Daily Occurrence Reporting System (CADORS) air safety database. The fee was based on a provision in the Access to Information Regulations what allows for a fee of $15 per minute of **central processing unit** (CPU) time. The provision dated from the Access to Information Act's passage in the 1980s when processor time could still be a valuable resource. (Despite calls for reform, the act has not been subject to much substantial change since it took effect on Canada Day in 1983.) However, with the arrival of personal computers on nearly every desktop, things have changed. The *Spectator* pointed out that the Treasury Board does not allow for more than the actual costs to be charged. Transport's bill disappeared.[6] CADORS is now available online.

If we give it to you, you'll change the information. Politely explain that a database is no different from any other record—such as a document—that journalists obtain. Explain that a journalist, whose main asset is his or her credibility, is likely the last person who would then alter it maliciously.

If we give it to you, we'll have to give it to everyone else. That would be true if you were making a formal open-records request, but it's not so in an informal request. In fact, the agency may have more control over who gets the information if it keeps it informal than if it pushes you to go the formal route. It can't hurt to point this out.

If we give it to you, you'll be able to undo any redactions and unearth personal or sensitive information. This has actually happened, so don't scoff at the idea. One Canadian newspaper reporter, who shall go nameless, was once given a disk containing an Excel sheet that had been "redacted" by using the hide function to conceal a column. As anyone who knows Excel would tell you, hide is exactly as it sounds, and is not the same as delete. If an official makes this claim, it gives you an opportunity to educate your negotiation partner. Explain that if information is properly deleted, and the file exported out to a text format after the severing has been done, the redacted information simply won't be in the file. Some Canadian government organizations have argued they must release data in PDF-image formats in order to use special freedom-of-information processing software that performs redactions. In this case, you are dealing with a policy and not a technical hurdle: you will have to persuade them to alter the policy in the name of openness. Remember, the "open by default" principle we learned about in the previous chapter.

We can only give you 1 year's worth of data because anything more would take too much time. As noted earlier, there is little difference between exporting 1 year's worth of data and 5 or 20 years' worth. Refuse to accept the excuse of poor record management, which is a problem many departments and agencies experience. You should not be penalized for this through excessive fees or refusals.

Proprietary software. Bureaucrats may refuse to release data, arguing that the software is **proprietary**; in other words, it is licensed and cannot be shared. Well, you are not asking for the agency's software, only the data it stores. Any database program has the ability to export extracts. If the agency says it would take several hours, gently ask again why officials bought the system, or point out that it's difficult to believe that a cabinet minister would be told that she had to wait several hours—or days—for information that she needs for that day's legislative session or news conference.

Armed with these tips, you may well be successful in persuading an agency to release a dataset without being forced to go through the formal process. If so, go celebrate, and ask if you can have a sample of the data so you can start exploring the file structure. If not, you may have to move to the third part of AND, demand.

Demanding

We use the term "demand" because it can be rolled into an easily remembered acronym, but also because it accurately reflects what is happening when you move to using a formal open-records process. You are now making what is a legal demand for information, one that the agency is obligated to fulfill, within the constraints of the particular open-records laws.

There are dozens of open-records laws in the world, including in leading Western countries such as the United Kingdom, Canada, and the United States. The first was actually in Sweden. These laws are similar in that they give you a legal right to obtain records, and as a result, they substantially shift the balance of power between requesters and governments. Especially in countries such as the United Kingdom and Canada, which did not traditionally have openness as a trait of government, they represent a sea change in thinking. Not surprisingly, government bureaucrats are not always as open to releasing records as the laws suggest they should be.

In Canada, the Newspapers Canada's freedom-of-information audit, led by one of the authors of this book, has shown repeatedly that governments, when faced with requests for data, are not always as open to its release as their open-data policies suggest they might be.[7] So know that when you resort to the formal records laws, especially if officials are reluctant to release the data (and you will know this because negotiations were not successful), it may be a challenging process. Don't be lazy and skip the A and N parts of AND and go straight to D. It might seem easier, but this is an illusion; the formal process is almost always more complicated.

If you do have to go this route, the first thing you need to do is get to know the law, and most importantly, what it says about the release of electronic records, particularly whether computerized data is considered to be a record under the law, under what circumstances officials must produce an extract for you, what kind of fees they can charge you, and the provisions to potentially waive those fees.

In the United States, the Electronic Freedom of Information Act Amendments of 1996 redefined the term "records" to include those maintained in computerized "electronic" formats.[8] Canadian acts have tended to include electronic records in the definition of a record. The federal act defines a record as "any documentary material, regardless of medium or form,"[9] while the act in Ontario, is even more explicit, stating that a record is

> any record of information however recorded, whether in printed form, on film, by electronic means or otherwise, and includes . . . any record of information however recorded, whether in printed form, on film, by electronic means or otherwise, and includes, a machine readable record . . .[10]

Similar provisions exist in Canadian provincial and territorial acts, while in the United States there are a variety of definitions in different state open-records laws. In the United Kingdom, the act provides a right to information rather than records, but the right to obtain data has been reinforced. So it's a good idea to learn the law of the jurisdiction that possesses the data you're after.

Knowing about these provisions is important because some officials will argue that computerized records do not constitute records. Other provisions exist in some acts that allow for the creation of records from machine-readable (computerized) records and give officials the right to refuse to create such a record if it's impracticable. But in fact, a database is in itself a record, and no new record needs to be produced. Exporting the data from a computer to a CSV or other file is simply making a copy of that data, not creating a new record, in our view.

Understanding the basis on which fees may be charged is also important, because if you start requesting datasets, you may eventually be presented with an estimate of fees. (In Canada, at the federal level, the government decided to stop collecting processing fees for requests in 2016). You need to know the basis on which fees can actually be charged so you can properly interrogate any estimate, and challenge it if necessary. We'll discuss that more later in the chapter.

Making an Effective Request for Data

As you already did your homework before making your first informal data request, and you've been through a round of negotiation, you have a strong understanding of the data you want, the system it's kept in, and how it can be provided. This research will help you make an effective records request.

A good request should be precise, should specify the format in which you would like to obtain the data, and should refer to the data in as specific terms as possible. If there are certain fields that you would like to obtain, indicate these in the request wording. If you want to limit the data you receive to a particular date range, put that into the request as well, but avoid limiting your options for analysis by choosing too narrow a date range.

There are two schools of thought about information that might be exempted, such as fields that would violate personal privacy. One school of thought suggests saying explicitly in your request that you are not interested in such information, and to exclude it. Another way of putting it is to ask for "anonymized" data; that is, data such as dates, times, and descriptions while leaving out information that could identify individuals. The other school of thought is to ask for all the fields you want, and then allow officials to apply the privacy exemption if they feel it applies.

Both approaches have merits. Asking to take anything that contains private information out of the scope of the request may make the process go more quickly and smoothly. However putting in such a provision means that you give up rights under the act. Once an official determines that a particular field might violate personal privacy, you have given that official permission to take it out of scope. If you disagree, and appeal, you may find that your decision to give that discretion to the official means that you are out of luck. On the other hand, by asking for the information and putting the onus on the official to remove it, you leave open the possibility of an appeal to the body that handles complaints or appeals under the particular open-records law.

Another important thing to do is to ask for a waiver of any fees that might apply, although fee-waiver provisions vary by province, state, and country. Again, this is an important reason to know your laws.

Finally, make sure you include your contact information, including your address.

Here is an example of how your request might read:

> I would like access to the data in the FileMaestro building standards database for the period 1 January 2012 to 31 December 2016, including but not limited to the inspection ID, civic number, street name, city, postal code, inspection date, inspection type, inspection outcome, charges, court outcome, fine, and inspector name fields. Please provide the data in a machine-readable electronic format, preferably a delimited text file or Microsoft Excel .xlsx format file. Please contact me at myname@emaildomain.com or at 555-555-5555 if you have any questions.

Some open-records laws may require that you file your request using a form. For others you may be able to simply use a letter. More and more agencies are accepting requests via the web. If you do file using the web, make sure you keep the receipt the web application provides as proof that you filed the request.

After You Make the Request

After you make the request, you may find yourself back negotiating. Officials will often contact you and suggest you modify or narrow what you are asking for. This provides an opening to once again negotiate to get what you need. For example, if officials say that there might be individuals' names in a free-text field and that to go through the data to remove the names could end up producing large fees, you may decide to allow that field to be removed.

If you are still waiting for an acknowledgement and the normal initial response period has passed, contact the agency to ensure your request was received and is being processed. Some requesters make a practice of following up with the agency a few days after the request is filed to ensure it has been received and to find out if there are any questions. You can also specify in your letter that you want to be contacted to review the request's wording before it is sent to the agency bureaucrats who will actually retrieve the data. Such a provision obliges the officer handling your request to make contact. This can also help build rapport with that official, who is, after all, human.

In jurisdictions that have them, fees are one of the most likely issues to crop up after you file your request. In fact, you may be asked to pay a lot of money, on the basis that much effort will be required to extract the information. As discussed earlier in the chapter, these claims can be ill-founded, and officials may try to take advantage of a perceived naiveté or lack of knowledge about things technical. In some cases, a simple conversation may be enough to knock such fees down. If you do receive a large fee estimate, the first step is to contact the official handling your file to understand further the basis for the estimate. But as always with requests, be wary of offers to lower fees by removing certain elements. Be sure you can do without them.

Persistence is the key, even if it means that your data request will occur in stages. Remember, officials may be motivated by the hope that if they delay enough, you will give up access to potentially damaging information. So keep going.

If a fee is large, it is important to ask officials to give a breakdown of the costs, including each technical task and how long it will take. Querying a database to extract certain fields, for example, should be straightforward. If you see entries for hours of time to develop and run queries, it is reasonable to ask why this task would take so long. The same goes for charges for "run time" for computers. Today's computers are cheap to run; such charges may not be justifiable. The key point is that you need to understand the basis for fees, so you can test the logic behind them, and test the claimed basis for the fees against what is allowable in the legislation and regulations. Do not assume that because a public official proposed a fee that he or she has a legal basis for doing so.

The Answer

Typically, open-records laws provide about 30 days to give you an answer, extend the time limit, or issue a fee estimate. In some jurisdictions, such as at the federal level in Canada, it may take much longer than 30 days, but you will eventually get a formal response. Sometimes, the answer will be no, or you will be unable to obtain fields in the data that you need for your planned analysis.

At this point, you will have the option to appeal. In Canada, that usually means a complaint or appeal to a specialized body that will take a second look at the public body's decision, and depending on the jurisdiction, either make a recommendation, or issue a binding ruling that the organization must follow. All of the research you did earlier, plus your insistence that the public body document to you the reasoning for its decisions, will help you make your case.

In the United States, fighting a decision can mean a trip to court, which is also the follow-up in Canada at the federal level, and in certain provinces, where the appeal body is only able to make recommendations. Such appeal processes can be long and legalistic, which is another reason to try to avoid the formal legal process in the first place.

Study Questions and Exercises

1. Using the tips in this chapter, go find a database and document it as best as you can. What is the system called? What kind of data is stored and for what purpose? What is the system used for, and what, if any, access already exists?
2. Identify a dataset you would like to obtain. Gather information on it as discussed in this chapter, then go ask for it. Follow through the processes discussed in this chapter, and file an open-records request if need be.
3. Conduct research to determine which advocacy groups in areas such as the environment, health, and public safety routinely request data. Once you've made the connection and built up a trust, ask for a slice of the data to study the content and decide how it can be used.

Notes

1. Fred Vallance-Jones and David McKie, *Computer Assisted Reporting: A Comprehensive Primer* (Toronto: Oxford University Press, 2008), 253.
2. Ibid., 252.

3. Bob Warner, *NICAR Tipsheet: Negotiating for Data with Reluctant Local Officials* (Boston: NICAR, 1999).

4. Quoted in Vallance-Jones and McKie, *Computer Assisted Reporting*, 250.

5. Warner, *NICAR Tipsheet: Negotiating for Data with Reluctant Local Officials*.

6. Vallance-Jones and McKie, *Computer Assisted Reporting*, 252.

7. Vallance-Jones and Emily Kitagawa, *National Freedom of Information Audit 2015* (Toronto: Newspapers Canada, 2015), 4, http://newspaperscanada.ca/sites/default/files/FOI-2015-FINAL.pdf.

8. Electronic Freedom of Information Act (United States), Amendments of 1996, http://www.gpo.gov/fdsys/pkg/PLAW-104publ231/pdf/PLAW-104publ231.pdf, 3.

9. Access to Information Act (Canada), 1985, http://laws-lois.justice.gc.ca/eng/acts/a-1/FullText.html.

10. Freedom of Information and Protection of Privacy Act (Ontario), 1990, http://www.ontario.ca/laws/statute/90f31.

Part II
Analyzing Data

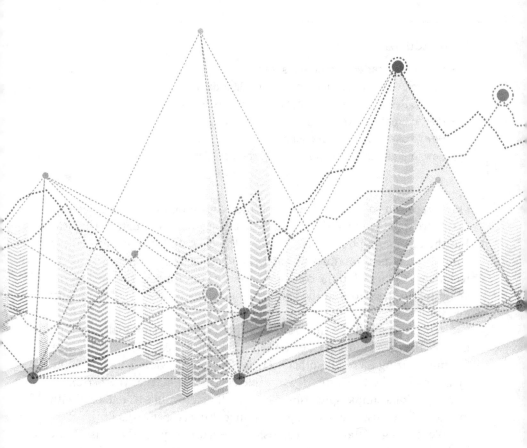

Chapter 4

Spreadsheets: The Basic Tool

What You Will Learn:

- How to get started in a spreadsheet
- How to use a spreadsheet to sort and filter data
- How to use formulas and functions to find patterns
- How to create a pivot table
- How to use advanced functions
- How to organize your material using chronologies

Our discussion so far has focused on the acquisition of data, and there's a reason we spent so much time on it; without data there is no data journalism. But there comes a point when you have the data, and you've cleaned it to eliminate misspellings, missing entries, and other inconsistencies using the techniques discussed in the companion website. It's time for the main event, analyzing the data to find the patterns and trends that can lead to insights and stories.

When journalists speak of analysis there are two main goals. The first is to see the big picture, the 30,000-foot view, so to speak. You get this view by summarizing data. The other view is the close-up view, which is found by narrowing the focus to a few notable cases. This is true whether one is working with a simple spreadsheet in a small dataset, an SQL database with millions of records, or a mapping program looking at spatial data.

We're going to start with spreadsheets because they are the Swiss Army knife of data journalism; pretty good at doing a lot of things, but with important shortcomings such as limitations on file sizes, and being (mostly) restricted to working with one data table at a time. Like the famous utility knives, they have tools that extend their capabilities beyond what you might expect, and if your main need is to organize and isolate information, do mathematical calculations on relatively small sets of data, or prepare data for online mapping or visualization, you may never need to look at the tools we introduce later in the book.

Spreadsheet programs, examples of which include Microsoft Excel, OpenOffice, LibreOffice, and Google Sheets, can be used to open, sort, filter, organize, summarize, and tidy data. They are particularly adept at doing math, and in that regard are superior to the other applications we discuss in this book. They can even be used to do more advanced statistical analysis, though this is beyond the scope of this book. Spreadsheets are an excellent training ground for the more complex tools we introduce later because they familiarize you with working with tabular data and doing simple analysis.

So What Exactly Is a Spreadsheet?

Conceptually a spreadsheet is based on the accountant's spreadsheet, a large sheet of paper on which calculations can be spread out across a grid of rows and columns. But unlike the paper spreadsheet, the electronic version can do calculations dynamically, so that as the numbers change, the calculations based on them can update automatically.

Today's spreadsheets are endowed with data-manipulation features unheard of in the first of their kind, called VisiCalc. The program was conceived by Harvard University business student Dan Bricklin, who imagined the idea while daydreaming in a lecture hall.

> I tried prototyping the product's display screen in [the programming language] Basic on a video terminal connected to the Business School's timesharing system in the spring of 1978 . . . That's when the desire for general placement of numbers, formula results, and text turned into rows and columns to give them human-friendly names. It also was when I decided upon the status line for displaying the formula and formatting behind the values being displayed.[1]

Bricklin teamed up with his friend Bob Frankston and Harvard MBA grad Dan Fylstra,[2] and VisiCalc became a nearly overnight success, selling up to a million copies in six years and becoming the first "killer app." You may have never heard of VisiCalc because innovative competitors overtook it, first Lotus Development Corporation's Lotus 1-2-3, and later, Microsoft's Excel. The modern spreadsheet was born, and as they say, the rest is history. Journalists have been an important part of that story.

Fundamentals of Spreadsheets

At their most basic, spreadsheet programs are designed to be calculators. This is evidenced in their design, a grid of rows and columns set up in such a way that each individual **cell** (the little rectangle formed by the intersection of a row and a column) can be populated with its own piece of data and individually referenced in mathematical or other formulas. Each column is labelled with a letter starting at A for the leftmost column and continuing rightward through to Z, then moving to AA through to AZ, BA to BZ, and so on, until the maximum number of columns is reached. The rows are numbered sequentially downward, until the maximum number of rows is reached. In the latest versions of Excel, the program can accommodate 16,384 columns, and 1,048,576 rows, meaning there are 17,179,869,184 individually addressable cells . . . otherwise known as a heck of a lot.[3] Here, you can see the top left corner of one sheet:

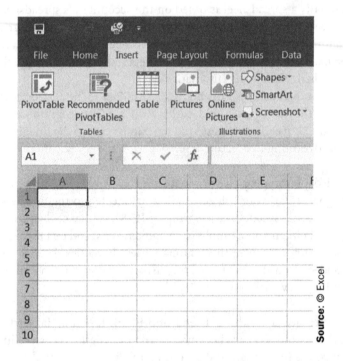

Source: © Excel

A spreadsheet program can accommodate more than one of these sheets; in fact you can have as many **worksheets** as you like in one Excel **workbook**, limited only by your computer's memory.[4] Be aware, however, that workbooks can be only so large before they slow your computer to molasses.

Tutorials Included with the Companion Website

You will find these tutorials on the OUP Companion Website(www.oupcanada .com/Vallance-Jones):

- Getting Data into Your Spreadsheet
- Sorting and Filtering Your Data
- Calculating Rates and Percentages in a Spreadsheet
- Specialized Functions in Excel
- How to Use Pivot Tables
- Doing Cool Stuff with Paste Special
- Creating and Using an Excel Chronology

The row, column, and cell layout makes a spreadsheet versatile. For example, it can be used to create a business's balance sheet, with formulas to add up annual revenue and expenditure figures. Just as easily, it can hold row-and-column data of the type we discussed in the last chapter, with fixed column headers, and one row for each line of data.

How Journalists Use Spreadsheets

Spreadsheets can help journalists find answers to some of the most important questions in journalism: who, what, when, how much, and, sometimes, where. Here are some typical questions spreadsheets might help you answer:

- Which public servant earned the highest salary in a given year?
- What age group contains the highest number of contributors to tax-sheltered savings accounts?
- How much money did the government spend on grants to a particular group?
- What time of year do people make the largest number of noise complaints?
- Which restaurant received the largest number of inspections?
- Which politician received the largest value of donations?

But how? Let's start diving in to find out.

Getting Data into a Spreadsheet

There are a number of ways you can get the data you want to analyze into a spreadsheet program. The most straightforward way is to simply type it in. Type the column headers in cells across the top and any row headers along the left, and start adding your information by hand. Click in any cell, and start typing. To advance to the cell to the right, hit the tab key. To advance downward, click the enter key. It's quick and easy so long as there isn't too much data to enter.

Unlike the database programs, which we will discuss in Chapter 5, spreadsheets are extremely forgiving in terms of the type of data that can be entered. Each cell in a spreadsheet can contain anything the user wishes, be that a formula, a number, a word, or a 5,000-word essay. (Technically, an Excel cell can hold up to about 32,000 characters and display around 1,000.) The program will adjust its **data types** and formatting based on what is entered, and will usually get it right. Underneath the hood, the program stores one of four data types: number, text, logical, or error. Here is what makes each unique:

- The **numeric type** stores numbers of any kind, including dates. All numbers are stored with decimal places.
- The **string or text type** stores any character, including numerals to be treated as text (you can't do math on numerals treated as text). While a number stored as text looks the same to human eyes as a number stored as a number, they are very different things to the computer.
- The logical type can be either TRUE or FALSE.
- The error type contains errors, which we discuss later in the chapter.[5]

Excel also applies formatting to the contents of cells. The default format for any cell is called General; it can handle text or numbers and will automatically adjust itself depending on the type of data entered. Numbers will show as many decimal places as space in a cell allows. Other formats include the number format, that shows the number of decimal places the user directs, percentages, dates, and currency. Excel will automatically apply whatever type and format it guesses the user wants. If you type in "$100," it will store

If you ever want to know what type of data is in a cell, type the formula =TYPE(cell-reference) into an empty cell on your sheet. You'll get back a number representing the type, with 1 for number, 2 for text, 4 for logical, and 16 for error.[6] We'll talk more about formulas and functions later in this chapter.

it as a number data type and then apply the currency format. If you type in some text, it will store the data as text. Sometimes things can get a little tricky with numbers stored as text. If you want to enter a number as a text data type, type in an apostrophe before the number. Some ID numbers have leading zeros, for example, and if you type them in without the apostrophe Excel will assume they are numbers and strip off the "unnecessary" leading zeros.

Sometimes you have the reverse problem, and will end up with numerals you want to be numbers, but are being treated as text. This can sometimes happen when tables of data are pasted in from the web, as discussed below, and the program "misinterprets" what kind of data is intended. This can require some creative corrective action. You can sometimes avoid the problem by pre-formatting the columns to the correct formats before pasting the data from the web. We have created a tutorial on cleaning up data to make it useable; you can find it on the companion website.

Spreadsheets can also import data that already exists, and depending on the program you use, a great many data formats can be accommodated, such as delimited text, HTML, XML files that have simple data structures, and the various proprietary spreadsheet formats of different manufacturers. Opening data in a spreadsheet program is just like opening a word-processed document. For example, if you open a delimited text file, such as a CSV file, Excel will recognize it as such, and open it in a new workbook, as with this table of tenders.

	A	B	C	D	E	F	G
1	Bid Number	Bid Type	Bid Description	Award Date	Vendor Name	Bid Amount	Awarded
2	PS20110699	Request For Proposal	PROFESSIONAL SERVICES - OWNER'S ENGINEER FOR THE POWELL STREET GRADE SEPARATION PROJECT	01-11-2012	MMM Group Ltd	$213,506.00	YES
3	PS20110445	Invitation To Tender	SUPPLY AND DELIVERY OF ICE RESURFACERS	01-13-2012	Crocker Equipment Co. Ltd	$400,250.00	YES
4	PS20110445	Invitation To Tender	SUPPLY AND DELIVERY OF ICE RESURFACERS	01-13-2012	Vimar Equipment Ltd	$412,447.00	No
5	PS20110558	Request For Proposal	DESIGN/BUILD OF REPIPING SYSTEMS AT 312 MAIN STREET	01-19-2012	Arete Mechanical Ltd.	$226,875.00	YES
6	PS20110602	Invitation To Tender	GENERAL CONTRACTORS FOR TENANT IMPROVEMENTS AT 312 MAIN STREET	01-20-2012	Ledcor Special Projects	$1,221,500.00	YES
7	PS20110602	Invitation To Tender	GENERAL CONTRACTORS FOR TENANT IMPROVEMENTS AT 312 MAIN STREET	01-20-2012	PCL Constructors Westcoast Inc	$1,360,200.00	No
8	PS20110602	Invitation To Tender	GENERAL CONTRACTORS FOR TENANT IMPROVEMENTS AT 312 MAIN STREET	01-20-2012	Graham Construction &	$1,473,731.00	No
9	PS20110634	Request For Proposal	SUPPLY OF E-LEARN SERVICES FOR MICROSOFT 2010 UPGRADE	01-24-2012	SkillSoft, Canada Ltd.	$19,374.11	YES
10	PS20110435	Request For Quote	SUPPLY AND DELIVERY OF BULK CEMENT AND FLY ASH	01-30-2012	Lafarge North America - Cement	$729,000.00	YES
11	PS20110448	Request For Proposal	CONSULTING SERVICES FOR VANCOUVER CIVIC THEATRES BUSINESS REVIEW AND STRATEGIC PLAN	01-31-2012	Kathleen Speakman & Associates	$96,758.00	YES

Once you have opened the file, you can then either continue working with the original file, or follow the much better practice of saving the file to the Excel format (there are actually two formats, the **xls** format that was used by earlier versions, and the newer **xlsx** format). In fact, a good tip is to always make a copy of any file you open, so if you make a mistake, you don't irreparably damage the original. Unlike in the database programs we discuss in the next chapter, in spreadsheets you work with the actual file, and any changes you make change the file itself, just as when you work in a word processor.

In Excel, you also have an option of using the **text import wizard**, which allows you to specify the delimiter and the data formats.

It is also possible to copy and paste data from tables in web pages directly into Excel and other spreadsheets. Often, you will find a table of data online and would like to apply some of the techniques we describe in this chapter, but you don't want to open the entire web page. Just highlight the part of the page you want to copy, in the same way you would select text in any other program, copy the material, put your mouse in cell A1 of the spreadsheet, and paste the data. You may have to use the "**paste special**" feature, rather than a simple paste, and select "text" as the type of material being pasted. With a bit of trial and error, you can usually get the data from the web pasted in and start doing analysis. The type of browser that you're using can matter, because some of them perform this task more seamlessly than others. So you might have to experiment.

This ability to simply copy and paste data from web pages makes it an excellent tool for quickly grabbing data or statistics and doing some "quick and dirty" analysis on deadline.

Once you have the data in your spreadsheet, it's important to ensure the data has made the transition without being corrupted or acquiring weird formats. For example, if you intend to use a column of numbers for calculations, make sure that the numbers are flush to the right side of the cells; in the normal configuration of these programs, that indicates that they are being read by the program as numbers, not as text that happens to look like numbers (which would be flush to the left). Also, if you have taken the data from the web or the data was converted from a PDF or image file, check to be sure that the content is identical to the original and that the columns have lined up properly. If not, you'll have to fix them manually, or use the more advanced techniques covered in the data-cleaning tutorial on the companion website.

Before doing anything with the imported and properly formatted table, it's a good idea to paste the URL (**Universal Resource Locator**) of the dataset's online location somewhere in your sheet, with the top left corner a good choice. You should also always work with a copy of the original data. That way if anything goes wrong—it can and does—you always have a backup.

You'll find a tutorial on "Getting Data into Your Spreadsheet" on the companion website.

Getting to Work

With their relative ease of use, their simple and intuitive table structure, and their Swiss-Army-knife versatility, it's no wonder spreadsheets are such a popular choice for basic data analysis. Depending on the spreadsheet you choose, you'll find slight differences in the user interfaces. The starkest differences are between the most recent versions of Microsoft Excel and most other spreadsheet applications, either desktop or online. Starting with Excel 2007, Microsoft introduced what it calls its "ribbon" interface, a kind of combined menu and toolbar that is supposed to make it easier to discover features. Other products, such as OpenOffice, LibreOffice, the cloud-based Google spreadsheets, and Corel's Quattro Pro use the standard menu

Microsoft Excel Menu

Source: © Excel

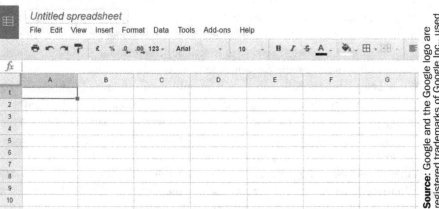

Google Spreadsheet Menu

Source: Google and the Google logo are registered trademarks of Google Inc., used with permission.

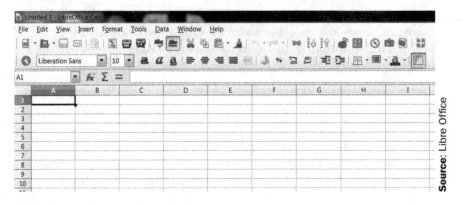

LibreOffice Menu

and toolbar interfaces you will be familiar with from traditional desktop software. In these images, you can see the ribbon interface compared with the standard menus of Google spreadsheets and LibreOffice. Note that for the desktop programs, we are showing you Windows versions but the Mac versions are similar.

All of the spreadsheet programs will show you a context-sensitive menu if you right-click (<ctrl> + click on a Mac) in the area where you are working. The options offered will differ depending on what you are doing at the time.

In Excel, OpenOffice, LibreOffice and similar progams, you can work with spreadsheets on your desktop. With Google Spreadsheets or Microsoft's Office Online you can work in the cloud. Both services allow you to work with online sheets offline, when you don't have an Internet connection. You can also download a table from the cloud, save it on your computer, and continue working on it, or conversely, you can upload a desktop version to the cloud. The advantage of working in the cloud is that several people can add data to a spreadsheet, which comes in handy if it is being used by many people in different locations. Be aware, however, that the cloud versions of these programs work best with small datasets. If you want to analyze hundreds or thousands of rows, you're best to work on the desktop. Throughout this chapter, we will use examples from the desktop version of Excel, but rest assured that the simple techniques shown in this chapter will work on other spreadsheet programs and in-cloud spreadsheets. We'll point out the few differences that do exist. The images shown here are from the Windows version, but you'll find things work the same way on Mac and Linux versions.

Sorting and Simple Analysis

For this example, we're using data that was obtained from the Elections BC website, which is the agency that runs elections in British Columbia. The site has a search interface that allows searches for contributions of $250 or more made to political parties, local constituency associations, leadership candidates, and so on. The database tracks contributions made from 2005 on.

We will begin with analysis that uses no math. This is not to dissuade you from using math. Indeed, the point has been made that journalists who avoid numbers are more susceptible to being spun by public figures—business people or politicians, to name a few—who may use numbers to mislead, distort, bend the truth, or outright lie.

A good first step in any data analysis is to simply "eyeball" the data. Scroll up and down and across the sheet and familiarize yourself with the columns and the data in them, considering as you go what questions you might want to ask of the data. Many researchers will keep a list as ideas occur to them.

The simplest analysis you can do in a spreadsheet is to **sort** the data based on key columns. In the contributions data from Elections BC in the image below, you might sort the amount given in what is called descending order, from largest to smallest, to see who gave the most money.

In Excel, the simplest way to sort data in this example is to place your mouse in the column in which you would like to sort, then click the appropriate icon on the "home" ribbon to sort in ascending or descending (reverse) order:

In other programs, you will usually find sorting under the Data menu. This is what a sample of the Elections BC contributions data looks like once sorted in descending order:

Source: © Excel

Here, we see the BC Patriot Party made the largest single donation recorded in the dataset. But what on earth is the BC Patriot Party? And what is the Advocational Party? Our curiosity is piqued. The $1.8-million donation dwarfs values from the more established parties of the BC NDP and BC Liberals, although the latter raised more than twice as much money that year from much smaller contributions. The answer isn't in the dataset, of course, but it has given us an intriguing question to ask.

Excel and other spreadsheets are capable of sorting by more than one column at a time. This is done by opening the sorting dialogue box, and choosing the columns on which you would like to base a sort. The sort will be based on the first column selected, then if there are duplicate values in that column, those data will be sorted by the next selected column, and so on. In the BC data for example you could sort first by party, then by the amount given to that party.

Filtering

Filtering is another first step in analyzing data, a process that allows you to show only those rows that have values you choose in columns that you specify. When filtering, the spreadsheet adds a drop-down menu to the top of each column that allows you to indicate the values by which you would like to filter. In Excel, you turn on the filter by clicking on the filter icon, which looks like a funnel.:

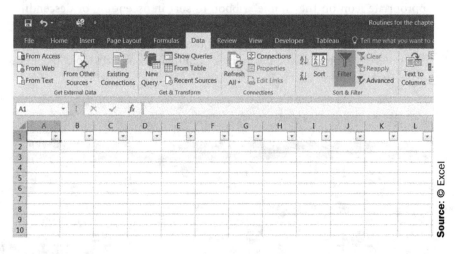

Source: © Excel

Other programs may have a similar icon, or put the filter feature under the Data menu. Here is the previous sheet with the filter turned on:

	A	B	C	D	E	F
1	AFFILIATION	DATE	AMOUNT	BOUNDARY_S(	CLA	CONTRIBUTOR_NAME
2	ADVOCATIONAL PARTY	29/12/2006	$1,838,100		6	BC PATRIOT PARTY
3	ADVOCATIONAL PARTY	04/12/2007	$1,625,483		6	BC PATRIOT PARTY
4	ADVOCATIONAL PARTY	31/12/2011	$596,553		5	BC PATRIOT PARTY
5	BC NDP	07/01/2010	$465,996		1	OLIVE FAIRBAIRN (ESTATE OF)
6	BC NDP	16/05/2005	$300,000		1	ESTATE OF EVALYN M CHENEY
7	BC NDP	16/01/2007	$279,728		1	ESTATE OF EVALYN M CHENEY
8	BC NDP	25/03/2009	$278,400		4	BC GOVERNMENT & SERVICE EMPLOYEES' UNION
9	BC NDP	24/10/2012	$250,000		4	UNITED STEELWORKERS CANADA
10	BC NDP	16/09/2010	$210,858		1	ESTATE OF RUTH M HASS
11	BC NDP	13/03/2009	$210,000		4	BC FEDERATION OF LABOUR
12	BC NDP	05/05/2005	$200,000		4	BC FEDERATION OF LABOUR
13	BC LIBERAL PARTY	24/01/2013	$200,000		2	GOLDCORP INC
14	BC LIBERAL PARTY	03/11/2010	$200,000		2	GREAT PACIFIC CAPITAL CORP
15	BC LIBERAL PARTY	08/11/2010	$200,000		2	HAYWOOD SECURITIES INC
16	BC LIBERAL PARTY	17/11/2008	$200,000		1	MILAN ILICH
17	BC LIBERAL PARTY	23/11/2012	$150,000		3	2300 KINGSWAY RESIDENCES
18	BC LIBERAL PARTY	23/11/2012	$150,000		3	2300 KINGSWAY RESIDENCES
19	BC LIBERAL PARTY	28/11/2011	$150,000		2	GOLDCORP INC
20	BC LIBERAL PARTY	08/11/2012	$150,000		1	JOHN REDEKOP

Using the filter is an excellent way to get to know your dataset. If, for instance, you wanted to know how many contributions the BC Patriot Party made, you could filter for only those entries under "CONTRIBUTOR NAME," producing this filtered result:

Canada's Global News actually did this analysis for a story, and found that the BC Patriot Party only made contributions to the Advocational Party. From that article, we learned that the BC Patriot Party is a so-called fringe party that hadn't run a candidate since 2005. Initially, the party wanted to establish a federal party that would work to change Canada "to a republic, where the Senate is filled by a merit-based lottery."

You could also filter the dataset by specifying the donation amount. For instance, if you wanted to limit the selection to donors between certain amounts, or more than a certain amount, you can do using the filter for column C. Filtering for two or more criteria is also possible.

Sorting and filtering are excellent tools to get to know your data and as we've seen they can produce story ideas on their own. If you did nothing else but sort and filter, in substantial datasets from open-data portals, you'd produce an impressive number of stories to pitch to editors and producers. However, there is so much more that spreadsheets can do when we perform some basic math. You'll find live exercises in sorting and filtering on the companion website.

Doing the Math

Spreadsheets have been likened to calculators on steroids,[7] allowing users to perform hundreds, or even thousands, of calculations simultaneously, such as figuring out percentages and percentage changes.

Every calculation in a spreadsheet begins with an "=" sign or a "+" sign (not to be confused with the "+" operator for addition). By typing this into a cell, we tell the program that what follows will be a formula for doing something to data, rather than another data entry. If you need to edit a formula later, you can do so in the formula bar at the top of the sheet, or by double-clicking in a cell that contains a formula to open it for editing.

The magic of a spreadsheet, and the reason it is so powerful, is those individually referenced cells we discussed earlier in the chapter. Rather than having to write out long formulas containing the actual numbers we want to calculate, we enter references to the cells that contain those numbers. And if we want to run the same calculation repeatedly, we can copy the formula to other cells, rather than having to type it again. If the numbers used in the calculations change, the formulas don't have to be rewritten; the program will recalculate for us automatically.

The simplest formula is one that simply uses arithmetic operators such as the "+" sign to run a calculation on a number of cells. Operators are symbols that indicate the type of math operation you want to carry out, which in our example below is addition. Once you have finished plugging in the formula, hit the "Enter" key to get the total.

Let's say that we wanted to add up the dollar amounts the BC Patriot Party donated to the Advocational Party in our current example. We can write a formula like this:

Notice that the formula appears not only in the cell where we write it, but in the formula bar at the top of the sheet. Hitting Enter causes the calculation to be done. For simple subtractions, the calculation follows the same routine, using the "-" sign as the subtraction operator.

Multiplying and dividing cells is done in much the same way. You begin the formula with the "=" sign or a "+" sign, and then enter cell references that contain the values you want, using the multiplication operator "*" to multiply two cells, and the symbol "/" to divide them. Division comes in handy for calculating percentages, which we'll look at shortly.

Functions Big and Small

It would be tedious if we always had to use simple arithmetic to calculate values in a spreadsheet. For example, imagine if you had to sum up a column of 100 numbers. Writing B2+B3+B4+B5 and on to B100 would not only take a long time, it would be error-prone. What if you missed one cell along the way? Similarly, working out an average by first manually adding up all the values, then dividing by the total number of values (which you would have to count manually), would wipe out most of the advantages spreadsheets give us. Fortunately, Excel has built-in functions that replace endless tedium with single entries.

One of the simplest functions, and most commonly used, is the SUM function. It uses this **syntax**: SUM(range of cells to be summed). Instead of writing B2+B3+B4+B5+B6+B7+B8 we can write SUM(B2:B8). The colon in between the cell references means "everything in between." If you want to skip some cells, say B5, you can write SUM(B2:B4,B6:B8).

All functions follow the same pattern: the name of the function followed by a set of brackets in which you enter whatever the function needs to do its magic. These entries within the function are called its "**arguments**." Many functions have one or two arguments. The SUM function can have up to 255.

Function Argument Types and Examples

1. No arguments. With no argument in the bracket, this function returns the current date: **=NOW()**
2. One argument. Here, the formula will produce the average of the values in the range identified by the cell references: **=AVERAGE(A1:A3)**
3. Several arguments. The following example adds up the values in between A1 and A3, and then in A6, and then in A8, and then between A14 and A16: **=SUM(A1:A3, A6,A8, A14:A16)**.[8]

Arguments can be cell references, numbers, text, or even other functions, depending on the calculation you'd like to do. The arguments are separated by commas.

If you are familiar with the function and know the correct spelling and the types of arguments it takes, you can use the function in your formula. Spreadsheets also have function builders, which allow you to use an interactive dialogue to pick the function and write in the arguments.

Spreadsheets contain far more functions than we could ever use. For the most part, journalists are interested in just a few, such as SUM, AVERAGE, MEDIAN, MIN, and MAX functions for numbers, the WEEKDAY, MONTH, and YEAR functions for working with dates, and the LEFT, RIGHT, LEN, and MID functions for working with text.

Some functions are used so commonly that Excel and other spreadsheet programs provide a tool called the AUTOSUM button. For example, click in a cell below a column of numbers, click the AUTOSUM button (symbolized by the Greek sigma character) and the program will suggest a SUM function and populate its arguments for you. You have the option to change the suggested formula before pressing Enter. In more recent versions of Excel, the AUTOSUM button can also be used for common mathematical functions such as AVERAGE.

Math and Trig Category Functions contain a wide variety of functions that perform mathematical and trigonometric calculations. Please consult the companion website for a tutorial on the use of a variety of Excel functions.

Calculating Percentages

One kind of calculation journalists perform frequently is calculating a percentage, be it a straight percentage or a percentage change. It helps the audience understand big numbers and makes it easier to compare different numbers against each other. Let's say we wanted to see which of the top-10 earners received the largest slice of the total donations in the BC contributions data we looked at earlier. The formula for calculating a percentage is to divide the subtotal by the total, or the part by the whole. Back in math class we used to also multiply the result by 100, but spreadsheets take care of that by changing the format of the result to a percentage. The first thing we would need to do with the donations data is add up all the donations to provide a total. For that, we can use the SUM function, by either writing it in manually or using the AUTOSUM button.

With a total in place, we can then write in the formula, which for the first line of data would be B2/B12, the subtotal divided by the total:

	A	B	C
1	Political Party	Amount	Percent of Total
2	BC LIBERAL PARTY	4964699.8	=B2/$B$12
3	ADVOCATIONAL PARTY	1839251.18	=B3/$B$12
4	BC NDP	1229292.51	=B4/$B$12
5	BC GREEN PARTY	87544.71	=B5/$B$12
6	BC YOUTH COALITION	18750	=B6/$B$12
7	B.C. PATRIOT PARTY	13393.15	=B7/$B$12
8	PARTY OF CITIZENS	6060.7	=B8/$B$12
9	COMMUNIST PARTY OF BC	4568	=B9/$B$12
10	WORK LESS PARTY	3919.01	=B10/$B$12
11			
12	Grand Total	8182029.17	
13			

Notice that in the formula, visible in the formula bar, the denominator is written as $B$12 rather than B12. This is because we always want to divide by cell B12 to find the percentage. The "$" sign tells Excel to make the reference to row 12 absolute, rather than relative. Relative cell references allow the source cells to change when the formula is copied down or to the side. For instance, "=A2+B2" written in cell C2 will change to "=A3+B3" if copied into cell C3. The references change exactly the same number of cells down and/ or to the right or left as the formula itself moves. This is desirable, because we want our formula to adjust itself as we copy it to a new location, but when we want part or all of the reference to remain static, or absolute, the "$" sign takes care of that. In our current example, when the formula (visible here in the formula bar) is copied down column C, the value used as the numerator from column B will shift down as the formula shifts down, but the total (B12) is always the denominator; in this way, one copied formula produces the correct result for each of the parties.

By the way, to copy a formula to a new cell, either highlight and copy the cell containing the formula, and paste it in a new location, or hover over the bottom right-hand corner of a cell until the cursor becomes a small black plus sign. Now, either click and drag that small plus sign over the range of cells you'd like to copy the formula to, or double-click in the bottom right hand corner of the cell to have the formula copy down until there are no longer any populated cells to the left.

In the example we have been using, we can see that the Advocational Party, through that one $1.8-million donation, comprised 22.5 per cent of the total money raised by political parties for the year, putting it second in the top 10. That's a pretty interesting story.

To calculate a percentage change, use the formula (NEW-OLD)/OLD. That is the new value minus the old value (which gives the difference or change), divided by the old value. An example would be =(C2-B2)/B2. Make sure you put the parentheses around the part to the left of the "/" (division sign), so the difference between new and old will be calculated before the result is divided by the old value. Without the parentheses, the spreadsheet would first divide the old value by the old value, and then subtract that from new value, reducing it by one, definitely not the intended result. The standard order of operations in mathematics divides or multiplies first, then adds or subtracts. Parentheses override the standard order, allowing you to indicate which operation should be done first. Many readers will remember the acronyms BEDMAS ("Brackets then Exponents, then Division/Multiplication, then Addition/Subtraction") or PEDMAS ("Parentheses, Exponents, Division/Multiplication, and Addition/Subtraction") used by math teachers to drill home the order of operations.

Calculating Rates

Percentages are great when you are comparing two instances of the same **variable**, but sometimes you need to calculate a **rate** based on two variables, such as the number of cases of a disease in the population, or the number of meltdowns compared to the total number of nuclear reactors (you never know!). Rates are useful in this regard because they allow you to compare the rate in one population with that in another. To calculate a rate, divide the number of cases of the phenomenon you are looking at by the other variable, such as the population. Normally in these instances, you are looking at something that happens rarely, so you will then want to multiply the result by something like 100,000 or 1 million, to get the rate per 100,000 or per million people or reactors, etc. For example, if B2 has the number of cases of a rare type of cancer in a state and C2 has the population of the state, the formula to get the rate per 100,000 would look like this: =(B2/C2)*100,000. Be aware that factors such as the age of the population can affect the rates in different localities, and statisticians tend to correct or control for such variables. It is wise to consult with an expert if you are unfamiliar with this kind of calculation to make sure your results are valid.

Dealing with Errors

Error messages are inevitable when working with spreadsheets. The messages indicate that the program is incapable of performing the task you are asking it to, possibly because you made an error in the syntax of a function, or entered impossible values. For instance, when we were calculating the BC party donations as a percentage of the $8,182,029.2 million total, the spreadsheet would have produced a divide by zero error message ("as we also saw in the image on page 63") had we neglected to anchor the B12 with the "$" sign before copying the formula:

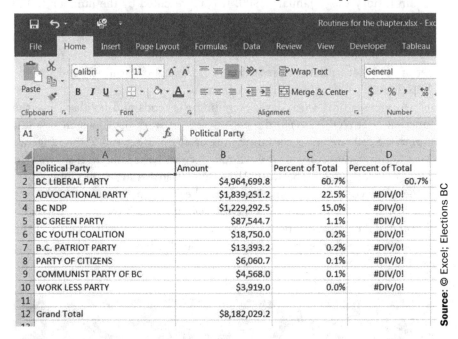

Source: © Excel; Elections BC

Other Error Messages

#N/A This is short form for "not available." Usually, it means that the spreadsheet was unable to return a legitimate result. Typically, you will see this when you make a mistake in your formula or one of the functions we will learn later in this chapter.

#NAME? You see this when Excel fails to recognize the name that you've used in the formula or when it identifies the text—characters justified to the left—as an unidentified name. As was the case with the #N/A error message, there may be a typo or some other error in your formula.

#NUM This means there is a problem with the number in the formula, usually when you are performing math.

#REF This one is telling you that your formula contains an invalid cell reference. It might be referring to a blank cell the spreadsheet is attempting to use, or a cell that has been deleted.

#VALUE This means that part of your function is incorrect. Perhaps you have used the incorrect data type, such as a number instead of text.[9]

Working with Dates

The key thing to realize about the dates displayed in spreadsheets is that they are really just numbers, as we discussed earlier. In spreadsheet land, the first day in history was 1 January 1900. It is represented by the number 1. The second day of January 1900 was number 2. The first of September 2016 was 42614, and so on. Hours and minutes are represented as decimals, so 42614.5 means 12 noon on 1 September 2016. So if you wanted to calculate the number of days that lapsed between 1 June 2015 (entered in cell A1) and 15 June 2015 (in A2), you would subtract A1 from A2.

To include only work days, excluding weekends and holidays, use the function NETWORKDAYS (the net number of work days), which in addition to the cell references containing the dates on either end of the range we want to count, also contains the cell reference with the holiday. If we want to count the working days between 21 December 2015 and 28 December 2015, we need two columns: column A contains the Christmas reference in the second row and column B contains the cell references with the two dates on either end of the range, B2 and B3. As you can see below, the NETWORKDAYS formula also needs the specified holiday as its third argument, which in this example is A2:

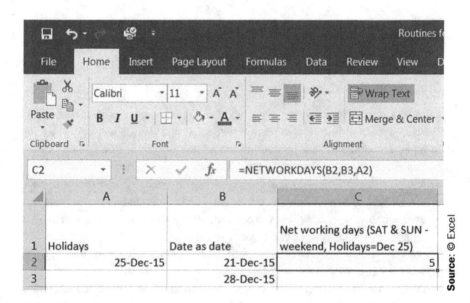

To learn about other common date functions, please see the tutorial on the companion website.

Concatenation

There are times when you want to combine the contents in two or more cells. Combining, or **concatenating**, the contents can be desirable when creating a pivot table, which we will cover in a little while, or when combining address fields in a table with geographic coordinates you want to map using a web-mapping service, which will we discuss in Chapter 6. The ampersand (&) can be used to concatenate two cells, as can the CONCATENATE function.

As an example, let's look at this table of political donations in Quebec. We've inserted a formula in cell C2 to hold the combined contents of cells A2 and B2.

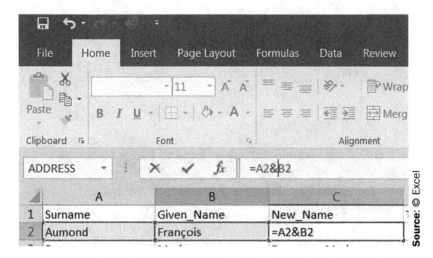

Here is the result:

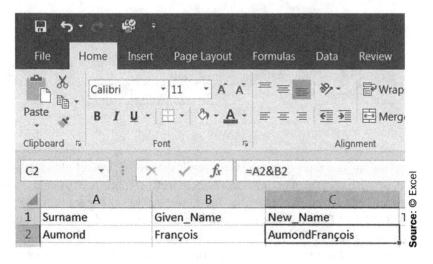

To add a comma and a space between the two names we do this:

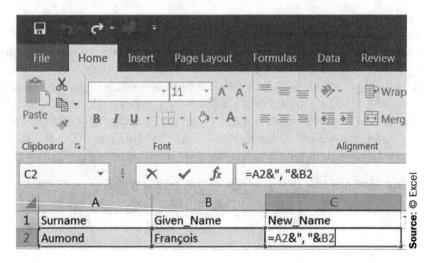

Here is the result:

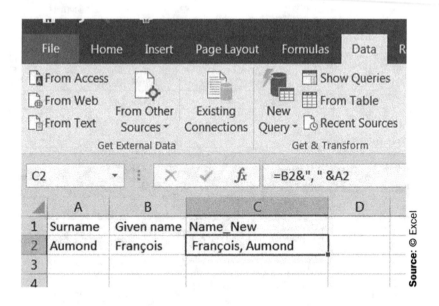

You can also accomplish the same result with the CONCATENATE function, which has the syntax CONCATENATE(cell1,cell2). You can concatenate as many cells as you like, as well as literal text such as the space we inserted. CONCATENATE(cell1," ",cell2) would combine cell 1 and cell 2, and add a space in between.

You'll find more examples of text functions on the companion website.

Summarizing Information with Pivot Tables

Pivot tables are arguably one of the most powerful and useful tools for journalists looking for patterns and stories in data. Given their importance, it's worth spending a bit of time explaining and showing how they operate. We'll use Excel for Windows for our examples, but the functionality is almost identical on a Mac. The OpenOffice free spreadsheet has this feature, called the **Data Pilot**, and Google's cloud-based spreadsheet application also incorporates pivot tables. They allow you to take a table of row-level data such as in this image:

	Home	Insert	Page Layout	Formulas	Data	Review	View	

	A	B	C	D
1	Date	Vendor Name	Description	Value
2	2015-10-01	3GA MARINE LTD	0675 Repair of Ships and boats	$23,700.00
3	2015-10-01	DONALD EINARSON	1310 Marine installations	$184,100.00
4	2015-10-01	HARBOUR AUTHORITY FERMEUSE	1245 Safety and sanitation equipment and parts	$27,500.00
5	2015-10-01	KEYSTONE ENVIRONMENTAL LTD.	0423 Engineering consultants - other (specify)	$46,145.70
6	2015-10-01	VILLHOLTH JENSEN & ASSOCIATES	0423 Engineering consultants - other (specify)	$13,800.00
7	2015-10-01	ANDERSON ENGINEERING CONSULTANTS LTD	1310 Marine installations	$23,443.00
8	2015-10-01	AZIMUTH CONSULTING GROUP INC	0499 Other professional services not otherwise specified	$13,825.00
9	2015-10-01	BAYLEAF SOFTWARE INC	0491 Management consulting	$9,525.00
10	2015-10-01	QUANTUM	0447 Tuition fees and costs of attending courses including seminars not elsewhere specified (specify)	$9,537.50
11	2015-10-01	TIDELAND SIGNAL CANADA LTD	1244 Radar equipment and parts	$86,440.20
12	2015-10-01	CHEVRON CANADA LIMITED	1124 Diesel fuel	$17,690.49

And summarize it like this:

	A	B
1		
2		
3	Row Labels	Sum of Value
4	1256 Ships and boats	$ 44,473,203.39
5	0675 Repair of Ships and boats	$ 22,946,489.62
6	1124 Diesel fuel	$ 6,702,066.89
7	0601 Marine installations	$ 5,936,956.18
8	1310 Marine installations	$ 5,103,427.80
9	0422 Engineering consultants - construction	$ 3,435,497.88
10	0430 Scientific services	$ 2,742,405.08
11	1261 Road motor vehicles	$ 2,481,263.00
12	0473 Information Technology and Telecommunications Consultants	$ 2,105,044.79
13	1286 Operating System and Utility Software related to servers, storage, peripherals and components	$ 1,905,497.71
14	1339 Other engineering works	$ 1,839,579.30
15	0628 Other engineering installations	$ 1,631,868.61
16	0859 Other business services not elsewhere specified	$ 1,453,833.64
17	1242 Electric lighting, distribution and control equipment and parts	$ 1,408,704.82
18	1249 Other equipment and parts	$ 1,313,518.20
19	0491 Management consulting	$ 1,051,620.66
20	0431 Scientific consultants	$ 969,168.40
21	1243 Measuring, controlling, laboratory, medical and optical equipment and parts	$ 815,145.39

The "pivot" in pivot tables refers to the fact that not only is the data summarized, but one of the data columns can be "pivoted" to the top of the sheet with its entries becoming column headers. You do not have to enter any formulas to make a pivot table. Instead, the summary is created using a drag-and-drop interface. With it, journalists can answer questions such as these:

- What department spent the most money during the most recent fiscal year?
- Which political party received the most money?
- What day of the week sees the highest number of drunk-driving accidents?

The ability to answer these kinds of questions, and the ease with which they can be asked, are two key reasons why pivot tables have earned the undying love of many journalists who work with data.

To create the pivot table, go to the "Insert" menu of the ribbon. Selecting the Pivot-Table option produces a dialogue box that identifies the range of cells to be included. The program should automatically choose all the cells in the table, but it's always a good idea to double-check cell ranges to make sure everything is included. If not, then you'd have to manually adjust the range to cover the entire table. In other programs, the equivalent feature is often under the Data menu.

The Pivot-Table dialogue box will give you the option of producing the pivot table on the same worksheet or a separate one. The latter option is generally preferable for a number of reasons, including the fact that it's simply easier to read, and work with, the contents.

The Pivot Table Field List is normally located on the right side of Excel's window, though you can change its location by dragging the title bar. Clicking outside the pivot table hides the Pivot Table Field List, which will reappear with a click inside the pivot table, or on the "Field List" icon on the top right.

You can set up the layout of the pivot table by using one of two techniques. The first method is to select a field name in the "Choose fields to add to report" section and use your cursor to drag it into one of the four boxes at the bottom of the "Pivot Table Field List." Alternatively, you can right-click a field name and choose its location from the shortcut menu that appears. Please consult the online tutorial on pivot tables to learn how to format the data. Once the information from the field list appears in one of the four boxes, the information will appear in the table to the left.

Pivot Table Terminology

Column labels: A field that has a column orientation in the pivot table. Each unique item in the field produces a column.

Grand totals: A row or column that displays totals for all the cells in a row or column in a pivot table. You can specify that grand totals be calculated for rows, columns, or both (or neither).

Group: A collection of items treated as a single item. You can group items manually or automatically.

Item: An element in a field or header that appears as a row or column header in a pivot table.

Refresh: Recalculates the pivot table after making changes to the source data.

Subtotals: A row or column that displays subtotals for detail cells in a row or column in a pivot table.

Table filter: A field that has a page orientation in the pivot table.

Values area: The cells in the pivot table that contain the summary data. Spreadsheets like Excel offer many ways to summarize the data. The most common methods used by journalists are SUM, COUNT, and AVERAGE.

Source: Walkenbach, John(2007). *Excel 2007 Bible*. Indianapolis:Wiley Publishing. pp. 598-599

Let's revisit the Elections BC data to see what kinds of results the pivot table can produce.

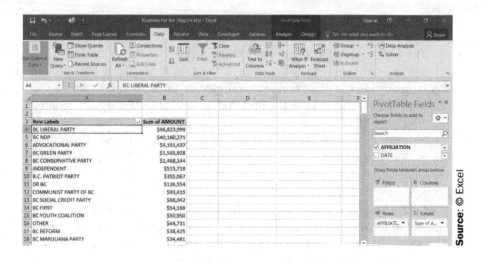

Source: © Excel

In this table, we have dragged the affiliation into the "Row Labels" section, and the donation amounts into the "Values" section. The table on the left contains the result, which can be sorted and filtered just like a regular table.

Pivot tables summarize the values by using functions such as SUM and COUNT. In this case, the pivot table can SUM or add up all the amounts to reveal the highest donors; using the COUNT function, the table can count the individual donations. The pivot table is also capable of showing both calculations at once, as you can see here:

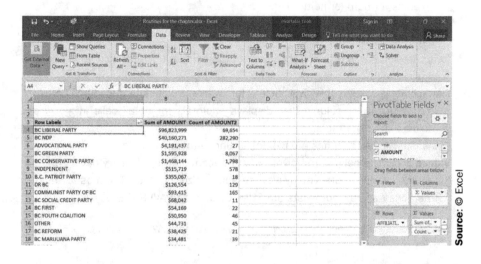

Source: © Excel

We have hidden the pivot table's grand total column to make it easier to see the results of summing and counting. We can see how many donations made up the total in any given year. In this case, 282,290 donors gave the BC

NDP more than $4 million Only 27 donors gave money to the Advocational Party during that same year.

The number of political donations can often be a different story than the amount each party raised. For instance, the BC Liberal Party had fewer than the NDP donors, but raised more money. There are many possible stories. Perhaps the Liberals appealed to donors with deeper pockets. Or maybe the NDP did a better job of attracting individual donors. By adding subsequent years, we can use the pivot table to count the donations to see how the parties are doing.

Logical Functions and IF Statements

Journalists use basic calculations, functions, and pivot tables to produce stories that either complement what's already making the news, take those leads on stories in new directions, or explore uncharted territory. However, what we've covered so far only represents a fraction of the spreadsheet's power. In order to squeeze more potential stories out of datasets, we can use a powerful category of logical functions and IF **statements**.

You'll recall that Excel has a logical data type, in addition to numbers, text, and errors. The logical data type can contain the values TRUE or FALSE. To see it in action, type either of these words into a cell in Excel (if you type an apostrophe first, you'll end up typing in the word rather than the logical value). Sometimes, you will want to test two values, to see if they meet some condition, such as being equal to one another. For example, you may need to check if two cells contain identical spellings (or cells in two entire columns). To do so, simply enter this formula:

```
=A2=B2
```

If A2 and B2 are identical, the formula will return the logical value TRUE. Otherwise, it will return the logical value FALSE. Similarly, you could write =B2>A2. In this case, the formula would return TRUE if B2 were greater than A2, and otherwise would return FALSE.

Such logical tests are fundamental to computing and are used a great deal in computer programming.

Excel's IF function is also drawn directly from the world of programming. An IF function allows your program to make decisions, and return different values depending on whether a condition you set evaluates to TRUE or FALSE. A basic IF statement requires three arguments.

1. What we are going to measure as being true or false
2. What to do if it is true
3. What to do if it is false[10]

If we were to use the logical comparator we just examined, an IF function could look like this:

```
=IF(A1<B1,"smaller","equal or larger")
```

Translated to English, the function would first test to see if A1 was smaller than B1. If it was, it would return "smaller." If not, it would return, "equal or larger." Similarly, we could use the function with our political donations example to populate a new column depending on whether a party raised more than a million dollars:

```
IF(A1>1000000,"More than a million","A million or less")
```

If you need to test more than one condition, you can put one IF statement inside another. You can also combine it with other functions, such as the AND and OR logical functions to create more sophisticated tests. We cover these functions with live values in the tutorial "Using Logical Tests in Excel" on the companion website.

Other Logical Category Functions using IF

Function: COUNTIF
What it does: Counts the number of instances something appears in your table according to one criterion.

Function: AVERAGEIF
What it does: Calculates a conditional average (similar to SUMIF and COUNTIF).

Function: AVERAGEIFS
What it does: Calculates a conditional average using multiple criteria.

Function: IFERROR
What it does: Returns a value you specify if a formula evaluates an error; otherwise, returns the result of the formula. You can wrap this around any function to provide error-handling capability. For example, in calculating percentage changes, you could use the IFERROR function to catch any divide-by-zero errors in instances in which the old value was 0.

Function: AND
What it does: Returns TRUE if all its arguments are TRUE.

Function: OR
What it does: Returns TRUE if any argument is TRUE[11]

Function: NOT
What it does: Reverses the logic of its argument

Using Paste Special to Convert Formulas to Values

In most programs you work with, there is one kind of paste in a cut-and-paste operation: you paste exactly what you copied. Excel vastly expands the capability of pasting with the Paste Special command. It is often used in instances in which you have used formulas to calculate values, and would then like to convert the values to their equivalent text or numeric entries. For example, you could convert the text created by the example we just looked at with the IF function. To do this, highlight the cells you wish to convert to their values, and copy the cells. On the home ribbon, click on the small arrow beside the Paste icon and choose Paste Special (in other spreadsheet programs, you'll find Paste Special under the Edit menu). This will open a dialogue box. Chose the Values radio button, and click OK. The values will be converted.

Paste Special can do a lot more than this. Please see the tutorial "Doing Cool Stuff with Paste Special" on the companion website.

Chronologies

Question period in the Canadian Parliament on 15 April 2013, was filled with heated rhetoric about a federal program that allowed businesses to bring in cheap foreign labour. The leader of the Official opposition was grilling the prime minister about a story the Canadian Broadcasting Corporation had broken about the Royal Bank of Canada using the program to replace Canadian workers.

The opposition wanted to know why the program had grown so rapidly when unemployment in Canada remained unacceptably high. The prime minister went on the attack, saying eight opposition members of Parliament had written asking "the government to approve additional temporary foreign workers for their ridings."

The PM was using the letters selectively. It turns out that 149 of his own MPs had been doing the same thing. That number came from an analysis of MP correspondence with the immigration minister about the temporary foreign worker program that the CBC obtained through an open-records request. A spreadsheet chronology was key in analyzing the 171 pieces of correspondence.

When you are working on a longer- or medium-term story, one of the challenges is organizing your material in a way to makes it easy to find specific bits of information or to spot patterns. In this case, the newsworthy pattern was the sheer number of letters coming from government MPs in Alberta, the province where employers used the program the most.[12]

Using chronologies is one of the most effective ways of organizing your material. While word-processing programs such as Microsoft Word can be used to accomplish this task, it is easier in Excel because dates can be sorted, categories that you have created (such as the MP's province) can be filtered, and key phrases from the letters can be highlighted using colours. In short, you can use many of the spreadsheet's tools we've discussed earlier in the chapter.

In this case, there were eight columns.

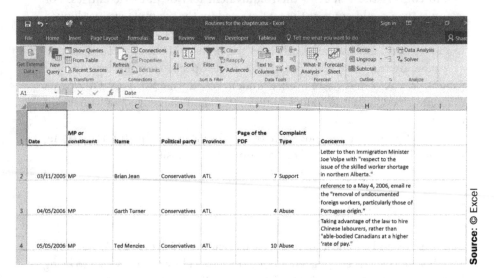

Source: © Excel

Once you have decided on categories and entered all the information, summarizing and grouping allows for powerful, definitive analysis. The beauty of using spreadsheets to build chronologies is that you can organize the material in a way that makes the most sense to you.

Conclusion

Due to their availability and the ease in learning how to use them, spreadsheets are the workhorses for journalists crunching data.

The key with spreadsheets, as with many of the tools discussed in this textbook, is to find an excuse to use them, even if the effort fails to pay immediate dividends. The eventual payoff—and there will be one—is an original story that your competitors will not have, or the context that adds deeper understanding to an ongoing issue such as the use of temporary foreign workers.

Remember, unlike a document that might contain one killer phrase, a good dataset contains several possibilities, making it worth the effort to find, clean, and maintain as many of them as possible.

Study Questions and Exercises

1. Download the BC elections donations and use pivot tables to see which party raised the most money over the most recent 10-year period, and which party attracted the largest number of donors.

2. Use your spreadsheet to construct a chronology of events for an issue that promises to be in the headlines for some time to come, or for a long-term project.

3. You'll find another exercise on the companion website that shows how data was used for a prominent published story. You'll have the opportunity to analyze the data yourself, perhaps finding new angles the reporter didn't pursue.

Notes

1. Dan Bricklin's personal website, http://bricklin.com/history/saiidea.htm.
2. Ibid.
3. "Excel Specifications and Limits," Microsoft Office website, http://support.office.com/en-nz/article/Excel-specifications-and-limits-1672b34d-7043-467e-8e27-269d656771c3.
4. Ibid.
5. John Atten, "Microsoft Excel Basics Part II: Data Types in Excel," 3 October 2011, http://typecast-exception.com/post/2011/10/03/Microsoft-Excel-Basics-Part-II-Data-Types-in-Excel.aspx.
6. "TYPE function," Microsoft Office website, https://support.office.com/en-us/article/TYPE-function-45b4e688-4bc3-48b3-a105-ffa892995899.
7. Eric Spellmann, *Amarillo Globe-News*, Saturday, February 09, 2002, http://amarillo.com/stories/2002/02/09/tec_spellmann.shtml.
8. Ibid., 180.
9. Mary Jo Sylwester, "My Favorite (Excel) Things," Investigative Reporters and Editors Tip Sheet, 2010, http://ire.org/resource-center/tipsheets/3346/. Page 9
10. Vallance-Jones and McKie, *Computer Assisted Reporting*, 102.
11. Sylwester, "My Favorite (Excel) Things," 8–9.
12. David McKie, "Temporary Foreign Worker Program Complaints Began in 2006," 23 June 2014, CBC *News*, http://www.cbc.ca/news/politics/temporary-foreign-worker-program-complaints-began-in-2006-1.2685056; McKie, "Temporary Foreign Worker Program Queries Came Mostly from Tory MPs," 25 June 2014, CBC *News*, http://www.cbc.ca/news/politics/temporary-foreign-worker-program-queries-came-mostly-from-tory-mps-1.2687159.

Chapter 5

Working with Databases

What You Will Learn:

- How database applications differ from spreadsheets
- How databases store information using different types of data for various purposes
- The difference between desktop and server database programs
- How to query databases using Structured Query Language
- When it makes the most sense to build your own database

Databases run the world.

Okay, maybe they don't quite run the world, but they do keep track of almost everything in it. Whether they be used by politicians tracking financial supporters, huge social networks recording the interests, relationships, and photos of their users, or local health authorities monitoring conditions in restaurants, the storehouses of data today are almost incalculably numerous.

That opens up huge opportunities for journalists who know how to dig into all that information. They can discover patterns and trends that even the owners of the data miss, find important stories, and produce raw material for visualizations and interactives.

We've already introduced spreadsheets, which are an excellent way to get started working with data. But spreadsheets are inherently limited, and eventually you tap out their capabilities. That's when you turn to a database program. Databases can handle much larger data files and they are able to work with complex multi-table datasets, something spreadsheets are at best clunky at. Along the way, they can help answer several of the classic journalistic questions: who, what, when, where, how much, and how many. They are a fundamentally important tool for in-depth journalism.

Tutorials Included with the Companion Website

You will find these tutorials on the OUP Companion Website (www.oupcanada .com/Vallance-Jones):

- Installing and Configuring the MySQL Server
- Exploring the Microsoft Access User Interface
- Exploring Navicat and Sequel Pro
- Backing up your Data in Access and MySQL.
- Making Tables and Importing Data into Access
- Making Tables and Importing Data into MySQL
- Getting Started Writing Queries in Access
- Getting Started Writing Queries in MySQL
- Indexing Tables in Microsoft Access
- Indexing Tables in MySQL
- SQL Queries to Add, Modify, and Delete Table Data
- Exporting Data from Access and MySQL

For Leslie Young of Global News in Toronto, analysis with the Microsoft Access database program was key to her series *Crude Awakening*. She embarked on the investigation of oil spills in Alberta after hearing a radio interview in which the interviewee said there were frequent spills in the province. "I wanted to see if that was true."[1]

Young went through a number of hurdles to get data, including an initial freedom-of-information request that produced hundreds of pages of printouts, obviously originating from a database. But it was incomplete. Eventually, she found she could purchase complete data from a government agency. "It contained all the information you could want—except the locations of spills in a readable form. Alberta has a unique geographic system, I discovered, called the Alberta Township System, and all coordinates were given under that system."

A sympathetic government official helped Young convert the coordinates to **latitudes** and **longitudes**, and she was able to proceed with the database analysis. "I chose Access because I was familiar with it, and it's an easy way to go through a dataset that is a bit too big for Excel. It also allows me to craft nuanced queries." As with any data project, two of the most important steps were to make sure she understood the data and to check that it was complete.

> I read through lots of data to get a good sense of how it was organized and what information was in there, and also double-checked that some known spills were recorded in the data as a way to make sure that it was a reasonably inclusive list.

Her data queries produced some startling figures. For example, there had been an average of two spills of crude oil every day from 1975 through 2013. Young did further analysis using a GIS program (see Chapter 7), and she and the Global team visualized the results. A map allowed readers to search for spills by company and other criteria, and there was a time-lapse animation that showed the frequency of spills. The stories were published online and on TV in May 2013 and were nominated for several awards, including a world data journalism award. It is an excellent example of how database analysis can reveal patterns that otherwise would remain hidden.

Screenshot from web version of *Crude Awakening*

Working with a Database

When you start working with database programs, you'll find that some aspects are quite similar to spreadsheets. For example, a table in a database program looks a lot like a worksheet in Excel. Both have rows and columns of information, can be sorted by one or more columns, and can be filtered to view only some of the rows.

But there are differences, too. You'll notice right away that instead of rows labelled with numbers, columns labelled with letters, and individual cells referenced by the intersection of the column and row labels (e.g. cell B2), a database table just has fixed column headers with names:

As well, while in a spreadsheet every single cell can hold anything you like, a database table has a more rigid structure, made up of columns called fields and rows called records. Each field normally contains one chunk of information, or data element, such as a restaurant's street name, a contract vendor, or a baby name. Each row is one complete instance of whatever that table records, be that restaurant inspections, government contracts, or births. Once a record has been added to the table, the different data elements within it stay together until you explicitly change the table structure. It's not possible to sort one column so it no longer matches up with the others, and make nonsense of the table, as you can in a spreadsheet.

Another big difference is that databases are organized in a hierarchy. At the top is the database itself. Inside a database you will find tables, and tables are further subdivided into fields. Inside each field, the data has to all be of one type. While a spreadsheet can have different data formats and types in the same column, a database requires each column to be of one data type. Because of this, it is far more important to understand data types and there is a much greater variety of them. Below is a table with fields for a database of political donations, with different data types. The table is shown in the table design view of Microsoft Access.

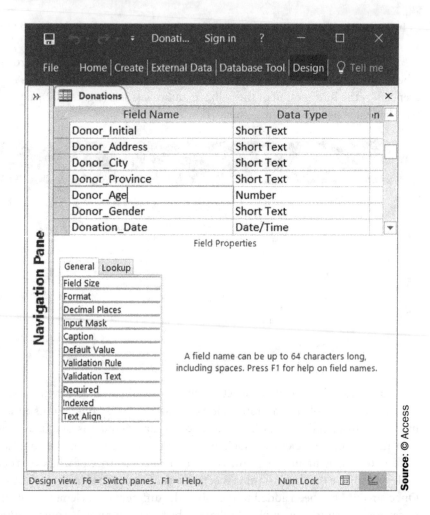

The names of data types in different database programs may differ slightly, but the basic types are all pretty much the same. Table 5.1 on page 83 shows some of the more common types. You can consult the documentation or help file for the program you are using to confirm the exact names of the data types you will need to use.

There are things to keep in mind about choices of data types. Some are obvious: text goes in a text type, dates go into date types, and time into time types. One tricky thing that trips up many newcomers is the requirement to put numbers that you want to behave as numbers in field with a number data type. You can put numbers in a text field—in fact a text field can hold any character—but they won't behave like numbers; instead the database program will treat the "numbers" as text, which means you can't do any math using them, and if you sort them, the numbers will be sorted

Table 5.1 Common SQL data types

Data type	What it can contain
Char, varchar, Access short text type	Any character at all; 255 character limit
longtext, memo, **MySQL** text type	Longer strings of text, such as long narratives
Integer or Int	Integer values (no decimals); if unsigned, values cannot be negative
Long integer or Bigint	The same as integer, but can hold bigger numbers
Single or Double floating point	Numbers with decimal places
Decimal	Similar to floating point, but slightly more accurate when the greatest precision is required.
Currency (Access only)	A special type formatted for currency values
Date, time, and datetime	Dates and times
Boolean or yes/no	Boolean values, true or false, yes or no

in alphabetical order, so that 1 is followed by 200 which is followed by 3, 42, 5, and so on.

Of course, a number field won't accept anything other than numbers. And when you start writing queries, if you try to join a number field to a text field, it won't work and will return an error.

Building Relationships

One of the most powerful features of database programs is that they can connect data contained in more than one table. This saves storage and memory and cuts down on data-entry errors by allowing information that would otherwise have to be recorded repeatedly to be stored only once. Imagine a database that keeps track of orders for an online bookstore. You could put all the data in a conventional spreadsheet or put everything in a single database table (called a "flat-file" database). But if you did, you would need to enter such details as the customer's name, address, phone number and customer number, along with the information on each book sold, its price, author, and title, its ISBN number, its date, and so on, into a new row, every time you sold a book. It might end up looking like this:

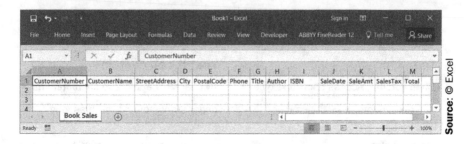

Source: © Excel

It wouldn't be long before you, the bookstore manager, would be tearing your hair out. If a customer moved, you'd have to re-enter all of the customer information for every previous sale. What if you entered the information incorrectly sometimes, perhaps misspelling a name? Suddenly, you wouldn't be able to track the customer's purchases properly.

A relational database aims to solve these kinds of problems by putting information into different tables, and then **joining** them, whenever needed, using unique identifiers called keys. So now, we can have a table for customers, a table for books, and a table for the individual sales information, with the tables joined by way of a unique customer ID number and a unique book number. When a new sale is made, the customer number and the book number connect the sales table back to the customers and books tables. Here is how our three database tables might look:

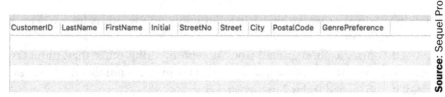

Source: Sequel Pro

Table for customers

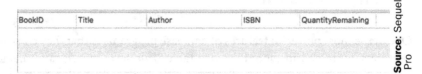

Source: Sequel Pro

Table for books

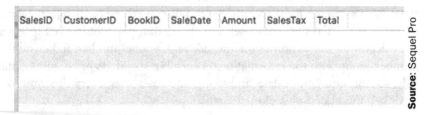

Source: Sequel Pro

Table for individual sales information

The theory and terminology around the structure of databases are beyond the scope of this book, but there are some basic principles illustrated by this example. There should never be any completely duplicated records in a table. So each customer should be recorded in the customers table just once, each book in the books table just once, and each sale in the sales table just once. The same last name might appear, even the first, but the unique combination of ID and all of the other customer information should appear in the table just once. If a database table design is such that it tends to produce duplicate entries, the information should be further divided.

In our case, we would still end up with duplicated entries because we would have to have a new sales record for every book sold. To solve this, we could create a fourth table for items sold, so that the main sales table could just contain the unique information about the sale, such as the date and time, and the items sold table could store the details. This process of reducing duplication is called **normalization**, and entire books have been written about it.

It is also preferable to divide information into the smallest reasonable chunks within the same table. So in an address, the street number and the street name will be recorded in separate fields, as will the zip or postal code. This allows for easier querying later as it is possible to look up all the customers in one postal code, for example.

Whether you are building your own database or trying to understand the structure of a complex multi-table database you got from a government agency, understanding these principles will make your job easier.

Desktop and Server Database Programs

There is a pretty standard workflow when you use a database program: obtaining data, making sure it is clean and free of errors, importing or entering the data, analyzing it, and, as necessary, exporting it for use in other applications. We cover obtaining data in Chapters 2 and 3 and cleaning data in Appendix A on the companion website, so here we will focus on the nitty-gritty of using database programs.

For the purposes of this book and the online tutorials, we have chosen to focus on two database programs that have been around for a long time and likely will be for years to come, the Microsoft Access desktop database and MySQL, an open-source, enterprise-scale **server** database maintained by Oracle. Access runs only on Windows, while MySQL has versions for Windows, Mac OSX, and Linux.

Access is a self-contained product meant to be used by one person on one machine, and because it is part of the Microsoft Office Professional suite, its user interface will seem familiar to someone who has worked with Excel. It can be a good choice for someone just starting out with databases, and can easily handle datasets with hundreds of thousands of rows. For those looking for something more powerful, MySQL can handle datasets of millions of rows; and for those who want to work in a web development environment, MySQL is used as the database back end for countless web applications. It is, however, a little more challenging to install and use than Access. Because it is a server database, you can't just use the program directly the way you do with Access. Instead, you have to issue commands to the server, and receive replies using a **client** program, much the way you use your web browser to issue commands to a remote server on the web.

If you like, you can do this directly from the command or terminal window of your computer, but we recommend using a **front-end program**. Front ends such as Navicat, Sequel Pro (Mac only), and MySQL Workbench provide a graphical environment that allows you to interact with your MySQL database from a more familiar environment. The Sequel Pro front end is pictured, with a table of parking infractions open.

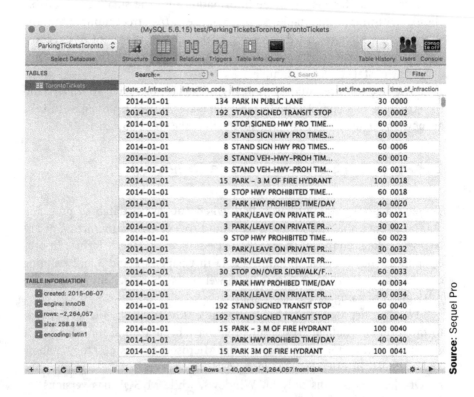

Source: Sequel Pro

We assume in the book and tutorials that you will be installing your MySQL server locally on your own computer, but you can just as easily use a remote server. The only thing that changes is the connection details and, of course, having permission to host your data on the remote server. We won't get into all the details of getting MySQL set up here. You'll find a complete installation and configuration guide on the companion website, including instructions on how to set up a connection between your choice of front end and MySQL.

Making Tables and Adding Data

If you're going to take advantage of the power of a database program, you first need to give it some data to work with. The process is a little more involved than using a spreadsheet because rather than just opening a file and starting to work, you need to create a database (if one doesn't already exist), add a new table to the database, and add the data to the table. After that, you can start to query the data.

In Access, a database is a file saved on your computer, in a location you specify, with the extension .accdb (prior to Access 2007, another format with the extension .mdb was used). It can be up to 2 GB in size, including all of the data within it. In MySQL, databases are stored in a location that varies by operating system.

Once you have created a database in either Access or MySQL, you need to create your table(s) within it, and then add the data.

The specific steps required to create tables and import data differ not only between Access and MySQL but between different MySQL front ends.

In Access, you can create a table separately in table design view— which you will find on the Create ribbon—then add data to it, or you can use the external data import wizard to bring in existing data and create the

It is always a good idea to back up your databases. In Access, this can be done by simply making a copy of the .accdb file. In MySQL, you can create what is called a MySQL dump file, using a utility called mysqldump or the backup functionality in a front end. The dump file can then be reloaded into MySQL if needed. As well as backing up your databases, it is good practice to use an external hard drive to back up the entire contents of your computer's hard drive. That way if your hard drive fails, you will be able to recover your files. Windows and OSX both have built-in routines that automate the backup process.

table automatically. The wizard will examine the external data and create the table structure and choose data types for you. You can change the names or types as part of the process. Access can import data from a number of sources, including delimited text files, Excel spreadsheets, and other Access databases. Complete instructions are in the Access data import tutorial on the companion website.

In MySQL, you also have the choice of creating the table first and then adding data manually, or using a wizard-type interface that is packaged as part of a front-end program to import external data. This is one of the best reasons to use a front end because it greatly simplifies what can be an error-prone process. Not all front ends have import utilities, but Navicat Essentials and Sequel Pro can both import delimited text files, and a more expensive Navicat licence can import Excel and other file types.

If you create the table first, then add data, you can also write the table-creation statement yourself, and then use the LOAD DATA INFILE command to suck in the data. One advantage of this approach is that LOAD DATA INFILE is extremely fast, so you may want to learn to use it if you want to import millions of records. Complete instructions for importing data into MySQL, using both methods, are on the companion website. These tutorials use the same sample data as we are using for the discussion on queries that follows; the data is available for download on the companion website, so you can follow along with the query examples.

If you are importing data you have obtained via an open-data site or from a government agency, make sure that you have obtained the record layout for each table you will need to create in your database, so you will know what the data types should be for each field.

As well, if your data is in a text format, such as CSV, it is a good idea to open and examine the data file in a text editor such as TextEdit on a Mac or Notepad on a PC, or in a text editor with line numbers, such as TextWrangler or Notepad ++. For really large text files of many megabytes or more you may need to use a large text editor such as UltraEdit or EmEditor. Becoming familiar with the structure and content of the data before you try to import it not only helps you understand the data better, but will cut down on import errors because you can ensure that the database tables into which you plan to import the data have the structure and data types that match the data you are trying to import.

The Main Course: Querying Your Data

Once you have successfully created your table(s) and imported your data, you can begin to query it. This is where you will start to see the real power of database programs. "Query" is another way of saying "question," and queries really are just questions you ask of your data. As with people, when you first meet a database you'll probably ask it general questions, to find out what data it contains, and determine what it can tell you. From there, you will ask ever-more specific questions, do summary calculations, and filter for specific instances that can lead to stories. By writing queries, you can get whatever result you need from one or more tables, in exactly the way you need it, as Leslie Young found when working on *Crude Awakening*.

> For the. . .question, how frequent are oil spills in Alberta, I had to first narrow down the data. There was data on spills of all kinds of materials from the oil industry. I decided I primarily wanted to look at crude oil, so I created a filter query on the data in Access to narrow it down to just incidents involving crude oil and crude bitumen.
>
> Then, it was easy to count the number of spills and calculate an average based on the number of days in the date range covered by the database. . .
>
> The data analysis was key to the story. It was the core of the piece—that spills are frequent in Alberta—and provided the jumping-off point for the rest of the series, which examined the oversight systems and alternatives.

Unlike in a spreadsheet, the act of analyzing data in a database program is non-destructive. What this means is that instead of the user opening the actual table and manipulating it, as in a spreadsheet, the queries return a snapshot of the data. The snapshot exists only as long as it is open on the screen. Once written, the queries can be saved, and then run again the next time the user wants to see the same result. Even better, if the table data changes, the query will reflect those changes the next time it runs. All of this makes for far greater efficiency and less wasted time.

In Access you write queries in query design view, which you will find on the Create ribbon. Choose SQL view and begin writing your SQL. MySQL front ends all have a query window in which you write your queries. This is the one in Sequel Pro, showing a completed query:

Source: © Access

Complete details on how to get started writing queries, for both Access and popular MySQL front ends, are on the companion website.

The Language of Queries

While Microsoft Access, and some front ends for MySQL, allow you to create queries in a drag-and-drop user interface, we're going to focus here on learning to write queries in the native language of relational database programs, Structured Query Language, or SQL, properly pronounced *ess-cue-ell*. SQL is a data journalism life skill, and once you master it, you'll find you can use it not only for data analysis, but in other applications such as building web applications that have database back ends.

We'll start with the SELECT query, the type you will write most often. It gets its name from the first word in such a query, SELECT. SELECT queries are how you drill down into a dataset, make sense of it, and find the patterns and trends. There are six main clauses you will use repeatedly, beginning with these command words:

SELECT
FROM

[WHERE]
[GROUP BY]
[HAVING]
[ORDER BY]

The first two clauses are required. The others are used to refine the query.

SQL queries are properly written with the command words in uppercase and table names in normal or lower case, though it is not required. Also not required, but encouraged for readability, is to write each part of a select statement on a separate line. One thing that is crucial is the order of the lines; it can't be varied.

Let's look at each line in turn. So you can follow along, you can download the data we are using in these examples, in CSV format, from the companion website, import it into Access or MySQL, and then run the queries. The tables are, quite deliberately, small, so small you could work out the results by eyeballing the tables. This will help you understand what the query is doing, and give you confidence that it is coming up with the correct results when you move to larger datasets and eyeballing a table is no longer an option. You can download the complete text of all the queries from the companion website.

You are not limited to existing fields in the SELECT line. You can also create columns based on math calculations, such as a percentage calculation based on two other numeric fields, combine the content of two or more fields using concatenation, extract only some of the content of a field using a **string** function, or put text in quotation marks (the same text would then appear in a new field in every row). Think of the SELECT line not as a way to pick fields but a way to define what the columns will be.

The SELECT line is where you pick the columns you will see in your query output. Our main table is a table of political donations with 10 fields. If you wish to see all of the fields, just write SELECT *. If you want to see only some of the fields, you can use the SELECT line to choose the ones you need, such as this line which selects five fields:

```
SELECT Donor_Last, Donor_First, Donor_City, Donation_Amount,
Partycode
```

The query won't actually do anything yet because the SELECT line can't sit on its own. A valid select query must have at least the SELECT line and the FROM line. The FROM line is where you declare the table(s) you are using in the query. So, to continue our example, we'll get our data from a table called Donations. If we add that to our query, it will look like this:

```
SELECT Donor_Last, Donor_First, Donor_City, Donation_Amount,
Partycode
FROM Donations
```

This query would return only the five selected fields, as shown here:

Donor_last ▾	donor_first ▾	donor_city ▾	donation_an ▾	partycode ▾
Smith	Joanne	Calgary	$1,500.00	Red
Jones	Steve	Toronto	$3,000.00	Blue
Leblanc	Carole	Dieppe	$2,000.00	Orange
Johnson	Gerald	Calgary	$1,750.55	Red
Stephenson	Brenda	Brandon	$1,900.00	Orange
Tremblay	Monique	Montreal	$3,700.91	Blue
Calhoun	David	Hamilton	$1,800.00	Red
Mills	Harold	Halifax	$1,200.00	Orange
White	Mel	Charlottetown	$1,375.28	Blue
Silvers	Wanda	Winnipeg	$2,700.00	Red

Source: © Access

That's good, but so far our query gives us every record (row) in the table. We can use the WHERE line to start narrowing that down, so only certain rows are returned. For example: WHERE Donor_city = "Calgary" would limit the output to only those rows where the donor's city was the Stampede City.

So in our developing query:

```
SELECT Donor_Last, Donor_First, Donor_City, Donation_Amount,
Partycode
FROM Donations
WHERE Donor_City = "Calgary"
```

And the result:

Donor_last ▾	donor_first ▾	donor_city ▾	donation_an ▾	partycode ▾
Smith	Joanne	Calgary	$1,500.00	Red
Johnson	Gerald	Calgary	$1,750.55	Red

Source: © Access

By the way, fields included in the WHERE line do not have to be in the SELECT line and will nonetheless narrow down the records included in the query, as in:

```
SELECT Donor_Last, Donor_First, Donor_City, Donation_Amount,
Partycode
FROM Donations
WHERE Donor_Gender = "F"
```

Which produces this:

Donor_last ▾	donor_first ▾	donor_city ▾	donation_an ▾	partycode ▾
Smith|	Joanne	Calgary	$1,500.00	Red
Stephenson	Brenda	Brandon	$1,900.00	Orange
Tremblay	Monique	Montreal	$3,700.91	Blue
Silvers	Wanda	Winnipeg	$2,700.00	Red

Source: © Access

We don't see the gender field in the results, but the WHERE line narrows the result to only those records in which the gender field contains "F". Much of the action in a query takes place in the WHERE line, and you can do a lot more than just find exact values. As well as the "=" sign, you can use the following operators in defining WHERE conditions:

- LIKE allows you to search for text within a field, using the % sign as a wildcard meaning any number of characters from 0 upward, and _ (underscore character) as a wildcard meaning a single character. In the Microsoft Access' version of SQL, the % wildcard is replaced by the * (asterisk), and the _ is replaced by the ? (question mark), when the database is set to its default variant of SQL. See the tutorial Getting Started Writing Queries in Access, for a longer explanation. So, in Access, **Donor_zip LIKE "902*"** would return all records in which the donor zip code begins with 902. Note that while some zip codes are just numbers, they are numbers that are treated like text, so are typically stored in a field with a text data type.
- You can use the standard mathematical symbols > (greater than), < (less than), >= (greater than or equal to) and <= (less than or equal to) with numbers. **Donation_Amount >= 1000** would limit the output to records in which the amount of the donation was equal to or greater than $1,000. Curiously, these operators work on text fields as well, producing alphabetical order.
- The BETWEEN operator lets you look for numbers between one value and another. For example, **Donation_Amount BETWEEN 1500 AND 2500** would find all records in which the donation was $2,500, $1,500, or anything in between. BETWEEN also works alphabetically on words. We'll look more at the AND operator in a moment.

If you want to test whether a field is empty, i.e. has **null** values in it, use this syntax:

```
SELECT Donor_last, Donor_First, Donor_Gender, Donor_City,
Donation_Amount
FROM Donations
WHERE Donor_Gender IS NULL
```

That would produce this output:

Donor_last ▾	donor_first ▾	donor_gender ▾	donor_city ▾	donation_amount ▾
Leblanc	Carole		Dieppe	$2,000.00
White	Mel		Charlottetown	$1,375.28

Source: © Access

Note that a text field can sometimes look empty, but actually have zero-length strings in it. They look the same on the screen as null values but are not the same to the computer. To find those, use this construction:

```
SELECT Donor_Last, Donor_First, Donor_Gender, Donor_City,
Donation_Amount
FROM Donations
WHERE Donor_City = ""
```

(Note that two quotation marks with no space between them denotes a **zero-length string**.)

The WHERE line uses **Boolean logic**, in which statements evaluate to either TRUE or FALSE. When a statement evaluates to TRUE, records are returned, and when it evaluates to FALSE, they are not. It also uses the Boolean operators AND, OR, and NOT. These allow you to string several conditions together to create extremely precise queries. For example, you could write:

```
SELECT Donor_Last, Donor_First, Donor_Gender, Donor_City,
Donation_Amount
FROM Donations
WHERE Donor_last LIKE "%Smith%" AND Donor_City = "Calgary"
```

Only records matching both conditions would be returned by the query. In other words, with AND, both conditions must evaluate to true.

Donor_last ▾	donor_first ▾	donor_gende ▾	donor_city ▾	donation_amount ▾
Smith	Joanne	F	Calgary	$1,500.00

Source: © Access

OR has the opposite effect. Only one of the conditions must evaluate to TRUE and any row that evaluates to TRUE for either condition will be returned. For example, this statement:

```
SELECT Donor_Last, Donor_First, Donor_Gender, Donor_City,
Donation_Amount
FROM Donations
WHERE Donor_Last LIKE "%Smith%" OR Donor_City = "Calgary"
```

would result in this:

donor_last ▾	donor_first ▾	donor_gender ▾	donor_city ▾	donation_amount ▾
Smith	Joanne	F	Calgary	$1,500.00
Johnson	Gerald	M	Calgary	$1,750.55

Source: © Access

If you find you would be constructing a query with a lot of OR operators, you can use the IN operator instead, with the following syntax:

```
SELECT Donor_Last, Donor_First, Donor_Gender, Donor_City,
Donation_Amount
FROM Donations
WHERE Donor_Last IN("Smith", "Jones", "Leblanc")
```

This is the same as writing:

```
SELECT Donor_Last, Donor_First, Donor_Gender, Donor_City,
Donation_Amount
FROM Donations
WHERE Donor_Last = "Smith" OR Donor_Last = "Jones" OR
Donor_Last = "Leblanc"
```

The IN operator can also be used with NOT, in which case it acts as a substitute for AND. For example,

```
SELECT Donor_Last, Donor_First, Donor_Gender, Donor_City,
Donation_Amount
FROM Donations
WHERE Donor_Last NOT IN ("Smith", "Jones", "Leblanc")
```

is the same as writing

```
SELECT Donor_Last, Donor_First, Donor_Gender, Donor_City,
Donation_Amount
FROM Donations
WHERE Donor_Last <> "Smith" AND Donor_Last <> "Jones" AND
Donor_Last <> "Leblanc"
```

The NOT Boolean operator reverses the meaning of any statement. So, NOT Donor_Last = "Jones" would return any record that did not have "Jones" in that field. The combination NOT = is so common, it can be written as <>, as you saw in the previous example.

You can mix and match the statements in the WHERE line to create extremely precise queries. For example, you can put an OR statement together with an AND, like this:

```
SELECT Donor_Last, Donor_First, Donor_Gender, Donor_City,
Donation_Amount
FROM DONATIONS
WHERE (Donor_Last = "Jones" OR Donor_Last = "Smith") AND
Donor_City like "%Calgary%"
```

Notice the use of the brackets around the OR statement. This ensures that the OR statement will be evaluated first. Without the brackets, the AND would be evaluated first and the query would return all records with "Jones" in the Donor_last field, regardless of what was in the Donor_City field, as well as all records with "Smith" in the Donor_last field and Calgary in the Donor_City field.

The MySQL documentation explains in detail the order in which operators will be evaluated. It also has a complete listing of all operators available for SQL statements. Similarly, Microsoft provides an online table of operators for Access.

We'll skip over the GROUP BY line and the HAVING line for a moment, and look at the ORDER BY statement. ORDER BY determines how a query result will be sorted. To use it, choose one or more fields (or other elements) that were declared in the SELECT line, as in this example:

```
SELECT Donor_Last, Donor_First, Donor_City, Donation_
Amount, Partycode
FROM Donations
WHERE Donation_Amount > 2500
ORDER BY Donation_Amount DESC
```

This will sort the result by the contents of the donation amount field, in descending order.

donor_last ▾	donor_first ▾	donor_city ▾	donation_amount ▾	partycode ▾
Tremblay	Monique	Montreal	$3,700.91	Blue
Jones	Steve	Toronto	$3,000.00	Blue
Silvers	Wanda	Winnipeg	$2,700.00	Red

Source: © Access

This line can also be written as ORDER BY 4 DESC, with the 4 meaning the fourth element in the SELECT LINE (doing this is deprecated in the official SQL standard, but it still works in MySQL and many find it convenient). "DESC" means descending order, largest to smallest or reverse alphabetical order. "ASC" means ascending order, smallest to largest or normal alphabetical order. If you leave out this part of the ORDER BY clause, the sort will be in ascending order.

If you sort by more than one field (or other element from the SELECT line), the sort will first be done by the first element you choose, and then within that the next field or element will be sorted, and so on. The easiest example to demonstrate this concept is last and first names. If you first sorted by last name and then by first, in ascending order, the last names would be sorted in alphabetical order, and for any identical last names, the first names would then be sorted. This behaviour is the same as in spreadsheets, with sorting proceeding from left to right.

Writing Math Queries

SQL queries can also do math. Just as spreadsheets do, SQL includes various math functions (though far fewer). The ones you will use most often are COUNT(), SUM(), MAX(), MIN() and AVG(). There is no median function and most often when you want to do a lot of math, the best approach is to export summarized data and then do the math in a spreadsheet program.

Whenever you use these math functions, you will usually put a field name in the brackets, although with COUNT you normally use the * symbol, for reasons we will explain in a moment.

The math functions go in the SELECT line, and just as when you put a field name in the select line, the function will result in a new column in the output. The simplest math function counts all records in the table, as in:

```
SELECT COUNT(*)
FROM Donations
```

That produce a single number as output:

Source: © Access

You can also put a specific field name into the brackets of the COUNT function, but if any of the records has a null (empty) value in the field, that record won't be counted. This is why it is best to use *.

The most important thing to understand is that COUNT(*) counts the records in the table. Another way to think of it is that it counts up whatever thing the table records, so in this table of donations, COUNT(*) will give you the number of donations; if it's a table of crimes, it will count crimes.

Count is the only math function that behaves this way. The other math functions must be used on numeric fields as they do math on existing numbers. The most commonly used function is SUM(); it allows you to add up the values in a field. Here is an example:

```
SELECT SUM(Donation_Amount)
FROM Donations
```

This would add up the contents of the donation amount field, giving you the total value of donations recorded by the table.

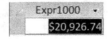

Expr1000 ▾
$20,926.74

AVG() does what you might expect it to do; it averages the values in a number field. MAX finds the largest value, while MIN finds the smallest.

These math functions can be combined with the WHERE clause. When this is done, the WHERE clause narrows down the records on which the math will be performed. Here's an example:

```
SELECT SUM(Donation_Amount)
FROM Donations
WHERE Donor_City = "Calgary"
```

This would only do the math on those records in which Donor_City was exactly equal to Calgary. Others would be ignored. You can use any combination of fields, operators, and Boolean operators in the WHERE line of a math query.

The GROUP BY Clause

The queries above would only provide one grand total. To generate subtotals you need to use the GROUP BY clause. The GROUP BY clause groups (or subtotals) on one or more fields that are declared in the SELECT line, as in the following example:

```
SELECT Donor_City, SUM(Donation_Amount)
FROM Donations
GROUP BY Donor_City
ORDER BY 2 DESC
```

This query would add up the donations. It would then generate subtotals of the results (grouped by Donor_City) and sort the results by the resulting sums in descending order.

donor_city ▾	Expr1001 ▾
Montreal	$3,700.91
Calgary	$3,250.55
Toronto	$3,000.00
Winnipeg	$2,700.00
Dieppe	$2,000.00
Brandon	$1,900.00
Hamilton	$1,800.00
Charlottetown	$1,375.28
Halifax	$1,200.00

Grouping is like counting the fruit in a basket, and then putting each variety of fruit into its own smaller basket. You end up with a subtotal for each variety of fruit—several groups of fruit, in other words.

A key thing to keep in mind: any elements, other than the math function, that you declare in the SELECT line must be included in the GROUP BY line. Otherwise, you'll get useless results. For example:

```
SELECT Donor_City, SUM(Donation_Amount)
FROM Donations
ORDER BY 2 DESC
```

Because there is no GROUP BY clause, this query would likely pick one donor city, almost at random, and group on that. Not good. Access prohibits this behaviour, but MySQL allows it.

The HAVING Clause

If you want to limit which of the calculated results are included in the query output, use the HAVING clause. While the WHERE clause in a math query filters or limits the records in the table(s) that will be included in the calculation, the HAVING clause filters the results after the calculation is done. So if a query is summing and grouping, as above, the HAVING clause can be used to determine which of the sums will be included in the output. Here's what it looks like:

```
SELECT Donor_City, SUM(Donation_Amount)
FROM Donations
GROUP BY Donor_City
HAVING SUM(Donation_Amount) >= 3000
ORDER BY 2 DESC
```

This would limit the query output to those results where the total value of donations equalled or exceeded $3,000.

donor_city ▾	Expr1001 ▾
Montreal	$3,700.91
Calgary	$3,250.55
Toronto	$3,000.00

Source: © Access

Aliases

You can rename any field or other element in the SELECT line using **aliases**. An alias is declared after the name of the field or element, using the AS command word. Whatever alias you use will then become the column name in the output of the query. So, continuing with the above example:

```
SELECT Donor_City, SUM(Donation_Amount) AS Total
FROM Donations
GROUP BY Donor_City
HAVING Total >= 3000
ORDER BY 2 DESC
```

Instead of Sum(Donation_Amount) appearing at the top of the second column in the result, it would be replaced by Total. Note that this doesn't change the names of the fields in the original table; it merely gives the column an alias when the query is run.

Joining Tables

Remember that we said that one of the powerful features of relational databases is their ability to join tables together. This is done so related information in separate tables that is intended to be combined can be brought together in a query. But it also provides journalists and others the ability to join tables together that were not intended to be joined. An example would be to compare the names of political donors to the names of individuals appointed to positions by the government.

Joining queries are a little different from one-table queries in that the join itself must be defined, in the WHERE line (failing to define the join will cause the database program to join every row in one table with every row in the other, a phenomenon called a **"Cartesian join"** that usually crashes the computer), and the names of all of the tables must be declared in the FROM line. The simplest join links two tables.

```
SELECT Donations.Donor_Last, Donations.Donor_First,
Donations.Donor_City, Donations.Donation_Amount,
Donations.Partycode, Parties.Party_Full
FROM Donations, Parties
WHERE Donations.Partycode=Parties.Partycode
```

As you can see, we've added a couple of other new things to account for the join.

Because we have more than one table in the query, we have added the table name joined by a dot to the field name (you can actually do this in any query and you could also put the database name before the table name, as in databasename.tablename.fieldname).

Adding the table name with the dot separator, as we have done in the query above, is only strictly necessary if the field name exists in more than one table being used in the query. However, it is probably easiest to get into the habit of always including the table name in a joining query.

If you find this produces more typing than you would like, you can replace the table names with aliases. In this case, they are declared in the FROM line. The previous query would look like this with aliases in place of table names:

```
SELECT a.Donor_Last, a.Donor_First, a.Donor_City,
a.Donation_Amount, a.Partycode, b.Party_Full
FROM Donations AS a, Parties AS b
WHERE a.Partycode = b.Partycode
```

If you like, to save typing, the "AS" can be omitted, as in:

```
SELECT a.Donor_Last, a.Donor_First, a.Donor_City,
a.Donation_Amount, a.Partycode,  b.Party_Full
FROM Donations a, Parties b
WHERE a.Partycode = b.Partycode
```

The aliases make it easier to write more accurate statements with fewer typing errors. This is what the result of the above three queries looks like:

donor_last ˅	donor_first ˅	donor_city ˅	donation_amount ˅	partycode ˅	party_full ˅
Jones	Steve	Toronto	$3,000.00	Blue	Big Blue Party
Tremblay	Monique	Montreal	$3,700.91	Blue	Big Blue Party
White	Mel	Charlottetown	$1,375.28	Blue	Big Blue Party
Leblanc	Carole	Dieppe	$2,000.00	Orange	Orange Crush Party
Stephenson	Brenda	Brandon	$1,900.00	Orange	Orange Crush Party
Mills	Harold	Halifax	$1,200.00	Orange	Orange Crush Party
Smith	Joanne	Calgary	$1,500.00	Red	Red Party of Canada
Johnson	Gerald	Calgary	$1,750.55	Red	Red Party of Canada
Calhoun	David	Hamilton	$1,800.00	Red	Red Party of Canada
Silvers	Wanda	Winnipeg	$2,700.00	Red	Red Party of Canada

Just as with non-joining queries, you can add as many conditions as you like in the WHERE clause, including conditions using Boolean operators. For example:

```
SELECT a.Donor_Last, a.Donor_First, a.Donor_City,
a.Donation_Amount, a.Partycode, b.Party_Full
FROM Donations a, Parties b
WHERE a.Partycode = b.Partycode AND (a.Donor_Last LIKE
"Smith%" OR a.Donor_Last LIKE "%Jones%")
ORDER BY a.Donation_Amount desc;
```

That produces this result:

donor_last ·	donor_first ·	donor_city ·	donation_amount ·	partycode ·	party_full ·
Jones	Steve	Toronto	$3,000.00	Blue	Big Blue Party
Smith	Joanne	Calgary	$1,500.00	Red	Red Party of Canada

Source: © Access

You can also do math, such as this query that totals up the amount of dona-tions to each party, and puts the result in descending order of the amount raised:

```
SELECT b.Party_Full, SUM(a.Donation_Amount) AS Total_Donations
FROM Donations a, Parties b
WHERE a.Partycode = b.Partycode
GROUP BY Party_Full
ORDER BY 2 DESC;
```

Some Notes about Joining

When two tables are joined, each matching row in the first table will match each matching row in the second table, producing a new row in the output of the query that has the information from both. It is a matter of good practice to make sure that when you do a join, there is only one matching record on one side of the join, even if there are many matching records on the other side of the join. Put another way, the joining field should be unique in one of the tables, which is exactly the relationship between a **primary key** in one table and a **foreign key** in a second table, and is called a **one-to-many join**.

You should try to avoid joins that have many matching records on both sides of the join, called many-to-many joins. This is because in the output of the query, the number of output rows will be the product of multiplying the number of matching rows on one side by the number of matching rows on the other side, for each matching value in the common field. This will produce wildly misleading results if you try to sum or count.

If you do find that you have more than one matching record on both sides of a join, it will be either because there are duplicate records in one or both tables, or because in both tables the ID number is a foreign key. In the first instance, you should eliminate the duplicate rows. In the second instance, you should use the WHERE statement to filter one of the tables so there is always only one matching record on that side of the join.

An easy way to get rid of entirely duplicate records on one side of a join is to use the DISTINCTROW command word in the SELECT line. The following query will select all unique rows in TABLE1:

```
SELECT DISTINCTROW *
FROM Table1
```

If you wish to create a new table with just the unique rows, use the CREATE TABLE syntax. Whatever is in the SQL statement will become the new table.

```
CREATE TABLE Newtable
SELECT DISTINCTROW *
FROM Table1
```

In Microsoft Access, the syntax is slightly different:

```
SELECT DISTINCTROW * INTO Newtable
FROM Table1
```

More Advanced Queries

Outer Joins

So far, we have looked at **inner joins**, with which only exactly matching rows appear in the query output. Sometimes, however, you would like to see all of the rows from one of the tables, including the ones that didn't match. For that, you can use a left or right **outer join**. With a left join, you get all of the records from the table on the left side of the join and only the matching records from the table on the right. The right join is the reverse.

The syntax for a left join is as follows. This query would show all current donations and those donations by the same people that exist in the Previous-Donations table.

```
SELECT Donations.Donor_Last, Donations.Donor_First,
Donations.Donor_City,
Donations.Donation_Amount AS Donation_2016, Donations.
PartyCode AS Party2015,PreviousDonations.Donation_Amount
AS Donation_2015, PreviousDonations.PartyCode AS Party2015
FROM Donations
LEFT JOIN PreviousDonations
ON Donations.Donor_ID = PreviousDonations.Donor_ID
```

You can see that the result includes everything from the donations table, plus in the Donation_2015 column, the donations from the previous year:

donor_last	donor_first	donor_city	Donation_2016	Party16	Donation_2015	Party15
Smith	Joanne	Calgary	$1,500.00	Red		
Jones	Steve	Toronto	$3,000.00	Blue	$2,100.00	Blue
Leblanc	Carole	Dieppe	$2,000.00	Orange		
Johnson	Gerald	Calgary	$1,750.55	Red		
Stephenson	Brenda	Brandon	$1,900.00	Orange		
Tremblay	Monique	Montreal	$3,700.91	Blue		
Calhoun	David	Hamilton	$1,800.00	Red	$300.00	Red
Mills	Harold	Halifax	$1,200.00	Orange		
White	Mel	Charlottetown	$1,375.28	Blue		
Silvers	Wanda	Winnipeg	$2,700.00	Red		

For a right join, substitute RIGHT JOIN in the third line. You can add WHERE, GROUP BY, HAVING and ORDER BY clauses as appropriate.

Union Queries

Sometimes you will want to put the results of two queries on top of each other, perhaps two queries that pull data from tables with the same fields, but for different time periods. A **union query** is ideal for this purpose. In a union query, the fields must be of the same number and in the same order of data types in both parts of the query. The result is a merge of the results of both. You can stack as many queries as you like this way:

```
SELECT Donor_Last, Donor_First, Donor_City,
Donation_Amount, Partycode, "2016" as DonationYear
FROM Donations
WHERE Donor_City = "Toronto"
UNION
SELECT Donor_Last, Donor_First, Donor_City,
Donation_Amount, Partycode, "2015" as DonationYear
FROM PreviousDonations
WHERE Donor_City = "Toronto"
```

When you run an UNION query, duplicate rows in the combined query are eliminated (or put another way, grouped together). If you don't want this to happen, replace UNION with UNION ALL.

With both variants, you can include an ORDER BY clause at the end of the query. Apply an alias to the field name(s) you want to sort on, in the first SELECT statement, then order on the alias name(s) as the last clause of the query.

```
SELECT Donor_Last, Donor_First, Donor_City, Donation_Amount as
Amount, Partycode, "2016" as DonationYear
FROM Donations
```

```
WHERE Donor_City = "Toronto"
UNION
SELECT Donor_Last, Donor_First, Donor_City,
Donation_Amount, Partycode, "2015" as DonationYear
FROM PreviousDonations
WHERE Donor_City = "Toronto"
ORDER BY Amount
```

Subqueries

Subqueries are queries within queries. One query is nested inside another. The nested query runs first and passes its result to the query on the outside. One use of a subquery is to pull all records from one table that do not match with records in a second table. In this example, we find donors who have not given before.

```
SELECT Donor_Last,Donor_First, Donor_City,
Donation_Amount,Partycode
FROM Donations
WHERE Donor_ID NOT IN (SELECT DISTINCT Donor_ID FROM
PreviousDonations)
```

In this example, the nested query first finds all the unique entries in DonorID in PreviousDonations. That list is then passed to the outside query, which uses the IN operator to find all records in Donations that do not match.

It is possible to nest more than one query, but with the provision that first query to run will always be the one most nested, proceeding toward the outer query. Go ahead, have some fun with subqueries!

Using Calculated Fields and String Functions

You aren't limited to working just with the fields that exist in your tables. You can also calculate new values in the SELECT line and they will appear in a column of the query output. You have already seen calculated fields as they are used in math queries, but you can also use calculated fields in non-math queries.

A **calculated field** can be a mathematical calculation, such as dividing one field by another to work out a rate per 100,000 or rate per 1,000,000. That might be written this way:

```
SELECT Field1, Field2, (Field3/Field4)*n FROM Tablename
```

(With **n** being a value for the rate such as 100,000 or 1,000,000.)
This technique can also be used to pull information from a text field using a string function. A string function is a function that performs an action

of text, such taking a portion of the text string. For example, if you wanted to grab the first five characters of a political donor's last name, you could write:

```
SELECT LEFT(Donor_Last,5) AS Fivechar
FROM Donations
```

Another function, called RIGHT, will do the same, counting backward from the end of a string. The MID function can grab a slice of text, starting at a position counted from the beginning of the string and continuing for a specified number of characters. For example:

```
MID("Computer",4,5)
```

would return "puter,"

This can be incorporated into a query, with a field name replacing a literal string:

```
SELECT MID(Fieldname,4,5)
```

Some functions return numbers, giving you information about a string. The INSTR function, for example, will tell you how many characters from the left you will find the first occurrence of a substring. We could find the position of the "p" in "Computer":

```
INSTR("Computer", "p")
```

would return 4. It can be used in a query this way:

```
SELECT INSTR(Fieldname,"substring")
```

The substring can be any character or series of characters. The number returned is always the position of the first character.

The LEN function (LENGTH in MySQL) returns the length of a string. So:

```
LEN("Computer") or in MySQL LENGTH("Computer")
```

would return 8. As with any string function, it can be incorporated into a query:

```
SELECT LEN(Fieldname) or in MySQL SELECT LENGTH(Fieldname)
```

The various string functions can be combined to manipulate a string in almost any way. A classic example is splitting an address into its street number and street name. Say we started with the address 123 Any Street. We could get the street number for donors in our donor database this way:

```
SELECT LEFT(Donor_Address, INSTR(Donor_Address, " ")-1)
FROM Donations
```

Here, we are nesting the INSTR function inside the LEFT function. The nested function returns the position in the field of the first space, contained in the quotation marks; 1 is subtracted from this to give the position of the last character in the street number. This result is then fed to the outer LEFT function, which then uses the number to grab all of the characters in the address number.

To grab the street name, we could use this syntax:

```
RIGHT(Donor_Address, LEN(Donor_Address)-INSTR(Donor_
Address," ")) FROM Donations
```

Here we first get the length of the address field and subtract from the whole length the position of the first space, using the INSTR function. That result is then fed into the RIGHT function, which slices off the requisite number of characters. Remember that in MySQL, the function name is LENGTH

In a query, it might all go together like this:

```
SELECT LEFT(Donor_Address, INSTR(Donor_Address, " ")-
1) AS StreetNo, RIGHT(Donor_Address,LEN(Donor_Address)-
INSTR(Donor_Address, " ")) AS Street
FROM Donations
```

Which produces this result:

streetno ▾	street ▾
22	Any Street
57	Moneybags Court
212	Tormentine Cape
55	Nonexistent Way
21	Anywhere Avenue
16	Rue Vide
99	Apex Landing
65	Atlantic Lane
27	Sandstone Bluff
55	Assini-Red Fork

Source: © Access

If you wanted to add new fields to the table, you could modify the table to add the two fields, and then use the UPDATE syntax to insert the street number and street name information.

```
UPDATE Donations
SET StreetNumber = LEFT(Donor_Address, INSTR(Donor_
Address, " ")-1), Street = RIGHT(Donor_Address,LEN(Donor_
Address)-INSTR(Donor_Address," "))
```

This is just one common example showing the power of string functions. Consult the documentation for the database program you are using for a full list of string functions and explanations of what they do.

Creating Views (MySQL)

In MySQL, you can create what are called "views." Views are quasi-tables that you can then run queries on. They are created using SELECT queries and the CREATE VIEW statement. One instance when you might want to use a view is if you want to run multiple summary queries based on a complex multi-table join. It can be easier to create the view with the joins, and then run the subsequent queries using the view as the source table. That way, the joins only have to be defined once. After being created, a view can be used just as a regular table can. Be aware, though, that when your subsequent query runs, the underlying query that creates the view executes. You can't create views in Microsoft Access. However, you can save a query in Access and run a new query using the saved query as the source table. This is the equivalent of using a view in MySQL.

To create a view in MySQL use this syntax:

```
CREATE VIEW NameofView
AS SELECT. . ... [remainder of select statement follows]
```

The view will then appear in your list of tables in your database.

Improving Query Performance by Adding Indexes

A database index is similar in concept to the index in a book. If you have to look through every page of a book looking for a term, it will take a long time. An index will guide you to the right page much more quickly. The same is true with SQL queries. An index will speed them up greatly, especially with very large tables and complex queries that join tables. You should index fields you plan to search or join on frequently. In Access, you normally create an index by altering the table in Table Design view. The syntax for creating an index in MySQL is as follows:

```
ALTER TABLE "databasename"."tablename"
ADD INDEX "indexname" USING BTREE ("fieldname" ASC);
```

Indexes can also be created in front ends such as Navicat, MySQL Workbench, or Sequel Pro.

Indexes can also utilize more than one field, if those fields will often be queried together. The companion website includes tutorials on how to index tables in Microsoft Access and using MySQL front ends.

It's important to be aware that while indexes speed up SELECT queries, they can actually slow down queries that change the content of your tables, such as UPDATE and INSERT queries, which are discussed next. This is because the index has to be altered at the same time as the table.

Queries to Alter Your Data

We have focused mostly on SELECT queries, because they are the queries you are bound to use the most when analyzing your data. From time to time you will need to change the data in your tables, and for this you use action queries. Note that once you run one of these, the change is not reversible (there is no undo command), so make sure that you have backed up and/or made a copy of your table.

To change existing data, use an update query:

```
UPDATE tablename
SET columnname = [string, string function, number, etc.]
WHERE [standard WHERE syntax to limit rows to which the
update will be applied]
```

When running an update query, it is best to add a new blank field to your table and update that. That way, if you make a mistake, you won't have affected your original data.

Here's how to add data to an existing table:

```
INSERT INTO tablename
SELECT [data with the same number of columns, and the
same data types]
WHERE [standard syntax to limit rows that will be added
from the other table]
```

To delete data:

```
DELETE FROM tablename
WHERE [WHERE conditions to limit which rows will be
deleted. Without WHERE, all are deleted]
```

Exporting Query Results

Sometimes you will want to export the results of your queries, for example to do further analysis in Excel, or to use as the basis for a visualization, online map, or map analysis in a GIS program. Microsoft Access can export queries and tables to Excel, delimited text, and other common formats. Go to the External Data ribbon, choose the kind of export you want to do, and follow the directions given by the wizard.

MySQL front ends such as Navicat, Sequel Pro, and MySQL Workbench also have easy-to-use dataexport functions, which export to text and a variety of other formats. The companion website has tutorials on exporting data in Access and MySQL.

Building Your Own Database

Sometimes you want to employ the power of data analysis, but there is no open dataset, nothing is available through freedom of information, and there's nothing to scrape online (see Chapter 9). That is when you turn to building your own database.

That is what Karen Kleiss, formerly of the *Edmonton Journal,* had to do when she was investigating the deaths of children in foster care in the province. The series *Fatal Care,* reported and written with Kleiss's colleague D'arcy Henton of the *Calgary Herald,* revealed that far more children had died in care than the provincial government had acknowledged. The story prompted changes to the law, including the elimination of a law that made it illegal to even name a child who died in care. The series won a bevy of journalism awards, including the Canadian Hillman Prize and the National Newspaper Award for investigations. *Fatal Care* was also nominated for Canada's top prize, the Michener Award.

It all began when Kleiss was reporting on the death of one child, and sought information from the government on how many other children had died in care. Officials couldn't give her an answer. "They literally didn't know how many children had died in foster care. . . . They hadn't made any effort to organize that list. . . .nobody knew anything about why these kids were dying."[2]

So began four years of work involving filing freedom-of-information requests, scouring court records, reading fatality inquiry reports, doing countless interviews, and creating the database the government didn't have. "The database was the most ambitious I had ever undertaken," she said in an interview. It also gave her what she described as "journalistic superpower," the ability to decide precisely what questions she wanted to ask of the data, and then enter the information needed to answer those questions.

For example, is the government more or less likely to do a fatality inquiry report when the case is the subject of a news report? And that was totally true . . . The government almost always did a fatality inquiry report when there were headlines involved. . .but where equally horrendous deaths would occur, there was not a fatality inquiry if the public didn't already know about it . . .

Kleiss's dataset, organized in one table, with one record for each child, ended up with more than 60 fields, from obvious ones such as the child's name and age, to whether there had been a fatality inquiry report or criminal charges, to details of lawsuits. As she scoured thousands of pages of records, the relevant data went into the dataset. Kleiss also included a notes field in which she could enter any outstanding questions or inconsistencies in her information, and through the depth of her research, developed an encyclopedic knowledge of the child-care system that helped her gain the trust of key sources. By the time she was done, "I knew more than anybody else in this province about how this system was working."

Kleiss's experience helps illuminate some of the most important aspects of building your own data. On the one hand, it is time-consuming to transcribe details from documents into rows and columns. On the other hand, the process gives the reporter fine-grained control over the contents of the database tables, which means they can be custom-built to support the analysis that is needed.

Here are some considerations for building your own database:

- Think about what it is you want to know. There's no sense in entering data you won't use. What summary information are you looking to derive from analyzing the data when completed?
- Consider whether it makes more sense to put all the data in a single table, as Kleiss did, or to create a multi-table structure.
- Is it more appropriate to make a table in a spreadsheet, or is a database with the power of SQL queries the most sensible choice?
- How will you enter the data? Will you do it yourself or should you hire others to do the data entry?
- How will you ensure the data is accurate? Should you perhaps have one person enter the data and another check it?
- What fields will you need? What data types and lengths will be needed? If you are going to do mathematical calculations, you'll need number fields. If you will have very large amounts of text, you may need a long-text type field.
- Perhaps most importantly, will the time and effort it takes to build the database yield stories significant enough to justify all the work?

Creating your own database can be a lot of work, but the effort can really pay off, as it did for Kleiss.

Conclusion

Databases are extremely powerful tools for manipulating and summarizing data. As with any data tool, the results are only as good as the data you use. Data cleaning and integrity checks are extremely important. As discussed in Chapter 11 with respect to reporting the data story, it is important to always check any data findings against real-world conditions.

If you can't find your great story in the wild, you should question whether it exists at all. When you do the legwork, however, data analysis can help you find patterns and examples that lead to amazing stories such as those we have discussed in this chapter.

It is also good practice to keep a record of everything you find while querying your data, as well as copies of the SQL queries themselves. One method that many find useful is to keep a query log. This can be as simple as a word-processed file but could also be kept in an application such as Evernote. In a log save the text of the SQL for each query you write (this is in addition to saving the SQL with a front end or in Access), as well as a description of what the query does and why you wrote it. This will be of great value when you need to run the query again and when you need to understand what you were doing weeks or months later. Make note of any new tables you created, and why, and the names of saved SQL queries. Also include a summary of your results and why they are important, and what further analysis needs to be done flowing from what you have found. This process can help keep your work focused, save you from having to repeat work you have already done, and provides you with a detailed record that will be of great value when you are doing follow-up interviews and starting to write a story or developing interactive elements and maps. In the next chapter, we turn to maps in detail.

Study Questions and Exercises

1. Find a flat-file (single table) database on an open-data website, import it into MySQL, and examine the data in a front-end program. Alternatively, use the import wizard in Access to import it into a new database. Consider the field structure, and the data content. Run some simple queries to determine if there are misspellings or other data flaws, such as fields not populated. Write up a plan to analyze the data.

2. Using your plan from question 1, analyze the data and write up a detailed data memo about what you find. What leads on stories are there, if any?

3. Repeat exercises 1 and 2 for a multi-table, relational database.

4. There is an additional exercise on the website that will allow you to use data that was the basis for a published story. You will have the opportunity to do your own analysis, and compare it with that done by the original reporter.

Notes

1. All quotes from Leslie Young in this chapter come from email correspondence with the authors, 9 July 2015.

2. All quotes from Karen Kleiss in this chapter come from a telephone interview with the authors, 26 September 2014.

Chapter 6

Introduction to Maps in Journalism

What You Will Learn:

- Basic principles of mapping
- How web mapping services work
- Layering and different types of map layers
- Common map formats

Maps are everywhere. From road maps to trail maps to transit maps to smartphone maps, we live in a sea of geographical information. We map out the plans for our week and work out the roadmap for our future. The idea of maps is embedded in our consciousness. So it's little surprise that maps have also long been a part of journalism, from locator maps to maps of the Santa Claus Parade.

But never has the technology and art of mapping been as accessible to journalists as it is now. Maps that once would have had to be created by skilled artists or designers can now be built in a few mouse clicks by anyone with a personal computer and an Internet connection. Maps with those little tear-shaped Google markers are everywhere; so are choropleth maps, which show geographical areas in different shades to represent changes in population density, crime rates, or the average price of ice cream. It's a powerful and alluring technology, one that simultaneously transmits information and engages readers, who explore the maps looking for details that matter to them.

Tutorials Included with the Companion Website

You will find these tutorials on the OUP Companion Website (www.oupcanada .com/Vallance-Jones):

- Building Maps with Google Fusion Tables
- Building Maps with ArcGIS Online
- Building Maps with CartoDB
- List of Online Geocoding Services and Costs

But maps can also mislead and outright lie, sometimes without us realizing they are doing it.

Mapping has become such a prominent part of data journalism that we are devoting two chapters to the subject. In this one, we'll explore basic principles, show you how to make simple online maps using web mapping services, and caution you about common mistakes. In the second chapter, we'll dive deeply into maps as an investigative tool, using geographical information service, or GIS, programs.

Let's start with some basics.

Maps Are Not Reality, but Representations of Reality

Maps take the real world of land, rivers, lakes and seas, roads, and highways, railways and pipelines, shipping routes and air corridors, daycare centres and hospitals, city, census, and election district boundaries, and just about anything else real or abstract that has a place in relation to the face of the Earth, and depict it on a two dimensional surface using **points**, **lines**, shapes, and colours. Maps make it possible to communicate a great deal of information using symbolic conventions that have been familiar to most of us since our earliest days in school.

Take for example this simple map of the boundaries of a piece of property, this one just outside the community of Sheet Harbour, Nova Scotia. The features it displays are straightforward, some lines, some shaded areas and very little else.

Now, let's look at the equivalent text-based description of the same parcel of land, as recorded in the province's computerized land registration system:

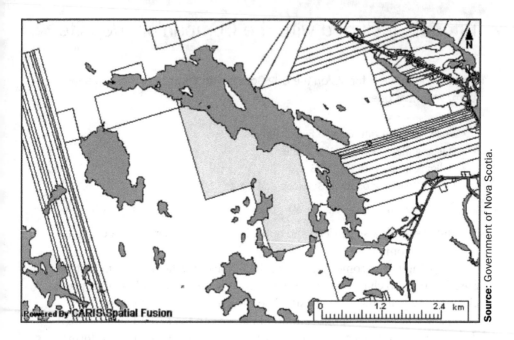

Map showing boundaries of a piece of property

ALL THAT CERTAIN LOT, piece or parcel of land situate, lying and being on the West side of Grand Lake, in Sheet Harbour, in the County of Halifax and Province of Nova Scotia, said parcel being more particularly described as follows:

BEGINNING at a stake standing at the Northeast angle of 10,000 acres granted to John Collier and Joseph Gerrish in the District of Sheet Harbour;

THENCE running South 05 degrees West, 160 chains and 75 links;

THENCE North 85 degrees West, 35 chains and 50 links to Two Bar Lake;

THENCE Westerly by the Northern side of said Lake, 18 chains to a stake;

THENCE North 05 degrees East, 64 chains and 50 links;

THENCE North 85 degrees West, 46 chains;

THENCE North 05 degrees East, 92 chains;

THENCE South 85 degrees East, 96 chains and 50 links to the PLACE OF BEGINNING;

SAVING AND RESERVING there out the land covered by the waters of Grand Lake, Slough Lake, Rocky Lake, Bear Lake and Star Lake;CONTAINING 815 acres, more or less;

BEING AND INTENDED TO BE the land as granted by the Crown to Nathaniel Curry and Nelson A. Rhodes by Grant Number 19814 and dated March 4, 1902 and being a portion of the original Crown Grant to John Collier and Joseph Gerrish escheated on May 6, 1898;

SAVING AND EXCEPTING the Southern portion of the island in Grand Lake and being a portion of the land as conveyed by Scott Worldwide, Inc to Cape Chignecto Lands Limited and described in Lot No. 2 (last description) under Schedule C in the Indenture dated June 6, 1994, and recorded in the Office of the Registrar of Deeds for Halifax County on June 8, 1994, in Book 5578, at Page 1, as Document No. 22975;

ALSO SAVING AND EXCEPTING that portion of the above parcel that lies East of Grant Lake and being a portion of the land as conveyed by Kimberly-Clark Worldwide, Inc to J. D. Irving, Limited by an Indenture dated December 18, 1998 and as recorded in the Office of the Registrar of Deeds for Halifax County on December 23, 1998, in Book 6324, at Page 744, as Document No. 41665;

ALSO SAVING AND EXCEPTING the two small islands in Grand Lake with the Northern-most island being located at Latitude 44 degrees, 55 minutes, 24.0 seconds North and Longitude 62 degrees, 36 minutes, 47.4 seconds West and the Southern most island being located at Latitude 44 degrees, 55 minutes, 21.7 seconds North and Longitude 62 degrees, 36 minutes, 39.4 seconds West and both islands being bounded on all sides by the ordinary high water mark of Grand Lake.[1]

It's not hard to see the great advantages of the map compared to the legal text as formulated from a legal survey. In a single glance, one can appreciate the approximate shape and size of the parcel, see it in relationship to neighbouring pieces of land and the nearby roadway, and even divine that the land is adjacent to a body of water. It's not hard to develop a mental picture of what this land might be like.

But there is as much missing from this map as is present. More, in fact. It gives us no idea of the elevation and topography of the parcel, the type of soil, the nature of the water frontage, and so on. The map-maker has chosen to display some aspects of reality, and leave others out. For the purposes at hand, it provides a perfectly reasonable approximation of the location and size of the parcel. Later on in this chapter, we'll talk about how maps can oversimplify and mislead, especially when one is not careful, but for now we'll accept that maps are a tremendously effective way of presenting what we call spatial information, information about things that is represented in physical space and in relation to other things.

The things shown on maps may be features that physically exist now or existed at some point, such as roadways or crime scenes, or completely abstract constructs such as boundary lines. Indeed all of these things can be present on the same map. The key is to always keep in mind the purpose and intended audience.

Sometimes, features are drawn on a map so as to represent their extent on the face of the Earth, such as with water bodies. Other times, a feature may take up far more space on the map than it does in real life, such as the line representing a highway or the location of a crime. If you tried to draw a road at its actual width on a small-scale state map, it would be invisible or nearly invisible, as would the location of a crime. Transit-line maps, such as the ones in subway cars, don't represent distance at all, because what is most important is the order of stations. The distance between them is less crucial.

People are so conditioned to viewing maps that they generally understand and accept these conventions. Motorists don't think twice about the width of a depicted road, and a news consumer doesn't question the point representing a crime scene nor think that it represents the spatial area occupied by the commission of the crime.

The important thing is that maps are representations of reality, not the reality itself.

While map users don't give much thought to these things, you as a maker of maps need to be more aware of them. How you depict features on your maps will affect how your audience interprets them. As with any medium, maps are essentially a means of communicating the abstractness and complexity of reality in a simple form. This means there will always be a limit to what can be done, and a potential result which may not convey exactly what we had intended.[2]

Web Mapping Services

Web mapping services take these long-established conventions of physical maps, and move them to the virtual world of our smartphone or computer screen. In doing so, they enable us as non-cartographer journalists to create remarkably accurate and useful maps, without having to worry too much at first about the finer details of how they go together. But it's useful to be aware of a few things.

While physical maps put real ink on real paper, web mapping services perform their magic through layering. A map is made up of at least one **layer**, and there may be several. When you work with Google Maps, ArcGIS Online, CartoDB, and similar tools, the foundational layer, or base layer, is provided for you. There may be choices as to which base layer to use, such as the map, hybrid, or satellite views offered by Google Maps and its close cousin Fusion Tables, but a map will always have one base layer. Everything else is shown in relation to it.

The base layer is made up of **tiles**, squares of base map that are stitched together by the web mapping service to give the appearance of a continuous map, a bit like a tile floor with invisible grout lines. Those tiles are served up to your web browser by the map service, as needed. If you have a slow connection, you may see some of the tiles loading. Using tiles takes far less time than having to send a whole map layer every time the user makes a change, such as panning sideways to bring new areas into view and take others out of view.[3] Only the newly visible tiles have to be sent again.

All web map services allow you to zoom in and out on the map. The tiles are different depending on the magnification, or zoom level, that you choose. So if you want to look at the whole world, the tiles may just show the oceans, some topographic differentiation in land areas, and prominent borders. As you zoom in, that is choose progressively greater zoom levels, the map server sends you tiles with greater and greater detail, until at the closest zoom level you may be looking at just a few blocks in your neighbourhood with the parks, trails, and road names visible. All of this happens so seamlessly that users are rarely aware of it.

Of course, the web mapping service needs to know where to put the tiles, and it does that through the use of coordinates referenced in latitudes and longitudes. We'll spend a lot more time talking about **coordinate systems** in the next chapter, but for now it suffices to know that the web mapping service is aware of where every latitude and longitude point is located in the world, and can locate any feature in relation to that. The magic of layering and tiles is that it now becomes possible to add additional layers of information, and thus the user can build on what the mapping service provides, creating a customized map experience.

Layers come in three different general types. A points layer depicts individual points that represent the location of something tangible or intangible that has as its primary characteristic a position at a specific latitude/longitude coordinate. While the feature at that location may occupy space in the real world, the point itself represents only the location. An example would be points representing crime scenes. Line layers represent tangible or intangible things that have as their primary characteristic being a line that connects at least two points. A line may be made up of many individual segments and through the use of many short segments, a line can be made to appear curved. Roads are very frequently line features, as are pipelines. A **polygon** layer depicts enclosed, many-sided areas. Polygons are also made up of many straight-line segments that run between points. Electoral districts are an example of

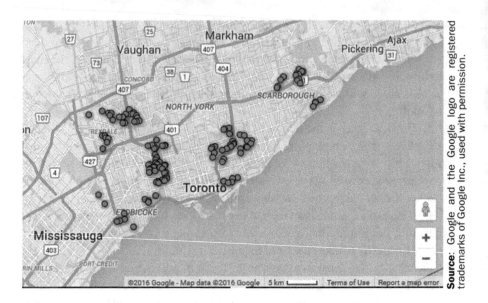

This map of Toronto is a simple points map layer on top of the basic road map base layer in Google Fusion Tables

polygons. On some maps, roads may also be depicted using polygons. While there are variations in terminology, these are the three main kinds of layers you can put on a web map.

Depending on the web mapping service you use, you may be able to add one or more layers. Google Fusion Tables allows you to add one layer of your own to a Google Map, although you can write code in the JavaScript programming language to add up to five. ArcGIS Online allows you to add many layers without having to use code. With all of these services, however, there is a practical limit as to the number of layers you can add to a map before it becomes cluttered and unreadable. A typical configuration might be a polygon layer depicting economic disparity in census tracts across a city, and a points file representing locations of banks. In some cases, you might add a few points layers, representing different kinds of things. But a useful rule in making maps is that less is often more.

Getting Your Data onto a Web Map

All right, so we understand the basics of how web maps work. Layers, made up of tiles, are served to our device and arrayed on the screen based on latitude and longitude coordinates. We can then add our own layers containing customized information we want to layer on top of the base map. But how do we get the information there?

The answer is we have to have our map layers in one of the map file formats that is supported by the particular web mapping service we want to use. A number of formats have been developed over the years, each with its particular strengths. Three you will encounter often will be KML files, shapefiles, and GeoJSON files.

A KML file is a Keyhole Markup Language file, the native map format of Google Maps and an open standard. A KML file looks just a bit like an HTML file, with the information needed to draw the layer contained in a single text file that uses tags around all of the elements. It's actually a subtype of XML, a markup language designed to transmit data between computers. Here is the very top of a typical KML polygon layer, this one depicting Statistics Canada census tracts. The pairs of numbers at the bottom are some of the latitude and longitude coordinates for the points that join the line segments that make up one of the polygons.

```
<?xml version="1.0" encoding="utf-8" ?>
<kml xmlns="http://www.opengis.net/kml/2.2">
<Document><Folder><name>HalifaxTracts</name>
  <Placemark>
        <Style><LineStyle><color>ff0000ff</color></LineStyle><PolyStyle><fill>0</fill></
PolyStyle></Style>
        <ExtendedData><SchemaData schemaUrl="#HalifaxTracts">
            <SimpleData name="CTUID">2050023.00</SimpleData>
            <SimpleData name="CTNAME">0023.00</SimpleData>
            <SimpleData name="CMAUID">205</SimpleData>
            <SimpleData name="CMANAME">Halifax</SimpleData>
            <SimpleData name="CMATYPE">B</SimpleData>
            <SimpleData name="CMAPUID">12205</SimpleData>
            <SimpleData name="PRUID">12</SimpleData>
            <SimpleData name="PRNAME">Nova Scotia / Nouvelle-Écosse</SimpleData>
        </SchemaData></ExtendedData>
        <Polygon><altitudeMode>relativeToGround</
altitudeMode><outerBoundaryIs><LinearRing><altitudeMode>relativeToGround</
altitudeMode><coordinates>-63.624374566999904,44.653497210000069
-63.624434651999927,44.653511941000033 -63.624895884999937,44.653639301000055
-63.625395403999903,44.653715849000037 -63.625740501999928,44.653741443000051
-63.626265412999935,44.653733604000081 -63.626471407999922,44.653718615000059
-63.626963385999936,44.653663692000066 -63.627720985999929,44.653593038000054
-63.628083710999931,44.653558398000087 -63.628963173999921,44.653540729000042
```

A shapefile is a map file format developed by Esri, makers of the most popular and successful commercial GIS program, ArcGIS. You will frequently encounter shapefiles on the open-data sites of national, state and provincial, and municipal governments.

A shapefile is actually made up of several separate files, including three required ones with the extensions .shp, .shx, and .dbf. The .shp file contains the geographical data, the .shx file an index, and the .dbf file the tabular data associated with the map. Whenever you work with a shapefile, you need to ensure that you have all of the files; they should all have the same name, with the various extensions.

GeoJSON is a specialized form of JSON, a text-based file format that is read easily by Internet browsers. GeoJSON adds additional information related to geography to the base JSON file type. Here is part of GeoJSON file from the site www.election-atlas.ca:

```
{
"type": "FeatureCollection",
"crs": { "type": "name", "properties": { "name":
"urn:ogc:def:crs:OGC:1.3:CRS84" } },

"features": [
{ "type": "Feature", "properties": { "NO_SV": "79", "POLLCODE":
"783079", "IND_OFF": "O", "RIDINGNO": "783", "RIDINGNAME": "Roberval",
"POLLNO": "79", "MERGEDWITH": null, "VOTERS": "351", "TOTALVOTES":
"218", "REJECTED": "0", "TURNOUT": "62", "PQPCT": "38.07", "LIBPCT":
"50.46", "CAQPCT": "6.42", "QSPCT": "4.59", "GRNPCT": "0.00", "ONPCT":
"0.46", "CONPCT": "0.00", "INDPCT": "0.00", "FIRST": "PLQ", "SECOND":
"PQ", "THIRD": "CAQ", "PTY1": "PLQ", "CAND1": "Couillard", "VOTES1":
"110", "PCT1": "50", "PTY2": "PQ", "CAND2": "Trottier", "VOTES2":
"83", "PCT2": "38", "PTY3": "CAQ", "CAND3": "Truchon", "VOTES3": "14",
"PCT3": "6", "PTY4": "QS", "CAND4": "NÃ©ron", "VOTES4": "10", "PCT4":
"5", "PTY5": "ON", "CAND5": "Cauchon", "VOTES5": "1", "PCT5": "0",
"PTY6": "PSP", "CAND6": "Boucher", "VOTES6": "0", "PCT6": "0", "PTY7":
null, "CAND7": null, "VOTES7": null, "PCT7": null, "PTY8": null,
"CAND8": null, "VOTES8": null, "PCT8": null, "PTY9": null, "CAND9":
null, "VOTES9": null, "PCT9": null }, "geometry": { "type":
"MultiPolygon", "coordinates": [ [ [ [ -72.3865, 48.90385 ], [
-72.41404, 48.89089 ], [ -72.42384, 48.8921 ], [ -72.4239, 48.89208 ],
[ -72.42413, 48.88824 ], [ -72.43726, 48.8816 ], [ -72.43985, 48.88395
1. [ -72.44072, 48.88412 ], [ -72.44081, 48.88494 ], [ -72.44206,
```

All of these map formats contain both the geographic information, based on latitudes and longitudes, and the attribute information, such as street or city names, of features that can be displayed on a map.

Different web mapping services have different requirements for the map formats they will allow you to upload and display. For example, CartoDB and ArcGIS Online permit you to upload shapefiles, so long as they are compressed using **zip**. Google Fusion Tables require geographic files to be in KML format. But you shouldn't be terribly concerned if the layer you want to add is not in the required format; it is generally possible to convert from one to another. One excellent tool for that job is the **open-source** GIS application QGIS that we introduce in the next chapter. Even if you never use it for anything else, it has an excellent built-in file conversion utility. ArcGIS can also convert from one format to another, and there are various online conversion services that come and go.

Data Not Already in a Map Format

Sometimes the data you want to add to your map isn't already in a map format. It may have street addresses, names of electoral districts, or zip or postal codes. There are two main approaches to adding such information to a map.

The first way is to connect or join the information to an existing layer that is in a geographical format. This is similar in concept to the joins that you can do in a database program, as discussed in Chapter 5. So if you have a file of election results with district names, you can join that table to a layer in a map format that depicts the district boundaries. You can now display the election results on your map. The major wep-mapping services, Fusion Tables, ArcGIS Online, and CartoDB all make this easy. You will find tutorials for building maps with all three of these services on the companion website.

The other way to turn non-geographic data into something that can be displayed on a map is a process called **geocoding**. In geocoding, the information in your non-geographic table, say the address field, is compared to reference data that contains all possible addresses for the area in question. The geocoding application looks for matches between the two, and assigns latitude and longitude coordinates to each row of your non-geographic data, making it possible to upload and add it to a map in a web mapping service. Most people working with a web mapping service will use some kind of online geocoding service. Some are free, some not so much. Google allows you to use its geocoding service, which you can access through Fusion Tables, to geocode up to 2,500 addresses a day at no charge, but the resulting address points must be used within a Google product. ArcGIS Online allows users of a free, public account to add up to 250 address points in a CSV file to a map; the geocoding happens automatically so long as the CSV has either street addresses or latitudes and longitudes for each point. More extensive geocoding requires an account, and the use of paid credits. CartoDB will geocode zip and postal codes for many countries, and computer IP (**Internet Protocol**) addresses, without charge, but uses a credit system for geocoding addresses. Accounts come with free credits, but after that, they must be purchased. Other, free alternatives exist, including Microsoft's Bing geocoding service. The array of services and the costs tends to change over time. The current available services and their costs, if any, are listed on the companion website.

Your Data Is Ready: How to Use It?

The underlying principles, and the technical tasks of getting data ready to map, are all important to know. Just as important is understanding how journalists use web mapping services. For the most part, they are used as an endpoint, to display the results of other analysis that might have been done using a spreadsheet or database program. Some vendors, such as ArcGIS Online and CartoDB are pushing more sophisticated analytical capabilities to the "cloud," as server-based services are often called. For example, CartoDB allows you to do a **spatial join**, which is a join between two map layers that compares the locations of features within the two layers. Esri is increasingly pushing analytical capabilities to the web as part of its ArcGIS Online service and the sophistication level is only going to increase (and this is evident from new platforms being released such as ArcGIS Earth). But part of the deal with online services is that if you go over use thresholds, you have to pay. And many journalists prefer to do this kind of work on their own desktops, using a GIS program, to protect their work from prying eyes. The latter approach has the benefit of costing nothing, once the software is acquired. Chapter 7 covers geographic analysis with a GIS in detail. This chapter will limit its focus to using web mapping services to create interactive maps that display data.

Chad Skelton, formerly of the *Vancouver Sun,* has been a prolific user of web mapping services, which he used to enrich his reporting for several years. In June 2014, he published online and in the paper stories on the rate of people registering as organ donors across British Columbia. He requested and obtained from the province's organ transplant agency, BC Transplant, the number of people registered in each forward sortation area in the province. Then, using the population of each FSA, he worked out the rate of organ donation in each area. As discussed below, an FSA is a geographical area that uses the first three characters of a six-character postal code, such as V5S. Skelton's analysis found the rate varied a great deal.

> People on Vancouver's west side were much more likely to be on the organ-donor list than those on the city's east side. And the differences are significant: People on the city's west side are several times more likely to be registered organ donors than in some neighbourhoods on the east side.[4]

Skelton also explored the connection between lower rates of organ donation and a higher presence of immigrants. The project was a relatively

Share of population on registry

under 15%   15-18%   18-22%   22-30%   30% or
more

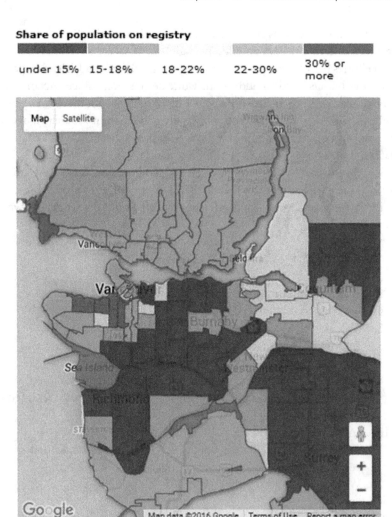

Choropleth map using diverging colour scheme to show rates of registered organ donors.
Source: Vancouver Sun. Interactive map created by Chad Skelton.

straightforward one, reflecting the ease with which journalists can use web mapping services to quickly convey information to readers. "I made a choropleth map using Google Fusion Tables to show the differences between neighbourhoods," he said, using a diverging colour scheme (see page 126). "I find that diverging palettes are more effective in quickly communicating data to readers. Readers can see at an instant which areas are higher than average, or lower than average." He used an online tool called ColorBrewer (see pages 132–3) to select an effective palette.

Skelton says one regret was not using a colour-blind-friendly palette, something he has tried to address in work he has done since. According to the National Institutes of Health, about 1 in 10 men have some form of colour blindness with the most common forms being the inability to distinguish between red and green and blue and yellow.[5] Chapter 8 discusses visualization in greater detail.

Except for some routine data cleaning, Skelton said there were no particular issues with the data, which BC Transplant provided without requiring a freedom-of-information request. His complete workflow was as follows:

1. Requesting the data from BC Transplant.
2. Getting the data.
3. Doing some simple cleanup on the data.
4. Getting population counts by FSA.
5. Calculating a rate for each FSA.
6. Importing the data into Fusion Tables.
7. Merging the data to a KML file of FSA boundaries.
8. Colour-coding the areas based on the rate of organ donation.
9. Formatting the Fusion Tables pop-up windows so they presented the data cleanly.
10. Interviewing experts with BC Transplant.
11. Talking to Karen Rai, a South Asian woman who waited several years for a kidney.
12. Writing the story.

Skelton's use of a web mapping service allowed him to turn around an important story with public policy implications in a relatively short period of time.

What Kinds of Maps Can You Make?

Web mapping services make it possible to create several different map styles, but they can be divided into two broad categories. The first are maps based on points.

Point maps serve a wide range of purposes, from simply showing the locations of all of the coffee shops in a given area to showing clusters of crimes. Each point may represent a single event or location, or it may represent an aggregation of many individual events that occurred at the same location, with the aggregate value given as a number. Either way, you will probably prepare your data first in a spreadsheet or database program, and the points may well be the result of extensive analysis that then produces a table of data with associated addresses, latitudes and longitudes, and so on.

If your points already have latitude and longitude coordinates, you can immediately put them on your map (though you should check the points for accuracy when you map them because problems such as flipped latitude and longitude coordinates can place your points in the wrong places). The same goes if the points come to you already plotted in a shapefile, KML, or Geo-JSON file. With at most a file conversion, the points are ready to upload to the web mapping service.

In many cases, though, the points probably won't already be geocoded, and you will need to use a geocoding service to put them onto your map. Be sure to check the accuracy of the geocoding job when it is completed and correct any incorrectly placed points. One easy way to check is to zoom far out and see if any points are in some other state, province or country (or indeed, appear in the middle of the ocean somewhere). Manually check a few of the ones that appear correctly positioned, to make sure there isn't some repetitive error cropping in. If you have only a few points, you could easily check them all.

Once your points have been uploaded to the web mapping service, you can do many things with them. For example, if your points represent aggregate data, you can give them different colours depending on a numeric value attached to each point. Intersections with greater numbers of accidents could be given different colours from intersections with lower numbers of accidents. Or, you can use the capability built into all of the web mapping services to create a **heat map**. A heat map averages values in areas around clusters of points, and produces an output that shows "hot" areas where many points are concentrated and "cool" areas where fewer are concentrated. This is a great alternative to choropleth maps when the latter aren't feasible. We'll talk about choropleth maps in the next section.

You can also make a heat map using points that represent individual values. Such points can also be used to illustrate locations, and can be given different colours depending on categories. For example, Tim Hortons coffee shops could be given one colour and Starbucks another, a project that was actually done by then *PostMedia* data journalist William Wolfe-Wylie, who used a web scraper written in **Python** to download the locations of Tim Hortons and Starbucks stores, including their geographical locations, from the companies' "find a location" pages.[6]

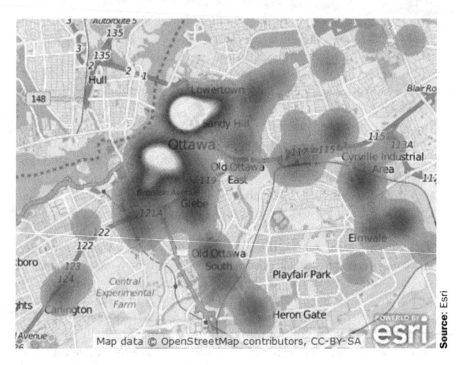

Heat map made in ArcGIS Online

Yet another kind of map uses proportional circles to represent values of different sizes. After a meteor exploded in the skies above Chelyabinsk, Russia, in February 2013, creating a huge fireball and a shockwave that broke windows and caused hundreds of injuries, the *Washington Post* used a proportional circles map to show the sizes of impact craters all over the world.[7] In that case, the map showed literal circles, but a proportional circles map can be used to compare many kinds of raw values, or rates. In March 2016, *Maclean's* magazine used a proportional circles map built in Leaflet to show the total number of Syrian refugees in each community across Canada, as well as the rate of refugees accepted per 10,000 residents.[8]

Boundary Maps

Journalists also routinely make maps that are based on the boundaries of polygon layers. These fall into two categories, categorical, and aggregate or quantitative.

A map using categorical data simply shades different polygons with colours that vary depending on the category. A map showing which party won each electoral district is an example of a **categorical map**.

A map using quantitative data is called a choropleth map, the type used by Skelton for his organ-transplant story. These are probably the most commonly used (and abused) category of online maps. When you create a choropleth map, you shade polygons in different colours depending on some numeric value, which should be some kind of rate or percentage. Your reader can then easily see how the values vary across the different polygons.

Some Important Design Principles

As we discussed earlier, maps make sense to people. We are all familiar with them, and understand intuitively how they represent tangible and intangible things from the real world on a 2-D surface. As such, maps are an appealing feature of twenty-first-century online journalism. They also have tremendous potential to be confusing or misleading. Decisions such as what style of map to make, what boundaries to pick, and what colours to use can influence whether our map informs or befuddles.

A Choice of Styles

Let's start with map styles. For our purposes, we will limit our discussion to the choice of making a map of points, a choropleth map that groups values into ranges, or a map that displays categorical data in boundaries.

The choice of points, choropleth, or categorical has a lot to do with the type of data you want to map.

If you are mapping individual instances, such as crimes, motor vehicle accidents, or polluting factories, a point map is probably going to serve your needs best. These kinds of things tend to be unevenly distributed and occur at discrete locations. You want to tell the story of "where are the factories; where are the crimes?" Even if you roll up the instances into aggregated statistics on the total number of crimes or accidents a point map will be more useful. From the points you can make a heat map to show concentrations of crimes, or vary the size of the aggregated points to show the crime hotspots. For your readers, this will be a useful map. It will allow them to see where the crimes occur relative to where they live, making the story individual. It is almost as if the map can tell a number of stories limited only by the number of individuals in your audience.

If you are mapping rates or percentages, the choropleth map may become a useful storytelling tool. But be aware that this type of map is overused, possibly because it is seen so often and users may begin to see it as the norm. The key considerations driving your decision to use a choropleth map are whether the data you want to map is intrinsically tied to the boundaries you intend to use, and whether it tends to be distributed across the whole map.

Broadly speaking, it's best to avoid using a choropleth map to display raw numbers. Without some kind of rate or percentage calculation, a choropleth map is not going to have real meaning. Let's say Chad Skelton had simply mapped the number of people on the organ donation registry in each FSA in British Columbia. This would have been as easy to do with a web mapping service as he did. But without considering the populations of the FSAs, the map wouldn't have given a true picture of the variations in organ donation across the province. The map would have told a half truth, never a good thing in journalism. This is why, if you are going to make this kind of map, you need to have data that calculates whatever numbers you are showing as rates, perhaps rates per 1,000 residents. Chapter 4, on spreadsheets, explains how to calculate rates.

It's also important that the data be intrinsically tied to the defined areas you are going to use to make your map. When you map election results in electoral districts, household income by census tract, or rate of organ donation by FSA, you are displaying data that has a close connection to the geographies. The voting took place in the electoral district and all the voters are represented by the same person in the legislature. The income is earned by people living in the census tracts. The organ donors live within the boundaries. Further, both Statistics Canada and the US Census Bureau set the boundaries of census tracts to represent coherent neighbourhoods.

The less the data is tied to boundaries, the less useful choropleth maps will be. Also, the numbers for each polygon will be directly affected by the decisions made on how to draw the boundaries. If the boundaries are, in effect, arbitrary, it may not be clear what you are really showing.

One of the commonly used boundary files in Canada is postal code forward sortation areas, the boundaries that Skelton used. FSAs were created by the post office to facilitate sorting and delivery of mail, but can be used as boundaries to display other data, if the data is closely tied to those geographical boundaries.

But let's say you wanted to map grants and loans to businesses from a government agency and the data showed the address of the organization that received the money, including the postal code. It would be easy to use a database or spreadsheet program to spit out the FSA and work out a rate, say total fgrants and loans per 100,000 people in each FSA.

But the map would be misleading. Just because the organization receiving the money has its address at a particular location, doesn't mean the money is going there or being spent there. The project on which the money is being spent may be in a completely different place. And the number of people living in the FSA is irrelevant, even though that data is available from the census. The residents have nothing to do with the loans and grants, though some might conceivably earn income at one of the businesses. At best, the map might be a good indicator of where company offices are located.

This may be an extreme example, but it's not hard to imagine other similarly misleading, even mendacious maps. If you had data on the number of traffic accidents that took place in each municipality in a large urban area, you could have two problems. First, the occurrence of some traffic accidents may have little to do with the boundaries of the municipality in which they occurred; they could just as easily have occurred a few kilometres down the road. Second, it may be difficult to work out a useful rate. Population of each municipality would not be particularly useful, because you can't be certain that the people driving the vehicles live in the places where they have the accidents, and it is drivers that have accidents, not the overall population. A more useful calculation would be the number of accidents taking place per the number of vehicles travelling on a particular section of roadway, say between two expressway ramps. But you wouldn't use a choropleth map to display that.

A similar problem would exist with a choropleth map purporting to show the incidence of crime by FSA. Since crime is not uniformly distributed, one crime hotspot could make a whole neighbourhood look less safe. Move an apartment block across the street into the next FSA, and another neighbourhood might suddenly be the unsafe one, even if the rest of the area were relatively quiet. In this case it would be fairer and more accurate to map using points, and then make a heat map.

Categorical maps are the simplest to make, and the easiest to understand. If you want to show categories, say which congressional districts voted for the Republicans and which for the Democrats, colour the districts appropriately. We'll be talking about colour next.

Choosing Appropriate Colours

Web mapping services make it easy to apply a rainbow of colours to a categorical or choropleth map, but that doesn't necessarily mean that you should. The use of colours again has a lot to do with your data and how you can make it easier for your audience to understand what the data means. Choose the wrong colours, or too many, and you may obscure your meaning or worse.

Categorical maps are a relatively simple exercise. You pick colours that contrast with each other, so as to highlight the differences. In some cases, the choice is almost made for you. In the congressional districts example, it's a pretty easy decision to make Republican districts red and Democratic blue.

Choropleth maps offer a greater challenge, because here the possibility for error is greater. The general rule is to use a colour scheme that allows the reader to discern easily the change in values across different areas, while not conveying unintended messages.

Let's start with an example from a real program. When you make a Google Fusion Tables map, you can colour polygons using what it calls buckets. Buckets are groupings of ranges of values, typical stuff for makers of a choropleth map.

But the default colours offered up are a mix of seemingly random colours. If you are trying to show variance, this is a problem because the reader will have no way to know, other than by reading a scale, which colour represents which value.

Of course, Fusion Tables makes it easy to change the colours to something more understandable, but it seems highly likely that a lot of users simply accept the offered array of colours, not realizing that they are hindering rather than helping storytelling.

But what is appropriate? That depends on what you are trying to show. If you are simply trying to show how values vary from boundary to boundary, use a range of shades of the same colour, for example light blue to dark blue. This is often referred to as a "sequential" colour scheme.[9]

The convention that light means lower values and dark means higher values is pretty well established, but make sure when you pick your colours that you don't inadvertently give the wrong message. Using varying shades of a red could be interpreted by the casual reader as meaning from good to bad, as more intense red is often associated with being worse. If you were showing the percentage of people who are visible minorities by census tract, you might not want to use reds. Something neutral such as greens or blues might be better.

On the other hand, if you were showing the percentage who voted Republican by district, a range of reds might be just fine, as the reader would associate red in that instance with the GOP.

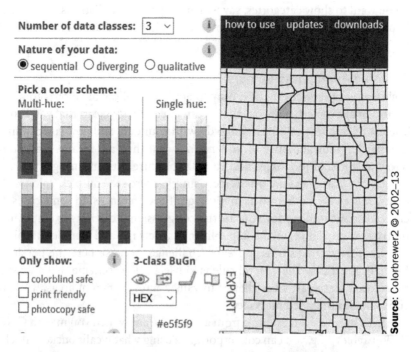

The ColorBrewer website makes it easier to pick appropriate colours for your maps

Sometimes, you want to emphasize certain boundaries that have extreme data values, which are called **outliers**. That can be accomplished by simply using very dark and light shades of one colour, but you can also use a divergent colour scheme like the one Skelton used for his organ donation story. It uses two contrasting colours for the extreme values, and then goes through lesser variants of those colours to a neutral colour for the middle of the range.[10]

Sometimes, if your storytelling purpose is to show something that varies from good to bad, such as the rate of cancer in each health district, using a colour scheme that is familiar can be effective. One well-understood convention is going from green to yellow to red to indicate go, slow down, stop, or "everything's good, some problems, serious problems here." This can be an effective scheme for journalists, but be careful that you aren't making qualitative judgments. Not everyone would agree, for example, that having low incomes makes a neighbourhood "bad."

An excellent tool that can help you pick effective colour palettes is Color-Brewer. You can find it at ColorBrewer2.org. Not only will ColorBrewer help you see if the colours show the pattern you intend to show clearly, it will also help you find palettes that are colour-blind friendly, as Skelton now does.

Setting Breakpoints

It's also important to be careful about the breakpoints that you use to separate the different ranges of numbers. GIS programs such as ArcGIS and QGIS can do mathematical calculations to produce breakpoints that accurately convey genuine differences between the different regions displayed (see Chapter 7). But you can do the same thing using a spreadsheet program. This can help reveal, in a visual way, where the groupings are within your data, so you can cluster together values based on actual groupings and not simply arbitrary divisions.

In journalistic contexts we often want to use even numbers for breakpoints, and there is even a temptation to always use equal ranges, but many readers will look at the map first and draw conclusions based on what they see, without even looking at the legend, making the choice of breakpoints more than a theoretical consideration.

If you are displaying socio-economic and similar data, where the goal is to see which areas fall into different tranches, quartile breakpoints can be an excellent and statistically valid way of showing differences. Quartiles, for example, divide the range of values into the first 25 per cent of values, the next 25 per cent and so on. Quintiles do this as well, but each slice is a fifth of the values. A GIS program can do this for you automatically, but you can also use a spreadsheet program to calculate the quartiles, then apply them to your map.

For those who would like to further explore these questions, one highly recommended resource is Mark Monmonier's classic, *How to Lie with Maps*. Chapter 10 of the second edition offers a detailed rundown of the hazards of working with choropleth maps, including choosing breakpoints and colours.[10] The book was important research material in developing this chapter.

Conclusion

We began this chapter by saying that maps are representations of reality. When you make a map for storytelling, you are putting yourself in charge of that representation of reality. Just as in conventional written journalism you need to strive to make your stories clear and accurate, with an appropriate tone, the same is true with maps. But if you apply some of the tools and principles we have discussed here, you can become a successful visual storyteller. In the next chapter, we'll discuss maps as analytical tools similar to the SQL databases we introduced in Chapter 5.

Study Questions and Exercises

1. Find two KML files on an open-data website and upload them to a web mapping service, using the methods in the tutorials on the companion website.
2. Upload a polygon KML file to a web mapping service, and some data with totals for the same polygons. Make a choropleth map, considering as you do the appropriate colour scheme to tell your story.
3. You will find an additional exercise using live data on the companion website.

Notes

1. Record contained in Nova Scotia land registration system, for PID 00486340: 870 acres of crown land on the shore of Grand Lake, Sheet Harbour, NS.
2. Many of the ideas in this section are drawn from this classic book: Mark S. Monmonier, *How to Lie with Maps*, 2nd ed. (Chicago: University of Chicago Press, 1996), 2.
3. John T. Sample and Elias Ioup, *Tile-Based Geospatial Information Systems: Principles and Practices* (New York: Springer, 2010).
4. All quotes from Chad Skelton are from email correspondence with the authors, 2 June 2015.
5. Dona M. Wong, *The Wall Street Journal Guide to Information Graphics* (New York: W.W. Norton, 2013), 44–5.
6. William Wolfe-Wylie "Starbucks Owns the Cities, Tim Hortons Owns the Highways," *Canada.com*, 21 February 2003, http://o.canada.com/business/tim-hortons-might-control-the-highways-but-starbucks-rules-the-city.
7. "Russia's Surprise Meteor and Earth's Crater," 15 February 2013, *Washington Post*, http://www.washingtonpost.com/wp-srv/special/world/russia-meteor/index.html.
8. Nick Taylor-Vaisey and Amanda Shendruk, "True North Refugees: Where 25,000 Syrians Have Settled in Canada," *Maclean's*, 2 March 2016, http://www.macleans.ca/news/canada/true-north-refugees-where-25000-syrians-have-settled-in-canada/.
9. "Color Theory and Mapping," *Mapbox*, n.d., http://www.mapbox.com/tilemill/docs/guides/tips-for-color/
10. Ibid.

Chapter 7

Working with GIS Programs

What You Will Learn:

- More key principles of mapping, including different types of coordinate reference systems
- The fundamentals of a GIS, a sophisticated type of program that can analyze location-based data
- How GIS data is structured
- Types of analysis in a GIS typically used by journalists
- Use of a GIS to alter and edit map data

In 1854, John Snow, an English doctor who helped establish the field of epidemiology, wanted to find the source of a cholera outbreak in London. So he drew a map. Using a small square to represent each case of the disease, he was able to trace the source to a communal water pump, which had become contaminated with cholera bacteria from human feces. In this way, Snow helped confirm his theory that cholera was a waterborne disease, showing the need for the kind of central water and sewer systems that today prevent the spread of it and similar illnesses.[1] Snow's map was one of the earliest examples of using a map to analyze spatial data and reveal otherwise hidden patterns.

Snow drew his map by hand, but today anyone who is willing to take the time to learn the tools and understand how they work can do similar analysis using what is called a geographic information system, or GIS for short.

Today, GIS applications are used for tasks as diverse as municipal planning, sales and marketing, and political campaigning. For data journalists seeking to answer the classic journalistic question, "where?," they allow for unprecedented understanding.

With a GIS, you can count crimes in police patrol areas, see how far chemical factories are away from schools, determine how many people have died

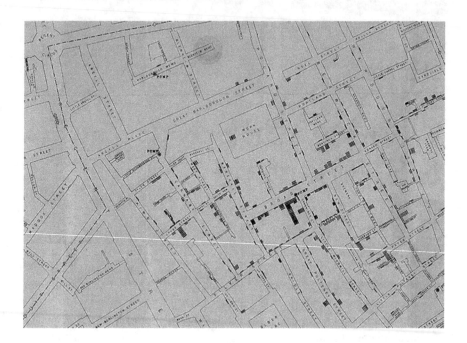

A portion of John Snow's map
Source: John Snow. Date: 1855. Copyright: By permission of the British Library Board

near crosswalks, find clusters of dilapidated buildings, and locate thousands, hundreds of thousands, or even millions of parking tickets on a map. It gives you the same kind of power to manipulate and understand spatial data as a SQL database gives you over tabular data. While a web mapping service, such as those we discussed in Chapter 6, can depict patterns, a GIS can help you identify them.

This chapter will give you enough knowledge of how GIS systems work to put them to work as journalistic tools, while avoiding some of the pitfalls that can get you in deep, spatial trouble. We're going to start by digging a little more deeply into how digital maps work.

The Inside Story

When we began our exploration of maps in Chapter 6, we posited that a map is a symbolic representation of features that can be located relative to specific locations on the Earth. We discussed maps mostly in the context of using them to display information, and looked at some of the ways maps can mislead if the map-maker is inept, careless, or mendacious. But we gave only passing attention to the way we actually build that model of reality. Partly, we wanted to keep things simple, but we approached it that way also because web mapping services such as Google Maps and Fusion Tables, CartoDB, and

Tutorials Included with the Companion Website

You will find these tutorials on the OUP Companion Website(www.oupcanada .com/Vallance-Jones):

- A Quick Tour of ArcGIS Desktop
- A Quick Tour of ArcGIS Pro
- A Quick Tour of Quantum GIS (QGIS)
- Joining Maps to Other Datasets in ArcGIS
- Joining Maps to Other Datasets in ArcGIS Pro
- Joining Maps to Other Datasets in ArcGIS QGIS
- Selecting by Attributes and Location in ArcGIS Desktop
- Selecting by Attributes and Location in ArcGIS Pro
- Selecting in QGIS
- Buffering in ArcGIS Desktop
- Buffering in ArcGIS Pro
- Buffering in QGIS
- Spatial Joins in ArcGIS Desktop
- Spatial Joins in ArcGIS Pro
- Spatial Joins in QGIS
- Making Choropleth Maps in ArcGIS Desktop
- Making Choropleth maps in ArcGIS Pro
- Making Choropleth maps in QGIS
- Geocoding in ArcGIS Desktop
- Geocoding in ArcGIS Pro
- Geocoding in QGIS
- Working with Projections in ArcGIS Desktop
- Working with Projections in ArcGIS Pro
- Working with Projections in QGIS
- Modifying Layers in ArcGIS Desktop
- Modifying Layers in ArcGIS Pro
- Modifying Layers in QGIS
- A Guide to Coordinate Systems

ArcGIS Online hide complexity by standardizing things such as map **projections**. The world is always modelled and depicted the same way, so there is no pressing need for the user to be concerned about how it's done. Since the main purpose of such programs is to display maps that look reasonably good at any zoom level, this arrangement produces acceptable results. By giving mapping a "paint-by-numbers" feel, it also makes the technology much more widely accessible.

A GIS program sets out to do much more, including sophisticated geographic analysis of features in relation to one another, and calculations of distances and areas. As a result, a better understanding of underlying concepts is necessary not only so you will understand the terms when you see them, but also so that you can avoid serious errors that can occur if you just start dropping map layers into a GIS and trying to analyze geographic relationships. Just as with the online mapping services, GIS programs assemble maps using layers, each one containing a set of features of the same type: points, lines, or polygons. A layer could represent locations of crimes, streets in a neighbourhood, or boundaries of police patrol areas, for example.

Ellipsoids and Datums: Modelling the World

We all know that the Earth is round, and many people are familiar with latitudes and longitudes, the numeric coordinates that allow us to pinpoint any position on that round planet or on a map. We probably learned in geography class that the equator is at 0 degrees latitude and the North and South Poles are 90 degrees north and south, respectively. If we really paid attention, we probably also remember that 0 degrees longitude has been standardized as a line running north-south through the observatory at Greenwich, England, called the prime meridian. Clear on the other side of the world, 180 degrees east or west is approximately the International Date Line, the point at which a person travelling westward jumps forward one day on the calendar.

The entire mapped world is covered by this grid of east-west parallels (circular lines of latitudes) and north-south meridians (semi-circular lines of longitude). Any single point can be identified by its unique latitude and longitude coordinates.

But unless we went on to advanced studies in geography or cartography, we probably didn't learn much about how map-makers decided where the latitudes and longitudes are, or how they managed to transform the globe on the teacher's desk into that oversized map hanging from the hook over the blackboard.

The detailed explanations of how these things are done lie in a great deal of mathematical modelling that is beyond the scope, and needs, of this book. But the basics are easy enough to grasp, and essential for understanding how to work expertly with a GIS. So here goes.

The first step to placing latitudes and longitudes is to figure out the shape of the world. Surprisingly, it's not the perfectly spherical ball that it appears

Our not-quite-spherical planet Earth viewed from space
Source: NASA

to be in those magnificent photos of our fragile blue planet floating in the black of space. If you were to take a giant measuring tape and run it around the equator, you would find that the measurement was slightly longer than you'd get if you ran your tape the other way around the world, through the poles. This is because the Earth is actually an **ellipsoid** or spheroid. Like a lot of people, it's a bit chunky in the middle.

Over the last century and a half, various mathematical calculations of the Earth's size and shape have been developed. The resulting models are called "ellipsoids."[2] Over time they have become more precise, as technology has advanced from railways, telegraphs, and ships to satellites in constant orbit. Today, we have a pretty accurate idea of the dimensions of our planet.

The actual grid of latitudes and longitudes is defined by a mathematical model known as a **datum**. Unfortunately for aspiring map-makers, there is more than one datum; in fact, there are a great many, each based on one or another of the ellipsoids. The WGS84 datum, used by all those online mapping services, was developed by the US Department of Defense, is global in scope, and can be used anywhere on Earth. GPS receivers use this datum. Other datums are intended for regional or continental use, and take into account local variations in the shape of the planet, literally areas of raised or depressed topography. A good example of this is the North American Datum of 1983, or NAD83, which is meant for use in North America and is fixed to the North American continental plate.[3]

Like the ellipsoids on which they are based, datums have become more accurate with time and technological advances. A good example is again in North America. The North American Datum of 1927, or NAD27, was based on an ellipsoid calculated in the nineteenth century, while NAD83 is based on the GRS80 ellipsoid, which used satellite measurements and is much more precise. Latitude and longitude coordinates in NAD27 and NAD83 can be out of alignment by up to hundreds of metres in some parts of North America, and yet you will still sometimes receive map files using NAD27.[4]

Even WGS84 and NAD83 are not exactly the same, despite both being developed at nearly the same time. When first rolled out, they were almost identical, but WGS84 was later refined to make it even more accurate, and the gradual shift of the North American plate since 1983 has slowly taken them further out of alignment.[5] NAD83 has itself been refined in both Canada and the United States, so there are several variants. If you are working in North America, you will often get map layers that use any one of them.

All of this is important because when doing precise journalistic work, you need to know where everything is in order to produce accurate results.

Projections

If an ellipsoid defines the shape of the Earth and a datum allows us to find any position on the Earth, a projection takes this 3-D Earth, and portrays it in 2-D on a flat surface. In doing that, distortion is the inevitable result. The science and art of creating map projections revolves around the decisions that need to be made about how it will be distorted.

Think of yourself out for a noon-hour walk on a sunny day. If it's the middle of June or you're near the equator, and the sun is nearly directly overhead, your body will cast a shadow that is quite small and nearly under your feet. The 2-D you will be about the same width from side to side as the 3-D you. Now, take that same walk an hour or so before sunset. Suddenly, you cast a shadow off to one side. The 2-D you is much longer than the 3-D you is tall because your shadow is being projected by the sun, onto the ground, at a much shallower angle.

The same kind of thing happens when we try to project a globe onto a flat surface. If we lined up a translucent globe straight up and down, north to south, and put a bright light in the middle of the globe, the line on the globe representing the equator would be projected onto an adjacent wall without much distortion, like our shadow at noon. But the lines toward the top, representing, say, the Arctic Circle, would be distorted in much the same way as our shadow is near sunset, because approaching the pole, each would be projected at an ever-steeper angle onto the wall.

Of course, map-makers don't make maps using translucent globes and light bulbs, but the distortions are just as real and can't be avoided. Some maps project the Earth out onto a virtual cylinder with the Earth placed inside the cylinder. The cylinder is then rolled out flat. These are called **cylindrical projections**. Other maps project the Earth onto a virtual cone, with the cone sitting on top of the globe. The cone is then rolled out. These are called **conical projections**. Yet others are like our translucent globe and the wall, in that the projection is made onto a surface that is already flat. These are called **azimuthal or planar projections**.[6] These descriptions are simplifications, but they give the general idea.

Each type of projection has advantages and disadvantages, and each has one or two lines running across it where there is minimal or no distortion, like our shadow at noon. Each can be manipulated to change the distortion that occurs to each of four properties: direction, area, shape, and distance.

Four Properties: Direction, Area, Shape, and Distance

Depending how the projection is created—within the basic types of cylindrical, conical, and planar there are hundreds and hundreds of variations—a particular projection will be effective at preserving one or a couple of these properties, but never all and sometimes none. Sometimes directions between continents will be correct, but the relative size of the continents will be wildly distorted. Sometimes they will be about the right size relative to one another, but straight directions will be skewed into curves. Sometimes area will be right, but continents will take on weird, elongated shapes. It all depends on what the map-maker wants to emphasize, or how the map will be used.

That map on the wall of your classroom is a perfect example. It was probably created using the **Mercator projection**. A straight line on a Mercator map equates to a steady compass bearing for a ship. But in keeping the angles

A world map projected in ArcGIS using the Mercator projection
Source: Esri

correct, and meridians all straight up and down, it expands the land area of land masses closer to the poles, creating the effect of Greenland looking nearly as large as Africa, despite being much smaller in reality.[7]

Interestingly, ArcGIS Online, Google Maps, and other web mapping services use the **Web Mercator projection**, a slightly modified version of the Mercator. Not only is Greenland gigantic but Antarctica seems as large as the rest of the continents combined. You might ask why anyone uses such a distorted projection, and that is a good question. The answer is that since angles are preserved, a user can easily zoom in from global scale to local scale, and satellite and other imagery can be incorporated into the map frame with the edges lining up properly.[8]

As well as being classified as cylindrical, conical, or planar, map projections are also known by the properties that they preserve. The Mercator and Web Mercator projections are said to be conformal, because they preserve the local angles and shapes of features. Other projections distort in different ways and preserve different characteristics. Equal-area or equivalent projections correctly display the relative surface areas of different features, equidistant

This is the same world map from the Mercator example, but in an equidistant conical projection
Source: Esri

projections preserve distances (at least to and from certain points on the map), and azimuthal projections preserve directions.[9]

Whatever projection is used, the distortion will be greater the smaller the scale of the map (in other words, the further it is zoomed out). When looking at the whole planet, the distortion will be clearly visible. When looking at a few blocks of your city, it may be negligible.

As you will see later in the chapter, this is not just an academic discussion. When using a GIS, you can change the projection used with a map to preserve those properties most important for a particular project and geographic area. So if you want to measure accurate distances, you can pick a projection that will preserve that quality for the area of the world and zoom level you are using. On the other hand, if area is most important, you can choose a projection that preserves that property.

The same map, in a cylindrical equal area projection

Source: Esri

How Datums and Projections are Incorporated in a GIS

In a GIS program, datums and projections are of central importance, and can impact not only how your map will look and how features line up, but the accuracy of the calculations you make using the program. The terminology used is slightly different, however.

A GIS uses two types of coordinate reference systems. The first is what is called a **geographic coordinate system** or GCS. This term is often used interchangeably with "datum," but they are not exactly the same. Instead, a GCS includes a datum and other references.[10] It locates points using latitudes and longitudes expressed in decimal degrees, and perhaps most importantly, has degrees as its unit of measurement. It does not include a projection; a map that is only in a GCS is often referred to as "unprojected." If you are not careful, this can cause serious problems if you are trying to calculate distances or areas.

A **projected coordinate system** (PCS) is based on a GCS and includes a projection. Points on the map are located using what is called a Cartesian coordinate

For the purposes of this chapter and the accompanying online materials, we're focusing on two GIS packages. The first is ArcGIS Desktop. It is the most widely used GIS, and has long been a favourite of journalists doing serious GIS work. It is also quite expensive, although at the time of this book's publication, a $100 annual license was available for non-commercial use. Nonetheless, many journalists doing GIS work will end up using it simply because it has already been acquired by their news organizations. It is a Windows program, but can be run on a Mac running OSX using VmWare, Parallels, or a dual-boot using Bootcamp. Esri, maker of ArcGIS, has recently introduced a new desktop application called ArcGIS Pro, which is meant to eventually supersede ArcGIS Desktop.

The second program we will talk about is **Quantum GIS**, or QGIS for short. QGIS is free, open-source software that has improved a great deal in recent years, and for many tasks it is a capable alternative to ArcGIS. There is a large user community, so most technical concerns can be addressed online. QGIS is available for Windows, Mac, and Linux operating systems, though the version available for a particular Linux distribution may not always be the latest and most up to date.

As we discuss the various tools journalists use most often, we will use illustrations from both programs, and indicate if one or the other of the programs is unable to perform a particular task. Please note that step-by-step instructions on how to use ArcGIS Desktop, ArcGIS Pro, and QGIS, for the tasks enumerated here, are on the companion website.

system of x and y coordinates, rather than latitudes and longitudes. A PCS has as its unit of measure an actual linear unit such as metres or feet, rather than degrees.[11] Very often, people use the term "projection" to refer to a PCS even though technically they are not exactly the same thing. At the very least, a map layer has to have a GCS to be displayed in a GIS program, because that is the minimum information needed to locate points on the Earth.

Later, we will discuss some of the issues that can crop up around different coordinate systems, and how you can avoid making serious errors. But for now, with the fundamentals under our belt, we'll turn to GIS programs.

Basics of a GIS

A GIS program is a sophisticated data and graphics management program. It does many things that will be familiar to users of relational databases, such as managing tabular data, running SQL queries against that data, creating new tables, working with delimited text files, joining tables, and so on. But instead of having only tables containing tabular data, a GIS can also work with data representing the geometries of geographic features, display those features, and query and manipulate that data using the location of geographic features as criteria. This means it is possible to do things such as count up the number of government infrastructure projects in each riding (in GIS terms, count points in polygons) or figure out how many daycare centres are within five kilometres of factories emitting toxic mercury (in GIS terms, drawing a **buffer** around points representing factories, and counting how many daycare centres are within the buffers). This creates great opportunities for journalists to examine almost anything that involves the spatial relationships between physical and/or abstract entities that can be positioned on the face of the Earth.

A GIS user builds a map by combining one or more of these layers containing points, lines, or polygons in an area of the user interface called the **data frame**. As discussed in the last chapter, a point feature is one that has no size or length, but simply exists at a particular map coordinate; a line is a feature that has length and is made up of segments that run between points; and a polygon is a closed, many-sided feature made up of line segments.

A GIS allows great flexibility in terms of how the user views these features. A user can zoom in and out to view the layer at any scale up to and including the full extent of the layer. (A scale is a ratio of how many units in the real world one unit on a map represents. For example, a 1:10,000 scale means that 1 centimetre on the map is equivalent to 10,000 centimetres on the ground.) The extent is the amount of the layer visible in the data frame and the full extent is the entire layer to its edges.

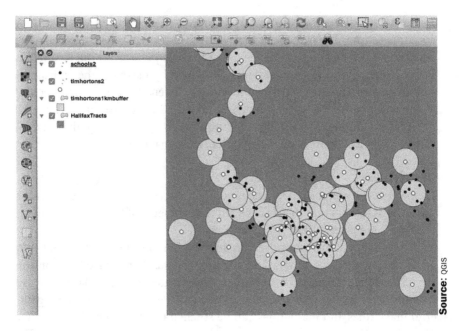

A buffer analysis in the data frame of QGIS. To the left of the computer screen, the table of contents/layers sidebar shows all of the data that is included in the map.

A user can make layers visible or not visible, change their order, make them transparent or opaque, add background colours to polygons, display or hide text labels, and much more. The online companion to this book includes downloadable "quick-tour" tutorials for ArcGIS Desktop, ArcGIS Pro, and QGIS that explain the user interface for each program.

Or course, you can't build a map without data, and we'll turn to that next.

How Spatial Data Is Structured

A map layer usually comes with a lot of information. Let's look at the typical elements.

Metadata
The first thing to know is that a map layer, if it is not a KML file, should come with information about itself, and most importantly, information about how it is to be displayed. This collection of data about data is called metadata, and in both ArcGIS and QGIS can be accessed by viewing the layer properties.

One property that is always important is the information about the geographic and projected coordinate systems the layer uses.

You'll recall the KML format is standardized on latitude and longitude coordinates and the WGS84 datum, but other formats make provisions to encode this information in the file. Most formats put everything in one file, but the widely used shapefile format developed by Esri puts the coordinate system information in a separate file with the extension .prj. Remember that a shapefile is actually a collection of files, all with the same file name, but with different extensions. The .prj file is not required to open the map file, but if it's missing you need to find out why. We'll discuss that later.

Geometries

Geometry is all about shapes. And since maps in a GIS display shapes of various sorts, it follows that these are called the geometry of the layer. Of course, the shapes are points, lines, and polygons.

Different map formats store this information in different ways, but they all come down to a common denominator, points. Points have locations on the face of the Earth, defined by their coordinates, either in latitudes and longitudes or the numeric coordinates of a PCS. Points can be joined together to make lines and many lines can be stitched together to make polygons. The information about these point coordinates is stored in the map file. The shapefile is again different in that the geometry information is stored in its own file with the extension .shp. Unlike in text-based formats such as KML, GML, and GeoJSON, the .shp file is a binary file, which means humans can't read it. A GIS program, however, can.

Attributes

As well as having the necessary geometric information to display the features contained in a layer, map layers typically come with attributes. These are like the fields in a database table and comprise information that tells us more about the features, such as the number of voters in an election subdivision polygon, or the number of people who died in a plane crash that is represented on the map by a point. The attributes also contain some basic information about the file itself, and in a shapefile has what is called a feature ID, or FID, which is the linking field that ties together all those different files that make up a shapefile. Without a FID, a shapefile won't display. In a shapefile, the attribute data is contained in a file with the extension .dbf. In other types, it is incorporated in the same file as the spatial information.

Attributes are an essential element of a map layer because they provide the information that gives the locations meaning and context. A whole lot of dots on a map won't tell you much, unless you understand what the dots represent.

This is what a typical **attribute table** looks like (ArcGIS Desktop pictured):

FID	Shape *	OBJECTID	FCODE	STR_NAME	STR_TYPE	FULL_NAME	
9672	Polyline M	8243	RRRD	GLEN EAGLE	WAY	GLEN EAGLE WAY	H
9673	Polyline M	8244	RRRDLI90	GULL ROCK	DR	GULL ROCK DR	H
9674	Polyline M	8246	RRRDAB60	HIGHWAY 107		HIGHWAY 107	P
9675	Polyline M	8248	RRRDLG60	UPPER LAKEVILLE	RD	UPPER LAKEVILLE RD	U
9676	Polyline M	8256	RRRDLJ60	SYMONDS	ST	SYMONDS ST	D
9677	Polyline M	2566	RRRD	CRAIGBURN	DR	CRAIGBURN DR	D
9678	Polyline M	2570	RRRDLG60	NORTH PRESTON	RD	NORTH PRESTON RD	N
9679	Polyline M	2589	RRRDCD60	MAIN	RD	MAIN RD	E
9680	Polyline M	2599	RRRDLJ60	PUDDLE	RD	PUDDLE RD	Q
9681	Polyline M	2601	RRRDLJ60	PUDDLE	RD	PUDDLE RD	Q
9682	Polyline M	2602	RRRD	BRUNSWICK	ST	BRUNSWICK ST	H
9683	Polyline M	2610	RRRD	VICTORIA	RD	VICTORIA RD	H
9684	Polyline M	2619	RRRD	BARRY ALLEN	DR	BARRY ALLEN DR	D
9685	Polyline M	8558	RRRD	LEEDS	ST	LEEDS ST	H
9686	Polyline M	8567	RRRD	RIVER	RD	RIVER RD	M
9687	Polyline M	8570	RRRDLJ60	WRIGHT	AVE	WRIGHT AVE	D
9688	Polyline M	8573	RRRD	MAJOR	ST	MAJOR ST	D

18 ▸ ▸∣ (0 out of 16733 Selected)

street

Source: Esri

Working with Layers

The layers are added one atop the other in the data frame. A reporter explor-ing the location of muggings in relation to parks might include one layer of line features representing streets, another of polygon features representing parks, and a third of point features representing the locations of muggings. Muggings that occurred in or within a certain distance of parks could then be easily identified.

Both ArcGIS and QGIS can simplify the use of map layers that have different coordinate systems through a convenient program feature known as "projection on the fly." In ArcGIS this is the default behaviour; the projection that will be used for the map frame is determined by the first layer that is added to the frame, unless changed manually by the user. In QGIS, this behaviour has to be turned on explicitly, and rather than use the projection of the first layer added, QGIS lets the user determine the coordinate system to be used. The default is WGS84, without a projection. **On-the-fly projection** saves having to change the projection for subse-quent layers if the projections are not the same and generally works very well, as long as the underlying GCS is the same. Because different GCS (based on different datums) may not line up with one another, adding layers based on different GCSs can cause alignment issues unless one of the layers is transformed to match the GCS of the other layer(s). ArcGIS warns you if you try to add a layer based on a different GCS and does not do the **datum transformation** automatically. QGIS does it automatically, but if a transformation method is not available, it will prompt the user to define a transformation.

Non-geographic data can also be added to a GIS, but it can't be displayed in the map frame. It can, however, be joined to a map layer. If it contains addresses, they can be geocoded to appear on the map.

How Journalists Use GIS Programs

As with database and spreadsheet applications, journalists turn to GIS programs when the applications can solve a journalistic problem, a question that needs to be answered. Journalists use this kind of software when they are looking for an answer to the question, "where?" This question can be paired with other journalistic questions to reveal the full scope of analysis that is required. For example, "how many where," "how much where," and "where in relationship to something else" are all examples of more complex questions one might set out to answer with a GIS application. These questions might in turn be trying to get at that central journalistic question, "why"; for example, "why do so many children get cancer in this neighbourhood?" In seeking an answer, the journalist might use a GIS to compare the location of schools to the location of factories using cancer-causing chemicals. So "where in relationship to something else" is then used to get at the why question. Similarly, "when" can also be introduced through the ability of GIS software to track changes over time.

Let's move from the abstract to a more concrete example.

In the spring of 2014, investigative journalism students at the University of King's College in Halifax, Nova Scotia, were analyzing a database of responses by the regional municipality's fire service. Using database software, they found a broad pattern that there are more major fires (those that burned beyond one room in a home) in areas away from the core urban area of Halifax than there were in the core. This led to that classic journalistic question, "why?" Many possible answers presented themselves. Perhaps buildings in these rural areas were built of substandard materials, and simply burned faster or more easily. Perhaps people in outlying areas took more risks with fire safety than those in the city; maybe they heated with wood more often, causing more chimney fires that then spread. Or maybe it had something to do with how long firefighters took to get to the fires; a faster response would mean knocking the fire down more quickly, perhaps preventing its spread.

As it turned out, there was no evidence that homes that burned in rural areas were notably worse constructed than urban homes, and chimney fires occurred in both rural and urban areas. An answer to the question of whether rural people were, as a class, more careless proved elusive and the prospect seemed unlikely. Response times began to look like a more likely explanation.

This meant answering the question, "how long, where?" and for that, a GIS program was perfectly suited.

The fire-calls data included a precise geographic position for fires in all years except the last year of the data. This was provided in UTM coordinates, which are x and y coordinates associated with the **Universal Transverse Mercator** projected coordinate system. This meant that, subject to any inaccuracy in those coordinates, the fires could be located with precision. Both ArcGIS and QGIS can easily place UTM coordinates on a map.

It was possible to calculate an approximate response time for each fire, as well as how long it took fire trucks to roll after the alarm came in, the so-called turnout time. The calculations were not perfect because sometimes firefighters are slow to report that they are on the road and/or when they arrive on scene. But there was no evidence that such late reporting was concentrated in any one area.

Simple data queries already showed that the longest response times were associated with the fires outside of the urban core. But the students wanted to understand the phenomenon more deeply, so they imported the calculated times into ArcGIS Desktop and added them to a map that already included a layer of the boundaries of the region's municipal election districts. They then used an analysis technique called a "spatial join" to associate each building fire (and its associated response time) to the electoral district in which it was located. Having done this, the students exported the new combined table to Excel, and calculated the median response time for each district. This figure was then mapped, and a stark pattern emerged: the districts away from the city had median response times that were longer than 10 minutes, a point beyond which a fire was often too far advanced to save the structure, according to experts. The visualization was further enhanced by colouring the dots representing each fire green, yellow, or red depending on whether the response was within 6 minutes, within 10 minutes, or longer than 10 minutes. In the rural areas, some of the red dots were often close to fire stations, indicating the closeness of the first station had little impact on the response time.

It turned out that a reliance on volunteer firefighters in rural and semi-urban areas, even though residents of those areas paid the same fire taxes, meant firefighters took longer to get to fires than in urban areas. In some areas nearer to the urban core, firefighters from distant full-time, paid stations got to fires before volunteers who were theoretically much closer.

The use of a GIS program allowed the investigative team to answer the questions "how long, where" with far more detail than would have been possible had they just relied on a blanket statement that responses were longer in non-core areas. And while the students could have achieved some of the same results by going through the table of fire calls one by one, coding each one as to which district it was in by looking up the address by hand, using the GIS program's spatial

Burned: the King's College journalism students' story on fire response times

Source: Helen Pike

join feature not only allowed the analysis to be completed in a fraction of the time, but allowed for far more extensive and complete analysis. Of course, all of this was accompanied by on-the-ground reporting to verify that the patterns identified in the data and GIS analysis held true in the real world.

The *Burned* example shows how powerful a GIS program can be in finding important patterns related to geography. We'll now unpack the most important capabilities. Programs such as these have deep feature sets and it's not possible to cover all or even a majority of the features in one chapter. At the end of the chapter, we'll recommend some further reading for those who may wish to take a much deeper dive into GIS. For now, we'll focus on the capabilities that have proven most valuable to journalists. For each of the major tasks below, you will find tutorials to complete them in both ArcGIS and QGIS, on the companion website.

Joining Non-geographic Data with Geographic Data

You'll remember from our discussion of web mapping services that the major services can join a map layer with another table based on common attributes. GIS programs are capable of the same kind of joins, and use the same method of making the join on a field that is common to the two tables. This kind of join is usually done as a prelude to using the combined table as part of a geographic analysis.

Both ArcGIS and QGIS are capable of importing and using a variety of external data formats. For example, you can add comma- or tab-delimited text to a map in either program. Both programs can also work directly with Excel spreadsheet files. Using a technology called **Open Database Connectivity** (ODBC), ArcGIS can work with multiple additional file formats, including Microsoft Access and Microsoft SQL Server data files.

Selecting Features That Meet Certain Criteria

As discussed earlier in this chapter, a GIS program is able to use queries to select geographic features in much the same way that a database program such as MySQL can select tabular data. These queries are of two general types.

The first type of query selects by attributes (called selecting by expression in QGIS). You write an expression similar to a database select query and the map features whose attributes match the query are highlighted (selected) on the map. From there, you can use them to create a new layer, or as the basis for further analysis.

The second type is what is called a **"select-by-location"** query. You select map features based on their location relative to other features. For example, a select-by-location query can be used to select features that overlap or intersect features in another layer or are contained within features that are in another layer. As of writing, ArcGIS's functionality in this regard was richer, and included the ability to select features based on their being within a distance of features in another layer. However, buffers (see page 154) can be used to recreate this functionality in a two-part workflow, first drawing buffers of a certain size around a feature, then seeing which points intersect the points in the other layer.

ArcGIS allows you to use select-by-location to create a new selection, add to a selection you have already made, or subtract features from an existing selection. Note that when doing any GIS operation that involves calculating distances, you need to be aware of the effects of different types of map coordinate systems on the potential accuracy of your analysis. An improperly chosen coordinate system can produce inaccurate results, and the GIS program may give no indication of the problem. More on that a bit later.

Source: Esri

A buffer drawn around a polygon in ArcMap.

Buffering

A **buffer** analysis can also be used to determine which features are within a specified distance of features in another layer. When you create a buffer, the GIS program draws a new polygon feature extending a specified distance from a feature. If the original target feature is a point, the polygon is a circle centred on the coordinates of the point feature. If it is a line segment, the polygon is a rectangle centred on the segment. If it is a polygon, the buffer will extend from the outside boundary of the polygon feature.

Once you have created your buffers, they will be independent polygon features, and you can remove the original features on which they are based from the data frame, if you like. You can now use the new buffer polygons in other analyses. For example, if you had created buffers of a certain distance around factories emitting toxic chemicals, and you had another layer containing the locations of public schools and the number of students per school, you could use a spatial join to count the schools and total up the number of students, adding a field for both to each factory's attributes. We'll turn to that kind of join next.

Joining Data Based on Geographical Location

One of the features that makes a GIS program so powerful is its ability to join tables not just on fields they have in common, but on geographical features that intersect or are near to one another in different layers in the same map frame. To give a very simple example, consider two map layers, one being a layer of crime locations, and the other a layer of neighbourhood boundaries in your city. Using a spatial join, you can use the GIS program to count up the number of crimes that took place in each neighbourhood and put the result in a new map that still shows the neighbourhoods but now has a new attribute column for the number of crimes. After that, you could join the map to a data table of the population of each neighbourhood, work out the crime rate per capita, and display the result on a web map.

Of course, the result will only be as accurate as the map layers and data that are used, but both ArcGIS and QGIS can do this type of join without any great difficulty.

You are not limited to just counting. If one of the tables contains numeric attributes, you can do math on these and apply the result to the other table. So, as an example, if the hypothetical crime table had an attribute field for the number of victims, you could use a spatial join to add up the number of victims in each neighbourhood and add that to the neighbourhood table.

Spatial joins can be performed between all different types of geometries, points, lines, and polygons. So you can use a spatial join to find which point in the other layer is closest, and how far away it is. The King's students working on the fire-calls story used this feature to work out the nearest fire hall, as the bird flies, for each address in the Halifax region. The result was then exported and made available to readers as an interactive feature on a web mapping service. Some spatial joins will also calculate how far features are from each other, and for these you should ensure the layers you are joining have PCS that are appropriate for use in the geographical area where you are doing your analysis.

Making a Choropleth Map

You will recall from Chapter 6 that a choropleth map is one that applies a number of colours to polygons to show variations in the values of a particular numeric variable. For example, a range of colours could be used to show variations in population density in census tracts. GIS programs are also capable of creating such maps, but the purpose for creating them is usually to help see patterns in the geographic distribution of data, rather than to present the results to the audience. For web presentation, it is much easier to simply use the web mapping service.

In a GIS program, a choropleth map can be made using any numeric variable as the input, including one created through previous tasks, such as spatial joins. Just making the choropleth map can reveal patterns in your data you might not have seen otherwise. A GIS can also create other types of maps, such as dot density maps and proportional symbols maps, that can reveal hidden patterns in your data, and categorical maps that show such things as which party represents each electoral district.

Geocoding

In the last chapter, we discussed the use of web-based geocoding services to geocode a limited number of addresses to then display on an online map. GIS programs can also geocode data, either via a web-based geocoding service or, in the case of ArcGIS, natively within the GIS program itself, using reference data stored on your own computer. In the earlier discussion, we mostly just took the details for granted. So let's spend a little time now discussing this in some more detail.

Geocoding is a process through which a map layer of point features is created based on a table of addresses or other geographic information stored in an ordinary spreadsheet or data table. This is done by comparing the spreadsheet or data table with an existing reference map or maps. It's one of the most important tools for a data journalist because you will frequently gather information on locations of all sorts of things—from dilapidated houses to crime locations to the best burger joints in town—that you will want to put onto a map. In a geocoding process, the application examines each address in the data, compares it to the known addresses in the reference table, and if it finds a match, creates a new point feature. When the process is complete, the user is either left with a new shapefile or **geodatabase feature class** (within ArcGIS) containing the geocoded address points and all of the attributes in the original data, or a text file containing the latitudes and longitudes of the geocoded points (with QGIS, using a web-based geocoding service). The geocoded addresses can then be used for further analysis.

Geocoding can be done at varying levels of accuracy, depending on the precision of the reference data, which can be to the single address level, ranges of addresses on either side of streets, zip or postal codes, or other unique geographies. Online geocoding services such as Google or Bing Maps are usually able to handle multiple variations in input addresses and can be impressively accurate in areas they cover. But if you are not careful, they can also put points in the wrong places without giving you any warning that there was an error.

If you are geocoding on your own computer with ArcGIS Desktop, accuracy will depend on the completeness of your reference maps and how up to date they are. However, the notable advantage of geocoding on your own desktop is that the work is all done on your own computer so you don't need to rely on an Internet connection. As well, ArcGIS can geocode hundreds of thousands of records an hour, meaning it is feasible to geocode very large datasets, such as the city of Toronto's parking-ticket data used by Steve Rennie for his stories on parking in Toronto and Ottawa (see Chapter 2), which amounts to almost 3 million records a year. You also have much more control over the accuracy of the end product, and addresses that won't geocode can be rematched manually.

As a side note, sometimes a dataset will come with latitude/longitude coordinates, or Cartesian coordinates for a projected coordinate system such as UTM. No geocoding is necessary for these as the necessary locational information is already in the file. Both QGIS and ArcGIS can add such data directly to a map. Just be careful when you add such data that you apply the correct coordinate system, or your points will be anywhere but where they should be. Tutorials on geocoding, and the other tasks we have discussed, are found on the companion website.

Common Problems and Solutions

GIS programs are amazing tools for analyzing geospatial data. But as you start using them, or using a web mapping service, you'll discover situations where you need to make changes to your data before you can work with it. GIS programs are chock full of features to do this.

Projecting and Re-projecting a Map Layer

Quite often, you will discover that a map layer you wish to use is in an inappropriate projection for your purposes, or is not projected at all. When this happens, you will need to either create a new layer that has the correct projection, or apply a projection to an existing layer. Both ArcGIS Desktop and QGIS come preloaded with a great many commonly used coordinate systems. Because of the complex mathematical calculations involved, the process of re-projecting can become quite complicated under the hood. If you wish to re-project a layer that has a different underlying geographic coordinate system it can become even more complicated because a datum transformation will be required. Both ArcGIS and QGIS can do this, but in some cases there may be no predefined transformation available. In this case you will need to research the correct transformation method and define the transformation yourself, a topic beyond the scope of this book. This will not be an issue if you are working with commonly used coordinate systems such as WGS84 and NAD83, but we want to flag it because it can be an issue if you receive a map layer in an obscure regional coordinate system.

If you receive a map layer that is not projected at all (for example, a shapefile that has no .prj file associated with it), you will need to find out what the coordinate system is supposed to be. This is best done by checking the source's website for the metadata, or contacting the source directly and asking. If you cannot find out, there are ways to identify the coordinate system. An excellent resource in this regard is Maragaret Maher's *Lining Up Data in ArcGIS* from Esri Press. Once you know, both ArcGIS and QGIS allow you to define the projection. When you define the projection, you'd don't create a new layer, but simply add the projection information to the existing layer. You'll find tutorials on re-projecting and defining projections on the companion website.

Converting File Formats

Even if you mostly create online maps for presentation, you will almost certainly need to make changes to map data along the way, and a GIS program is ideally suited for this kind of task.

One of the most common tasks is to convert a layer in one map format to another format. Probably the most common conversion is from one map format to a KML, or vice versa. This is because you sometimes need to create a

KML to use with a web mapping service, or you need to convert a KML file for use in a GIS program.

Often, open-source programs are able to deal with more file formats, both for opening and saving, than proprietary software. This is certainly true with QGIS, which can work with an impressive array of map file formats "out of the box." It can save to and from shapefiles, KML, GML, GeoJSON, GPX (GIS Exchange format), MapInfo Tab format, and others using the same menus for all of the conversions. ArcGIS can do most of these conversions as well, but requires the use of separate tools and in some cases the purchase of extra-cost plugins.

Simplifying Polygons

An important consideration to keep in mind when converting to the KML format is that Google in particular imposes hard limits on file sizes. For example, in Google Fusion Tables, no uploaded file can be greater than 250 MB, and there is a maximum storage quota of 1 GB per account (limitations current as of the publication date of this book). Perhaps the most important limit for any individual KML is that no single cell can contain more than 1 million characters.

You might think you'd never reach a million characters, but remember that a KML stores all of the geometry information for a feature in a single cell. Given that the geometry information for a polygon contains KML tags around each coordinate and each coordinate has two values that may have many characters each, mid- to large-size polygons contained in a shapefile, for example, can easily be converted to KML cells that exceed this limit. A good example are polygons of Canadian electoral districts, some of which cover vast, sparsely populated regions.

When this happens, you may need to use another of the tools in a GIS to simplify your polygons. **Simplification** refers to the process of removing some of the **vertices** (the points at either end of the line segments that make up the polygon). Both ArcGIS and QGIS can simplify polygons, though at the time of writing ArcGIS allows the user more control over the process.

Depending on the tolerance you set for the simplification, more or fewer of the vertices will be removed. If too many are removed, the polygon may appear jagged as in the on page 160, and adjacent polygons may not fit together neatly. The trick is to find the right balance between a polygon simple enough not to exceed the maximum file size permitted, and one that draws so jaggedly as to be aesthetically unpleasing or inaccurate.

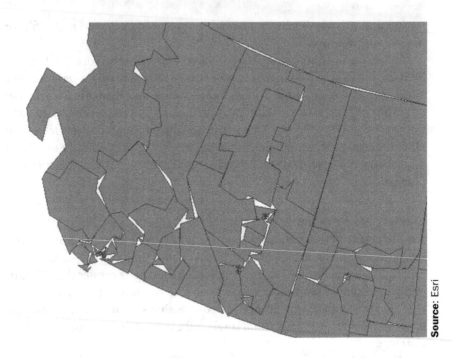

Source: Esri

Combining Layers into a Single Layer

Another frequent utility task is to combine two or more layers of the same feature type into a single new layer. This is accomplished in both ArcGIS and QGIS using the merge tool. In ArcGIS the input data can be a shapefile or a feature class in a geodatabase; in QGIS it can be a shapefile. Both create a new output dataset containing all of the features of the two input datasets. ArcGIS also has a tool called "append" that will add a dataset to an existing one, without creating a new layer. Once merged, the new or altered layer can be used for further analysis.

Combining Features within a Single Layer

Finally, if you want to combine features within a layer based on a field in the attribute table, you can use the dissolve tool. If you had a polygon layer of election polls that showed the number of votes won by each candidate in a mayoral election and the attribute table included a field for the ward name, you could use the dissolve tool to combine the poll polygons into polygons for the wards.

ArcGIS and QGIS contain additional tools for merging portions of layers that overlap: the union and intersect operations.

Special Considerations Relative to Coordinate Systems

Earlier, we discussed how maps are made, and introduced geographic and projected coordinate systems. Let's turn now to some of the special considerations we need to be mindful of when working with coordinate systems, to avoid making errors in our work.

While some users of GIS programs never explore these issues, we think that not understanding the impact that different geographic and projected coordinate systems may have on results is a bit like knowing how to operate a car, but not knowing the rules of the road. Pretty soon, no matter how technically adept you are at pressing the accelerator, changing gears, and steering, you'll make errors and possibly end up in an accident.

Let's look at a few of the specific errors you could make and how to avoid them.

Using a Map Layer That Has Only a Geographic Coordinate System

Especially with the explosion of web mapping services, it has become more and more common to find map files online that are not projected and have a latitude/longitude-based coordinate system. Such files will open fine in a GIS program, and at larger scales (zoomed in more) they may appear little different from layers that have PCS. But there is a fundamental difference.

Remember that a GCS uses decimal degrees as its unit of measurement (and latitudes and longitudes for map coordinates). This can cause huge inaccuracies if you try to measure distance as part of your analysis.

The problem with decimal degrees as a unit of measurement is that because a GCS still looks at the world as a spheroid that gets progressively narrower toward the poles, there is no consistent length for a degree. A degree running north or south along a **line of longitude** (meridian) is exactly the same length at the equator as it is at the poles. That's because all the meridians are semicircles running around the full north-south girth of the world and of about the same length. But a degree on a parallel running east and west, varies in length depending on where that **line of latitude** is in relation to the equator. At the equator walking along one degree of latitude would be a 111-kilometre hike,[12] but if you were to stand on the ice at the North Pole, you could walk the full 360 degrees around the world in a few steps because there a degree approaches a length of 0. All of this makes it difficult for a GIS application relying only on a GCS to accurately measure anything but north-south distances, with the size of the error increasing the farther you get away from the equator and the closer the measurement is to being east-west. This becomes extremely important when you start doing analysis that produces a measured distance as its output, such as when you measure the distance between daycare centres and factories emitting toxic pollution, to use a simple example.

You should make sure that you project your map and your map frame to an appropriate PCS before you try to measure distances in a GIS.

Attempts to calculate area are doomed to failure without a PCS because area is defined as length multiplied by width. Multiplying degrees this way makes no sense.[13]

As well, a map that has only a GCS will have wildly varying areas, with the distortion increasing away from the equator. So any map you might create that is meant to show something that has land area as a variable, such as population density, will be misleading. Again, this error can be corrected by projecting the map, using an appropriate PCS.

Using Maps Based on Different Geographic Coordinate Systems

Whether projected or not, combining map layers based on different geographic coordinate systems (for example, combining layers based on NAD27 with layers based on NAD83), can also be a recipe for trouble. Because different GCS are based on different datums, you can get misalignment of features on the ground. So say you were doing an analysis of the number and cost of government infrastructure projects in different election districts, misalignment could put some of the projects near the edges of electoral districts across the line and into the adjacent districts. Any resulting calculations would be wrong. It is crucial when combining layers based on different GCS to apply a datum transformation. Common transformations are built into both ArcGIS and QGIS. For the same reason, spatial joins could be inaccurate if misalignment placed features in different layers in the wrong relationship with one another.

Using an Inappropriate Projected Coordinate System

There are also important considerations around which PCS to use. You know now that depending on the coordinate system being used, and its underlying projection, it may distort different geographic characteristics (direction, shape, area, or distance) and preserve none, one, or maybe two of these. As well, some PCS are only meant to be used in specific areas, or at specific map extents (zoom levels). If you want to make accurate measurements of distance or length, you don't want to use a PCS that wildly distorts the desired characteristic. If you want to compute rates of deforestation by square kilometre, you don't want a coordinate system that distorts area. If you want to obtain accurate measurements over a wide east-west extent in the mid-latitudes, you want to use a projection that minimizes distortion in that dimension.

Let's take a look at a couple of examples.

The commonly used Universal Transverse Mercator (UTM) projected coordinate system is one that distorts east-west distances, but the distortion is minimal at closer zoom levels. In the UTM system, the world is divided into 60 north-south zones, each six degrees of longitude wide. High polar regions are not covered. The projection is designed such that distortion of distance will be minimal within any one of the zones and tolerable within the zones on either side. A slightly different projection is actually used for each zone, one that is optimized for that slice of the Earth. As soon as you try to look at more than three zones at the same time, the east-west distortion will be excessive.[14]

UTM is commonly used all over the world for maps that have limited east-west extent but may have a great north-south extent (for example Chile, Egypt, or some American states).

If your goal is to minimize distortion going east and west, especially at mid-latitudes, a PCS based on the **Lambert Conformic conic projection** will produce less of this distortion.[15] Coordinate systems based on Lambert Conformic are frequently used for maps that must show larger east-west extents in Canada or the United States. For example, the coordinate system used by Statistics Canada is based on this projection.

The main point to keep in mind here is that these slightly arcane concepts of datums and projections, and geographic and projected coordinate systems, really do matter if you want to do consistently accurate analysis with a GIS program, rather than relying on blind luck. It's easy to load map layers into a GIS and make extraordinary things happen, while actually producing garbage. This is especially true when you are trying to do spatial analysis that involves measuring distances or areas.

An interesting side note is that in ArcGIS Desktop, employing a GCS that uses decimal degrees as its unit of measure can actually produce more useful, accurate buffers if you are trying to draw very large buffers around points. This is because of the distortion introduced by projections.[16]

A tutorial on coordinate systems, where they are used, and how to pick appropriate coordinate systems, can be found on the companion site for this book.

Conclusion

A geographic information system, or GIS, is a powerful tool for journalists who want to move beyond simply displaying maps to understanding spatial patterns and relationships. As with any power tool, the learning curve is steeper and the potential for errors greater. Luckily, geographers and cartographers are often really friendly people. There are likely GIS experts in your region, often working for the local university or municipality. Don't be afraid to reach out and ask for help when you are stumped. Having an expert review more complicated work you have done can not only be a lifesaver if it catches an error, but it can help build relationships that are mutually beneficial. If you take care, you will not only learn, but you can follow in John Snow's footsteps and make amazing discoveries, and tell amazing stories, with a GIS.

Study Questions and Exercises

1. Using the web and your library, find out what projected coordinate systems and geographic coordinate systems are most appropriate for doing analysis in your province, state, or territory.

2. Find two shapefiles using the coordinate systems you identified in exercise 1. Build a layered map with them.
3. Using a polygon map layer and a point map layer, do a spatial join in ArcGIS or QGIS, to calculate the number of points in each polygon and sum up one additional attribute from the points table.
4. On the companion website, you will find an additional exercise with live data.

Further Reading

Law, Michael, and Amy Collins. *Getting to Know ArcGIS*, 4th ed. Redlands, CA: Esri Press, 2015.
Maher, Margaret M. *Lining up Data in ArcGIS: A Guide to Map Projections*. Redlands, CA: Esri Press, 2013.

Notes

1. S.W.B. Newsom, "Pioneers in Infection Control: John Snow, Henry Whitehead, the Broad Street Pump, and the Beginnings of Geographical Epidemiology," *Journal of Hospital Infection* 64 (2006), 210–6. Retrieved from http://www.ph.ucla.edu/epi/snow/jhospinfection64%283%29210-216_2006.pdf.
2. Francis Harvey, *A Primer of GIS: Fundamental Geographic and Cartographic Concepts* (New York: Guilford Press, 2008), 81.
3. "North American Datums," *ArcMap 10.3*, http://desktop.arcgis.com/en/arcmap/10.3/guide-books/map-projections/north-american-datums.htm.
4. Kang-tsung Chang, *Introduction to Geographic Information Systems*, 6th ed. (New York: McGraw-Hill, 2011), 230.
5. "North American Datums," *ArcMap 10.3*.
6. Geographic Information Centre, "Projections," http://gic.geog.mcgill.ca/projections/.
7. Margaret M. Maher, *Lining up Data in ArcGIS: A Guide to Map Projections* (Redlands, CA: Esri Press, 2013), 164.
8. Sarah E. Battersby et al., "Implications of Web Mercator and Its Use in Online Mapping," *Cartographica* 49.2 (2014): 85–101, http://cegis.usgs.gov/projection/pdf/Battersby_Implications%20of%20Web%20Mecator%20and%20Its%20Use%20in%20Online%20Mapping.pdf.
9. Chang, *Introduction to Geographic Information Systems*, 26.
10. ArcGIS Resource Centre, "Working with Spatial References," http://help.arcgis.com/en/sdk/10.0/arcobjects_net/conceptualhelp/index.html#//0001000002mq000000.
11. ArcGIS Pro, "Coordinate Systems, Projections, and Transformations," http://pro.arcgis.com/en/pro-app/help/mapping/properties/coordinate-systems-and-projections.htm.
12. Esri, "Why Are My Map, Distance and Area Measurements Wrong When Using WGS 1984 Web Mercator?" http://support.esri.com/cn/knowledgebase/techarticles/detail/39404.
13. Maher, *Lining up Data in ArcGIS*, 157.
14. Ibid., 156.
15. ArcGIS 9.2 Desktop Help, "Lambert Conformal Conic," 3 August 2007, http://webhelp.esri.com/arcgisdesktop/9.2/index.cfm?TopicName=Lambert_Conformal_Conic.
16. Drew Flater, "Understanding Geodesic Buffering," n.d., http://www.esri.com/news/arcuser/0111/geodesic.html.

Chapter 8

Visualizing Data

What You Will Learn:

- The history and origins of data visualization
- Doing your own visualizations using a number of techniques
- Dos and don'ts of visualizations

The term "data visualization" has gone from a storytelling format used mostly by obscure data analytics firms to a visual narrative form that is on the lips of journalists everywhere. Visualization makes it possible not only to display data in new ways, but also to tell stories with data, making it the main character rather than using it simply as a source to support traditional reporting methods. There has been an explosion of online visualization tools, from Google Maps and Google Fusion Tables to Tableau Public, Many Eyes, and other cloud-based tools. This chapter introduces the tools and journalistic thinking helping to make visualization the centrepiece of online journalism. It's a huge subject, to which entire books are devoted, so we'll stick with the simplest methods here and focus on some key principles that will help you produce better visualizations.

A History of Visualization: From William Playfair to the Present Day

Throughout history, visual abstractions have played a large role in helping us to see and understand the world: pictures from antiquity, maps from ancient Egypt, the geometry diagrams from Euclid, and, of course, the statistical diagrams of William Playfair (1759–1823).[1] The progress was steady, at least for a while.

Tutorials Included with the Companion Website

You will find these tutorials on the OUP Companion Website (www.oupcanada .com/Vallance-Jones):

- A Guide to Tableau Public Visualizations
- A Guide to Google Fusion Tables Visualizations

The seventeenth century witnessed measurement and theory with the growth in analytical geometry. The eighteenth century saw the birth of new geographic forms such as isolines and contours, along with the development of thematic mapping and abstract graphs.

Playfair is widely considered to be the inventor of most of the graphical forms that we use today and will discuss in this chapter. He used the first line graph and bar chart, eventually adding the pie chart and circle graph to his repertoire.[2]

By the mid-1930s, the enthusiasm for visualization appeared to wane. It would take another 30 years to come back into full force. The mid-1960s witnessed a significant development: computer processing of data, allowing for the ability to use computer programs to construct old and new graphic forms.[3] Fast-forward to the present day with the explosion of user-friendly software packages.

The introduction and continued development of spreadsheets such as Excel have made it possible for journalists to easily visualize their datasets with a few clicks of the mouse. And free visualization tools such as Google's Fusion Tables and Tableau Public have made it even easier to help bring to life the clichés "seeing is believing," and "a picture is worth a thousand words." In this new world of data visualization understanding and seeing become synonymous.[4] That is, to understand is to see, and to see is to understand.

The goal of this chapter, as it is with the book, is to stress best practices and fundamentals no matter what tools you are using. The idea is not to turn you into a graphic design guru. The most sophisticated visualizations may best be left to programmers and web developers, but journalists committed to learning the techniques can also create these. The goal of this chapter is to provide the tools to help improve your storytelling with simple visualizations. That is, to arm you with the concepts to help people see your story.

However, before we discuss those fundamentals, it is worth delving into the term "data visualization." Loose definitions are always helpful.

What Is Meant by Visualization?

Ideally, data visualization should increase our understanding of a particular story. If we accept this as a fundamental concept of data visualization, we can judge the merits of any example "above all else on how clearly, thoroughly, and accurately it enlightens."[5]

In his article "An Economist's Guide to Visualizing Data" in which he pleads with economists to keep it simple, Jonathan A. Schwabish uses a concept that is instructive for journalists. He says that an effective graph should "tap into the brain's pre-attentive visual processing," which allows the reader to perceive multiple basic visual elements simultaneously. To illustrate the point, he uses an instructive example, asking the reader to count the occurrences of the number three in the following set:

126954852361235698745824501240369857020695683127812439862012478136982173256

Now repeat the task with this set of numbers:

126954852361235698745824501240369857020695683127812439862012478136982173256

Source: Schwabish, Jonathan. "Economist's Guide to Visualizing Data." JOURNAL OF ECONOMIC PERSPECTIVES VOL. 28, NO. 1, WINTER 2014 (pp. 209–34)

The instances of number 3 in the second example are easier to find because they are darker, allowing the eye to quickly spot them. Or, to put it more technically, the numbers that we want people to recognize are "encoded using a different pre-attentive attribute—in this case, the intensity of boldface type." These attributes include hue, colour, text, etc.[6]

It is also helpful to leave you with this important thought before going any further: graphics are for your audience, not you. To that end, it is important to discuss some of the key principles that form the foundation of effective data visualization.

Basic Dos and Don'ts

Data visualization requires two sets of skills: first, the technical skills to create the visualization in a software program, and the critical-thinking skills to convey the essential information that matches your audience's numeracy level; and comfort with data visualization. We will stress both.

In his book, *The Functional Art: An Introduction to Information Graphics and Visualization*, Alberto Cairo reminds us that good design is not about mastering the technology but "about facilitating clear communication and the understanding of relevant issues."[7]

Keeping this in mind, it is instructive to consider the key elements we need to master in order to become clear communicators with data visualization. In *The Wall Street Journal Guide to Information Graphics*, Dona M. Wong, former graphics director for the *Wall Street Journal*, says there are three essential elements to good information graphics: rich content, inviting visualization, and sophisticated execution.[8]

Content Is King

Critical thinking produces the information that turns your research into a story worth your audience's attention. Or put another way, critical thinking is the mother of rich content. Ideally, the visualization should amplify and help that content spring to life, either by boosting the message the words have conveyed, or by adding context that gives the words or numbers more depth or context. For this reason the choice of what to visualize is critical.

To that end let's look at some data, in this case a table that shows property losses and damage by Canadian federal departments or agencies. The table shows that Parks Canada and the Department of National Defence had losses that dwarfed those of any other agency or department. But what is the best to way to help readers see the story? We could present a table that lists all the departments and agencies and their losses, like this:

	A	B
1	**Departmens and agencies**	**Sum of Amount of loss**
2	Parks Canada Agency	$32,284,261
3	National Defence	$20,125,190
4	Royal Canadian Mounted Police	$2,406,653
5	Agriculture and Agri-Food	$1,024,551
6	Correctional Service of Canada	$1,007,806
7	Employment and Social Development	$361,528
8	Environment	$299,452
9	Public Works and Government Services	$296,652
10	Canadian Food Inspection Agency	$190,761
11	Fisheries and Oceans	$130,022
12	Industry	$121,320
13	Statistics Canada	$116,905
14	Shared Services Canada	$109,389
15	Canada Revenue Agency	$108,298
16	Natural Resources	$51,748
17	Citizenship and Immigration	$48,004
18	Health	$44,377

While interesting, this fails to bring the data to life. Given that parks and defence suffered losses much larger than any other agency or department, why not simplify your list to three categories?

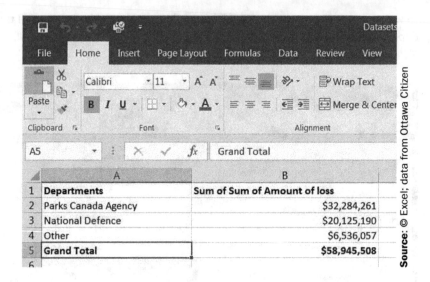

That's better. We created a third category for the aggregate of the smaller values and called it "Other." However, we can do an even better job of communicating this fact. In this case, a pie chart is an excellent option, as long as the number of data categories is minimized. So let's see what our data would look like in one.

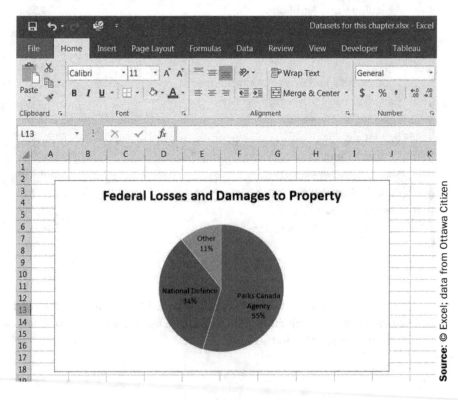

We can review the dos and don'ts for pie charts a little later in the chapter. For now it is sufficient to point out that the chart does a better job than the first two tables in explaining that two departments or agencies have suffered the bulk of the losses and damages.

The book *The Functional Art* points out that as journalists "we should strive for clarity because we are an interface between a chaotic world of information and the user who wants to understand something."[9] So by all means, spell out in your analysis that Parks and Defence are the main culprits, and then use the pie chart to show the percentages in play, something Excel does easily. Excel also calculates the percentages. In this example percentages explain the relative size of the problem at Parks and Defence.

Journalists are frequently confronted with the choice between using percentages and absolute values. While both are acceptable, it is key to think of the context, as we did when learning about mapping in Chapter 7. Absolute values state simple facts, while percent changes and ratios allow for comparisons, which line and bar charts can then illustrate.

For instance, if you are doing a story about the stock prices of two companies, and want to convey which firm is doing better, showing the percent change is more effective. In this fictitious example, Company A has revenue of $1 million. Company B has revenue of $100,000. During the same time period, the sales for Company A increased by $50,000 and the sales for Company B increased by $10,000.

	A	B	C	D
1	Company	Revenues	Sales	Stock Price Increase
2	Company A	$1,000,000	$50,000	$10
3	Company B	$100,000	$10,000	$10
4				

Source: © Excel

Using absolute values tells us that Company A made more revenue. However, that is to be expected because it is larger than Company B. Of more use to our audience is an assessment of which company is performing the best. For this, we need to calculate the sales increases as percentages of revenues.

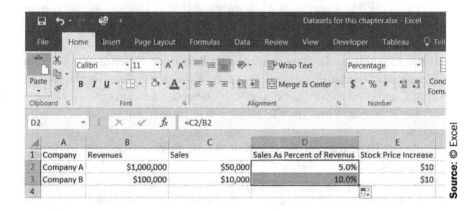

Now when we visualize the difference using a vertical bar chart, it becomes clearer which company is actually doing better.

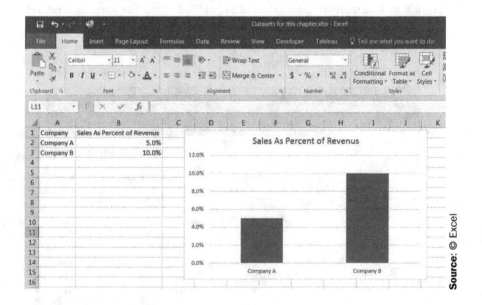

Absolute numbers can also obscure stories waiting to be told. Let's take this example from Statistics Canada of property crime numbers in Newfoundland and Labrador (NL), Nova Scotia (NS), New Brunswick (NB), and Prince Edward Island (PEI).[10]

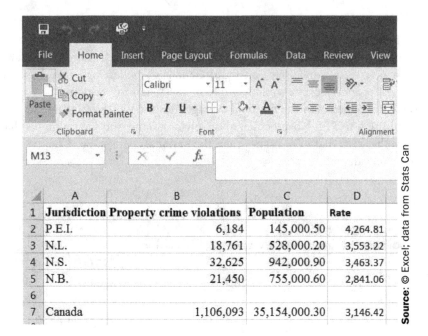

Source: © Excel; data from Stats Can

Given the relative sizes of the provinces, it is probably of little surprise that tiny PEI has the smallest number. So there is no real story, right? Not so fast. The numbers become more interesting when we calculate the rate using the population figures and a multiplier of 100,000, which Statistics Canada and police forces use when calculating crime rates.

	A	B	C	D
1	Jurisdiction	Property crime violations	Population	Rate
2	P.E.I.	6,184	145,001	4,265
3	N.L.	18,761	528,000	3,553
4	N.S.	32,625	942,001	3,463
5	N.B.	21,450	755,001	2,841
6				
7	Canada	1,106,093	35,154,000	3,146
8				

Source: © Excel

We divided the property crime violations by the population, multiplied by 100,000 to obtain a rate per 100,000 =(B2/C2)*100,000 and displayed the result in column D. Now if we sort column D in descending order, PEI takes on a new significance. Not only did Canada's smallest province have the highest property crime violation rate of the four provinces in 2013, but it was also higher than the national average. It's also worth pointing out that, in addition to PEI, Nova Scotia, and Newfoundland and Labrador also had rates that year that were higher than the national average. See Chapter 4 for more on calculating rates.

	A	B	C	D
1	Jurisdiction	Property crime violations	Population	Rate
2	P.E.I.	6,184	145,001	4,265
3	N.L.	18,761	528,000	3,553
4	N.S.	32,625	942,001	3,463
5	N.B.	21,450	755,001	2,841
6				
7	Canada	1,106,093	35,154,000	3,146

Source: © Excel

To help make those numbers stand out, we would want to use a vertical bar chart, which is ideal for comparing discrete quantities. Our visualization would look something like this if we created a quick chart in Excel. You can also see that we have given Canada a different shade to distinguish it from the rest. The companion website for this chapter will explain how to colour-code charts in Excel.

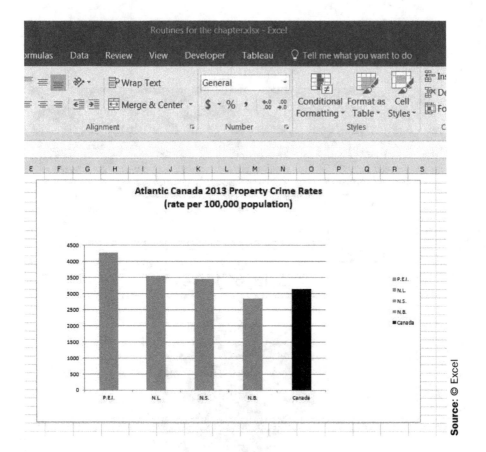

Choosing the Right Chart

The underlying principles used in selecting the right type of chart are crucial. The right visualization amplifies, adds context, or extra dimensions to your story. The wrong visualization muddies the message, or worse, distorts it or conveys the incorrect information. So it is worth taking some time to examine three of the most common charts journalists use: the pie chart, the bar chart, and the line chart.

The Pie Chart

Imagine reading a pie chart the way you would a clock. This is why it is important to place the largest segment at the 12 o'clock mark on the right to emphasize its importance.[11] Then, the best way to order the rest of the segments is to place the second-biggest slice to the left of the 12 o'clock mark; the rest would follow counter-clockwise, with the smallest and least significant slice falling to the bottom of the chart.

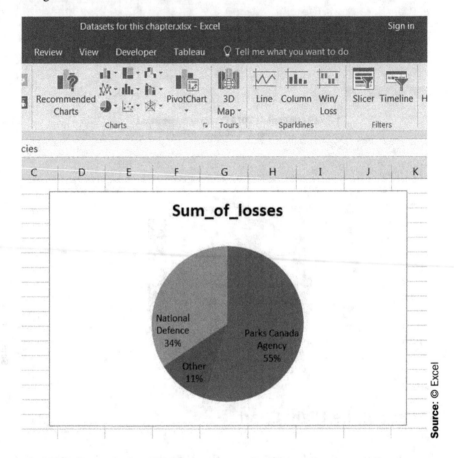

Given that Defence and Parks are relatively close together, we could make an exception, beginning at 12 o'clock on the right and continuing clockwise from largest to smallest.

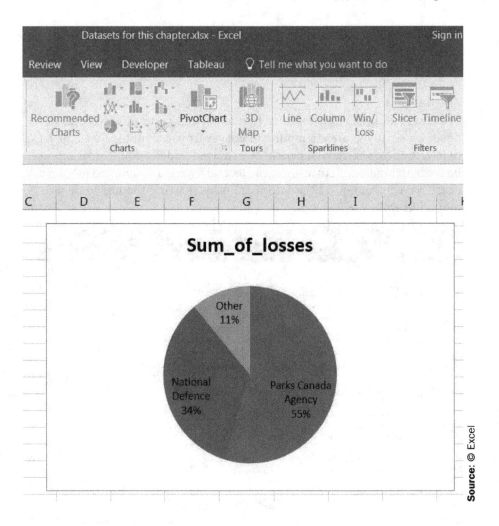

Labelling in charts is also important for two key reasons: the labels make it easy to understand the chart, and they can also turn your visualization into a standalone product that can be understood without having to read the entire story. This may be the case if someone's first introduction to the story is the graph. If the content is compelling and easy to understand, the person will, one hopes, be convinced the read the entire story.

Pie charts are at their most effective when depicting something as a percentage of a whole: in this case federal losses and damages as a percentage of the entire figure for the 2013–14 fiscal year. The fewer slices your pie has, the better. Experts advise that it should contain no more than five slices. A greater number makes the content too difficult to decipher. It is for this reason that we combined the remaining departments and agencies into the "Other" category. If you wanted to show more of these departments, then a bar chart would be better suited.

The Bar Chart

There are two kinds of bar charts: horizontal and vertical. The choice depends on what you are attempting to convey. If you want to show highest to lowest, then a horizontal bar chart, arranged in descending order might be the better option. Returning to the federal losses and damaged property chart, we can round out the information by charting the top 10 departments like this:

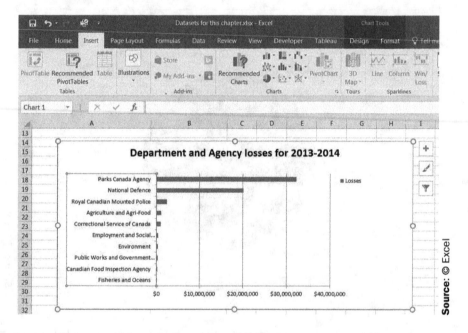

Source: © Excel

The losses for many of the other federal employers were so small in comparison to Parks Canada and National Defence that they barely register on the bar chart. However, for the purposes of this explanation, we can see how a horizontal bar chart allows the eye to quickly assess the two greatest losses compared to the others in our top-10 list. We could have also used a vertical bar chart, but it would not have been quite as effective.

By contrast, vertical bar charts may be better suited for showing how a value changes over time. For instance, if we had the losses for the departments and agencies during a five-year period, we could group the two of the largest departments side-by-side, and then plot them on the chart.

The Line Chart

In recent years in Canada, federal departments have often underspent their budgets. The practice is called "lapsed spending" in government lingo. That is, a department allows a certain fraction of its budget to remain unspent in a year, at which point some of it is carried forward to the next year. The rest is returned to general revenues. An undated and heavily redacted Finance Canada briefing note that CBC News obtained through the Canadian Access to Information Act explained that departments lapse spending if they carry out fewer of their planned initiatives, or have "lower-than-expected costs for programming."[12]

Of course, that was the official explanation. The suspicion of many was that departments were being forced to hoard cash in an effort to free up money for pre-election goodies for taxpayers. One Canadian Press story pointed out that National Defence, the RCMP, and CSIS (Canada's spy agency) were unable to spend $11 billion of their budgets starting in 2007, the year the Conservative Party came to power. The story quoted Jason Kenney, the defence minister at the time, who told reporters,

> Every department lapses funds every year. And they always have, and they always will. Departments don't blow out their budgets. That's irresponsible fiscal management. Departments submit budgets always with a little margin for error on the high side and they always have carry-forward provisions.[13]

Unfortunately, there were no charts to accompany the story, which would have helped compare the lapsed spending of the three government entities. But, as we have pointed out, it would make little sense to compare the raw numbers because they have different-sized budgets with National Defence being the largest.

It would make more sense to follow up on a point the defence minister made; that is, every year departments allow a certain percentage of their budgets to lapse. Calculating the lapse percentage for each entity from 2007 to 2013 would be a fair comparison that could be charted, just like we use rates to compare crime between different-sized cities.

The figures for the National Defence, the RCMP, and CSIS broke down as follows.[14]

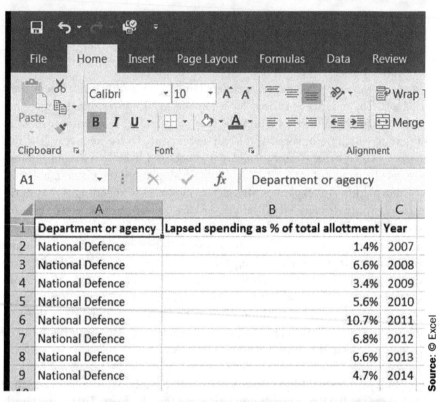

Source: © Excel

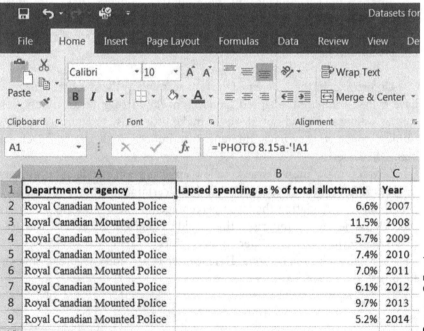

Source: © Excel

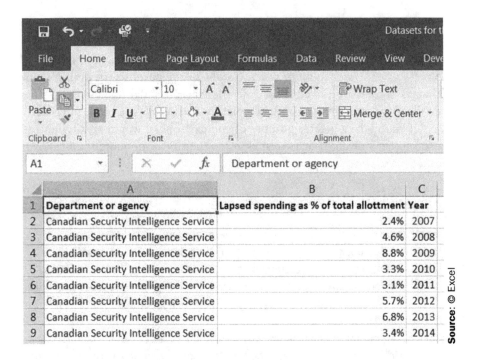

While the percentages are interesting, it's difficult to see the story; that is, which of these federal entities is lapsing the highest percentage of their budgets. Such a visualization plays into the strength of a line chart, which is at its best when showing how something behaves over time.

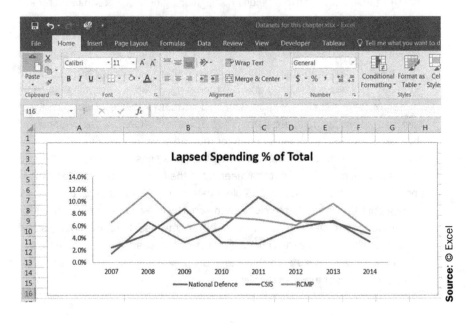

We can see that of the three, it is the RCMP that has been allowing a greater percentage of its budget to lapse in most years. When using a line chart, it is best to use no more than three or four lines. As Wong points out in *The Wall Street Journal Guide to Information Graphics*, "the purpose of a multiple-line chart is to compare and contrast different data series. Plotting too many lines on the same chart gives a confusing picture and defeats the whole purpose."[15]

If you make a greater number of comparisons, it would be advisable to use another line chart or two, sticking to the rule of no more than three or four for each one.

Best Practices

In addition to placing a lot of care into the chart you use, it is also important to remember some general guidelines that will help people see the story.

Legibility: There are literally thousands of typefaces in different styles and weights. Remember, the chart is meant to describe the information as simply as possible. Wong suggests that "typography should be chosen purely on the merit of legibility."[16]

Colour: As with everything else we have described so far, colour is also instrumental in conveying information. Choose your colours carefully. There are three main attributes to colour: hue, saturation, and value. Hue is how we describe the colour (red, green, black); saturation is the intensity of the colour; value is the darkness of the colour.[17] It is also important to keep in mind that about 10 per cent of the population has some form of colour-vision deficiency and many of those people have difficulty distinguishing between greens and reds.[18] It is for this reason that many visualization gurus suggest using black and shades of grey, rather than colours, especially for simple charts.

Avoid clutter: The cleaner the chart, the fewer distractions and the easier it is for the eye to concentrate on the message you are conveying. So avoid attributes such as heavy grid lines and 3-D rendering, which are tempting, given all the fancy options that Excel and data-visualization software offer. Do not get sucked in. Keep it simple. Remember the advice we offered at the beginning of the chapter: the data visualization is for the audience, not for you.

Legends and labels: It is difficult for readers to make sense of a chart if they are always struggling to figure out the meaning of the line or graph. This is why it is important to make the labelling as clear as possible. For instance, this means making sure that legends are close to the chart. Distance makes it difficult for readers to determine the relationship between the lines, bars, or pie slices and the legend. If you choose to label segments on the chart, be sure to keep the label concise. And make sure that the chart is properly titled and sourced, so that people know the information's origin.

Form and shading: Avoid creating shadows behind bars. The shadows contain no information and are merely distractions. The same advice applies to three-dimensional vertical or horizontal bars. Wong says they are "flat out wrong. Rendering the bars in 3-D adds no information."[19]

Zero baseline: A bar chart that does not begin at a zero baseline is misleading. "Truncation obscures the discrete total value of each bar and makes comparison of the data difficult."[20]

Ordering and grouping: Be sure to have a pattern that makes it easy for people to obtain the information. For instance, horizontal bars are the most useful when ranking numbers from highest to lowest or vice versa. Vertical bars are best when comparing groups of discrete values.

How Journalists Use "Data Viz" Tools

In a video presentation for the Knight Journalism Fellowship, data visualization expert Fernanda B. Viégas notes that "half of our brain is hardwired for vision."[21] That is, we are programmed to understand the world around us in terms of what we see. Perhaps this partially explains data visualization's increased popularity, which has been helped by free software. In using these data-visualization programs, journalists and their newsrooms are borrowing techniques from computer scientists, researchers, and artists.

Initially, data visualizations were designed largely to be viewed on desktop computers. As of 2014, smartphones and tablets represented roughly 50 per cent of the web's traffic.[22] This suggests that, while still essential for many stories, sprawling and ambitious interactive visualizations may be ill-suited for smaller screens. Simple charts like the ones we discuss in this chapter and that you can see on news sites such as Quartz (Qz.com) may often be the best choice.[23]

Charts came in handy for Allison Martell's train derailment story for Reuters, in which she showed an accident rate that had been steadily increasing in the wake of the tragedy in Lac-Mégantic, Quebec, on 6 July 2013, in which 47 people were killed when unattended runaway rail cars filled with crude oil careened down a hill and exploded in the town's centre.

"Trains operated by CN in Canada derailed along main lines 57 times in 2014, up 73 percent from 33 in 2013 and well above a 2009–2013 average of 39 accidents per year," she wrote. "On CN's full 21,000 mile (33,800 km) network, which also includes the Midwestern and southern United States, freight carloads rose 8 percent last year." The company was forced to concede that derailments were a problem.[24] To help tell the story, Martell used a simple line graph to compare the company's accident ratio to the Canadian average.

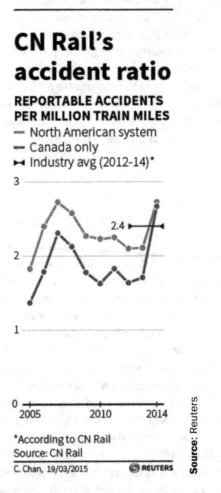

CN Rail's accident ratio

REPORTABLE ACCIDENTS PER MILLION TRAIN MILES
— North American system
— Canada only
⊢◄ Industry avg (2012-14)*

2.4 ►

*According to CN Rail
Source: CN Rail

C. Chan, 19/03/2015   REUTERS

Source: Reuters

Line graph that accompanied Allison Martell's story on the Lac-Mégantic disaster

Journalists also use data visualization to tell stories that provide context in the lead-up to large events affecting their communities. Such was the case with Radio-Canada's Valérie Ouellet, who told a story about the differing accommodation prices during Toronto's Pan Am Games in the summer of 2015. The process began when her colleague, CBC interactive developer William Wolfe-Wylie, one of the contributors to this book, scraped Toronto's Airbnb website for ads targeting Pan Am Games visitors (see Chapter 9 for a discussion of scraping). The results showed that the prices for people renting their rooms were generally higher than hotels, a counterintuitive result to be sure.[25]

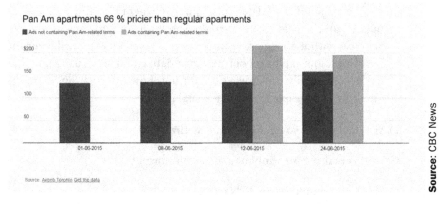

Bar chart accompanying story about Airbnb prices during the Pan Am Games

The vertical bar chart grouped and compared the ads, allowing the audience to see the difference between ads with Pan Am–related terms and regular advertisements for accommodations. Was this a case of price gouging? Perhaps. At the very least, it was a cautionary tale of renter beware.

"Data-visualization is essential for most of my data-related stories," says Ouellet. "I think maps, infographics, and graphs remain the easiest, smartest way to make numbers relevant and alive. But I also think finding strong characters to interview is just as essential."[26]

One Producer's View

One person who has noticed an increase in data visualization is the CBC's senior political affairs producer, Chris Carter. The following is a short question-and-answer session in which he explains why data visualization has become so popular, and what he looks for when editing stories, which is a large part of his job as the senior online producer in the CBC's parliamentary bureau.

David McKie: How has the prominence of data visualization grown over the course of your career?

Chris Carter: From an investigative point of view, the use of data to source stories or identify trends has exploded and opened up the possibilities to reveal stories from public records, data obtained by freedom-of-information, or records compiled from tedious hard work. From a presentation point of view, data visualization has gone from what used to be called "graphics," a label that implies a flat, one-way relationship, to a more interactive way of presenting numbers and information, particularly large amounts of related information that might have otherwise been too unwieldy or required hours of scrutiny to make sense of. The availability of data tools—many of them free and online—has opened up the field to all journalists, not just graphic artists and developers, although expertise in those areas is often responsible for the best work. The explosion of interest in data and data visualization has led to some really clever ways to consider how information intersects and how to translate that into a visual medium.

D.M.: How would you define data visualization?

C.C.: It is making sense out of a mass of information.

D.M.: When should journalists use it?

C.C.: Journalists should use data visualization to reveal trends, insights, or stories that would otherwise be obscured by the complexity or sheer volume of data. Ideally, it tells you something useful, even surprising, at a glance, and then reveals more complexity the more you look at it or play with it.

D.M.: What are three common mistakes journalists make?

C.C.: *Trying to do too much.* You have to choose to work with, or display, the information that is most important or necessary. Too much can lead to confusion—and missed deadlines.
A lack of clarity. You have to help the reader understand what he or she is seeing—that means knowing how to frame the visualization with titles, labels, and introductory text.
Forgetting about people. Data analysis can reveal important trends and interesting stories, but that shouldn't be where the journalism ends. In most cases, there are people behind the numbers or records and the analysis should help journalists tell their stories.

D.M.: When is data visualization at its best?

C.C.: When it tells a clear story and when it tells you something you didn't know or might have missed.

D.M.: When should a story use data visualization?

C.C.: When it can help make sense of what would otherwise be an overwhelming mass of information—or when it can simply make you go, "huh."[27]

Chad Skelton echoes Carter's views on data visualization. Skelton was a data journalist at the *Vancouver Sun* and is now a journalism instructor at Kwantlen University. These are some of the basics he stresses to his students:

- A good chart should make sense with the number labels removed. When you do this, you often realize the chart types that don't really communicate data very well and why certain practices can be misleading (i.e. using a baseline other than zero).
- Keep things as simple as possible. Remember that your user/reader is seeing this data for the first time.
- If your chart is interactive, be as explicit as possible on the chart how people interact with it (e.g. "Click on the name of a political party to see a breakdown of its donations").
- Try to "beta test" your interactives on your newsroom colleagues by getting someone who doesn't know about your story to try it out and see if they can figure out how it works (without you standing over their shoulder).[28]

The detailed how-tos of making visualizations involve many steps, and the tools are changing constantly. You'll find tutorials on current popular tools on the companion website.

Conclusion

Data visualization has become an important element in storytelling, allowing our audiences to understand the story.

There was a time when creating charts to supplement stories was the exclusive domain of graphic artists and web developers. However, as with so much of data journalism these days, the evolution of open portals, open-sourced software and online tools has made it easier to obtain data, analyze it, and use words and charts to tell stories.

The temptation is to want to impress our audiences with intricate visualizations, simply because they are easily available. Sometimes such visualizations can be stunning. However, more often, simpler is better. In this vein, perhaps it is best to use Chad Skelton's advice: test the visualization out with a colleague to see if what you are trying to say makes sense.

Study Questions and Exercises

1. Using data obtained from an open-data site, or from another source of your choosing, make a visualization using Google Fusion Tables, as shown in the online tutorial.
2. Using data obtained from an open-data site, or from another source of your choosing, make a visualization using Tableau Public, again as shown in the online tutorial.
3. An additional exercise using live data from a real story is available on the companion website.

Notes

1. Stuart Card, preface to *Information Visualization Perception for Design*, 2nd ed. by Colin Ware (Burlington, MA: Morgan Kaufmann, 2004), xvii.

2. Michael Friendly, "Milestones in the History of Data Visualization: A Case Study in Statistical Historiography," *Classification: The Ubiquitous Challenge* (New York: Springer, 2005), 5, http://www.datavis.ca/papers/gfkl.pdf.

3. Ibid., 5.

4. Stephen Few, "Tapping the Power of Visual Perception," *Perceptual Edge (blog)*, http://www.perceptualedge.com/articles/ie/visual_perception.pdf, 4 September 2004, 1.

5. Few, "Visual Business Intelligence, Data Art v. Data Visualization: Why Does a Distinction Matter?" *Perceptual Edge (blog)*, 18 May 2012, http://www.perceptualedge.com/blog/?p=1245.

6. Jonathan A. Schwabish, "An Economist's Guide to Visualizing Data," *Journal of Economic Perspectives* 28.1 (2014): 209.

7. Alberto Cairo, *The Functional Art: An Introduction to Information Graphics and Visualization* (Berkeley, CA: New Riders, 2013), 45.

8. Dona M. Wong, *The Wall Street Journal Guide to Information Graphics* (New York: W.W. Norton, 2013), 14–15.

9. Cairo, *The Functional Art*, 48.

10. All data used in this example is from Statistics Canada, "Crimes, by Type of Violation, and by Province and Territory (Newfoundland and Labrador, Prince Edwards Island, Nova Scotia, New Brunswick)," 22 August 2015, http://www.statcan.gc.ca/tables-tableaux/sum-som/l01/cst01/legal50a-eng.htm.

11. Wong, *Guide to Information Graphics*, 75.

12. Finance Canada briefing notes, "Lapse Forecast Methodology," 6 January 2015, https://www.documentcloud.org/documents/2179156-financecanadalapsedspendingbriefingnote.html#document/p5/a228615.

13. Murray Brewster, "DND, CSIS, RCMP Unable to Spend $11 Billion of their Budgets since 2007," *Canadian Press*, 19 February 2015, http://www.nationalnewswatch.com/2015/02/19/dnd-csis-rcmp-unable-to-spend-11-billion-of-their-budgets-since-2007/#.VOaIsPnF843.

14. Data used in this example is from Public Accounts of Canada, http://www.tpsgc-pwgsc.gc.ca/recgen/cpc-pac/index-eng.html.

15. Wong, *Guide to Information Graphics*, 55.

16. Ibid., 30.

17. Ibid., 36.

18. Schwabish, *An Economist's Guide to Visualizing Data*, 21.

19. Wong, *Guide to Information Graphics*, 62.

20. Ibid., 64.

21. Geoff McGhee, *Journalism in the Age of Data*, http://datajournalism.stanford.edu/.

22. James O'Toole, "Mobile Apps Overtake PC Internet Usage in U.S.," *CNN Money*, 28 February 2014, http://money.cnn.com/2014/02/28/technology/mobile/mobile-apps-internet/.

23. Mark Wilson, "What Killed the Infographic," *Co Design*, 5 June 2015, http://www.fastcodesign.com/3045291/what-killed-the-infographic.

24. Allison Martell, "CN Rail Derailment Numbers Soared before Recent Crashes," *Reuters*, 23 March 2015, http://www.reuters.com/article/us-canada-derailments-exclusive-idUSKBN0MJ0AZ20150323.

25. Valérie Ouellette and William Wolfe-Wylie, "Airbnb Renters Hope to Score Big Cash during Pan Am Games," *CBC.ca*, 2 July 2015, http://www.cbc.ca/news/canada/toronto/multimedia/airbnb-renters-hope-to-score-big-cash-during-pan-am-games-1.3133581.

26. Valérie Ouellet, interview with the author, 27 July 2015.

27. Chris Carter, interview with the author, 27 July 2015.

28. Chad Skelton, interview with the author, 21 July 2015.

Part III
Advanced Topics

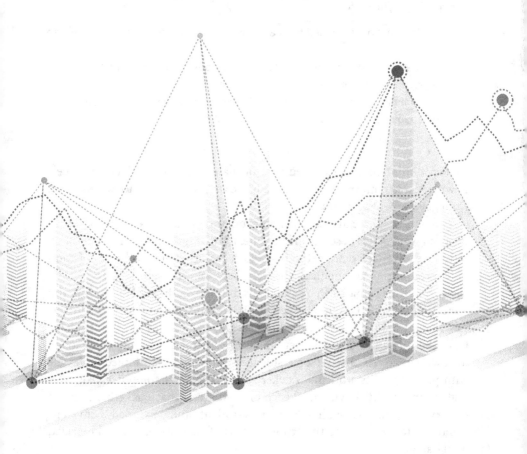

Chapter 9

Web Scraping

What You Will Learn:

- How information is passed back and forth between your computer and a web server
- How web scrapers emulate what a browser does, and how they process web pages to extract data
- How to build a simple scraper using the Python programming language
- The ethical issues surrounding web scraping

Earlier in this book, we explored how journalists can obtain data, be it freely downloadable data from an open-data site or data that has to be requested from government agencies.

Sometimes these avenues will not work, or will be closed to you, yet the data you want exists in some form online. In this chapter, the first of two that introduce advanced data methods, we look at web scraping, the use of computer programs to automatically harvest data from the web.

An early example of web scraping is dramatized in the Hollywood film *The Social Network* (David Fincher, 2010). A scene shows a Harvard University student named Mark Zuckerberg extracting pictures of other students from the university's web servers to run head-to-head beauty contests on his own site. Each "house" or residence at Harvard maintained a website with pictures of its students. Zuckerberg wrote small computer programs that automatically downloaded each one. So it was that Zuckerberg set out to harvest the images of all of Harvard's students and download them so he could create a site where the attractiveness of each student could be rated by classmates.

The beer-fuelled project got Zuckerberg in trouble with Harvard administrators, but ultimately inspired the creation by Zuckerberg and others of Facebook.

Tutorials Included with the Companion Website

You will find these tutorials on the OUP Companion Website (www.oupcanada .com/Vallance-Jones):

- Scraping Programs and Online Utilities
- Using Development Tools to Examine Webpages
- Choosing a Code Editor
- Getting Python Up and Running
- Running Your Python Scripts
- Dealing with Errors in Python
- Your First Multipage Scrape
- Scraping Sites with Search Form
- Scraping Sites That Use JavaScript
- Scraping Sites That Don't Want to Be Scraped
- Scraping Using Regular Expressions
- Using the Facebook API with Python
- Using the Twitter API with Python

Fortunately, web scraping is not limited in use to college frat-house antics. For data journalists, it's a powerful tool that allows them to assemble electronic records to find stories that could not be easily obtained otherwise, or would take much more time. Sometimes, it also affords the opportunity to obtain more complete data than that which is made available for easy download.

Take as an example the Elections Canada political contributions database. Using the site's point-and-click interface, you can see the town and postal code associated with each contributor:

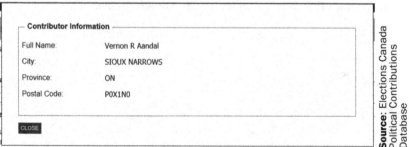

Source: Elections Canada Political Contributions Database

Unfortunately, downloadable data is limited to the donor name and the amount. The geographical information from the pop-up window is left out.

While not the easiest site technically to access programmatically, scraping the data allows for a much more precise analysis of who is giving, how much they give, and where they are located. Similarly, sites with searchable databases often serve up results in small chunks, broken into pages. This saves the web server from having to pass on large amounts of information that would slow it down, but makes it more difficult to assemble all the information at once.

The Underpinnings of Scraping

To understand how scraping is done, you need to know a little of how the web works. When you enter a web address (properly known as a Universal Resource Locator, or URL) into the address bar of your favourite browser, your computer sends a **request** to another computer, known as a server, located somewhere else on the Internet. That server responds by sending back the files required for the page you want to view. The browser assembles and displays the page. The same thing happens when you click on a link in a web page, click on the "search" button of a government's searchable database, click "download" to obtain a file, or touch a link on your mobile device. A request goes out, and files and/or data come back.

A web scraper works by sending automated requests, then extracting information out of the files that come back. Unlike a browser, it doesn't try to display the page, but just processes the raw information.

The main type of file that a scraper works with is called an HTML file. HTML stands for **HyperText Markup Language** and it's as old as the web itself. In fact, it's the foundation of the web. An HTML page contains the text of the page, plus the basic structures that hold the text. The various elements are set off by tags contained within angle brackets. Here's some basic HTML file containing a title, one line of text, and a two-row table.

```
<!DOCTYPE html>
<html>
  <head>
    <title>
      Some text and a table.
    </title>
  </head>
  <body>
    <p> Here is some text on the page. </p>
    <table>
```

```
<tr>
  <th> Column A heading </th> <th> Column B
  heading</th>
</tr>
<tr>
  <td> Data in column A</td><td>Data in column
  B</td>
</tr>
</table>

</body>
</html>
```

While this example is stripped down to its absolute essentials, you can see some of the key aspects of an HTML file. The first line, the doctype declaration, tells the browser which variant of HTML the file was written in. This one is written in HTML 5, the latest version at this book's publication.

There is a header section, set off by the <head> and </head> tags, a body section, one paragraph of text, set off by the paragraph tags, <p> and </p>, and a table, which has tags for the table as a whole, each row, the column headers, and each row of data. This table has only one header row and one row of data. More <tr> and <td> tags would be used to add more rows and data cells.

Notice that each tag in the file—the doctype declaration isn't really a tag—is first opened, then closed later with a closing tag using a / (forward slash) character. It is this structure of opening and closing tags that makes it possible for the web browser to render the page.

This is what our simple example looks like when rendered in the Google Chrome browser:

Here is some text on the page.

Column A heading Column B heading
Data in column A   Data in column B
Source: © Google

If you'd like to try making this HTML file for yourself, type the code above into a plain text file using TextEdit on a Mac or Notepad on a Windows PC, name the file, and give it the extension .html. You can then open the file in any web browser.

The tag structure in HTML files makes it possible for a web scraper to extract specific elements from the page, and save them as structured data. The scraper uses the tags as a roadmap to the information contained within the page.

Okay, let's look at a real-world example. Here is an excerpt of the HTML for a page of the Canadian federal government's "proactive disclosure" pages that list contracts greater than $10,000. We've started part way down a really long file so the top isn't visible.

```
<h1 id="wb-cont">2015-2016 - 1<sup>st</sup> Quarter (April to June)</h1><p class="note">N.B.: The
contract date represents the date that the contract is recorded in the departmental financial
system.</p><table class="wet-boew-zebra basic">
<caption class="font-small align-left">
<em>List of contracts for the trimester, which includes the date, vendor, description and value</
em>
</caption>
    <tr >
        <th class="secondary width20" scope="col"><a href="http://www.tpsgc-pwgsc.gc.ca/cgi-bin/
proactive/cl.pl?lang=eng;SCR=L;Sort=0;PF=CL201516Q1.txt" title="Reorder table by Contract
Date">Contract Date</a></th>
        <th class="secondary" scope="col"><a href="http://www.tpsgc-pwgsc.gc.ca/cgi-bin/proactive/
cl.pl?lang=eng;SCR=L;Sort=1;PF=CL201516Q1.txt" title="Reorder table by Vendor Name">Vendor Name</
a></th>
        <th class="secondary" scope="col"><a href="http://www.tpsgc-pwgsc.gc.ca/cgi-bin/proactive/
cl.pl?lang=eng;SCR=L;Sort=2;PF=CL201516Q1.txt" title="Reorder table by Description of
Work">Description of Work</a></th>
        <th class="secondary" scope="col"><a href="http://www.tpsgc-pwgsc.gc.ca/cgi-bin/proactive/
cl.pl?lang=eng;SCR=L;Sort=3;PF=CL201516Q1.txt" title="Reorder table by Contract Value">Contract
Value</a></th>
    </tr>
    <tr>
        <td>2008-04-22</td>
        <td><a href="http://www.tpsgc-pwgsc.gc.ca/cgi-bin/proactive/cl.pl?
lang=eng;SCR=D;Sort=0;PF=CL201516Q1.txt;LN=228" title="IGF VIGILANCE INC.;2008-04-22"><span
class="wb-hide">228</span>IGF VIGILANCE INC.</a></td>
        <td>420 - Engineering Services not Elsewhere Specified</td>
        <td class="alignRight">$500,695.10</td>
    </tr>
    <tr>
        <td>2008-04-22</td>
        <td><a href="http://www.tpsgc-pwgsc.gc.ca/cgi-bin/proactive/cl.pl?
lang=eng;SCR=D;Sort=0;PF=CL201516Q1.txt;LN=432" title="THE ARCOP GROUP  /  GERSOVITZ MOSS;
2008-04-22"><span class="wb-hide">432</span>THE ARCOP GROUP  /  GERSOVITZ MOSS</a></td>
        <td>423 - Engineering Consultants - Other</td>
        <td class="alignRight">$67,145,777.15</td>
    </tr>
```

And here is the same page rendered in the Firefox browser:

Government of Canada / Gouvernement du Canada		Canada.gc.ca | Services | Departments | Français

Public Works and Government Services Canada

Canada

PWGSC Services   Information for   PWGSC Resources

Home > Transparency > Proactive Disclosure > Disclosure of Contracts > Reports > 2015-2016 - 1st Quarter (April to June)

PWGSC Services
Transparency
Proactive Disclosure
Disclosure of Contracts
Disclosure of Travel and Hospitality Expenses
Disclosure of Annual Expenditures for Travel, Hospitality and Conferences
Disclosure of Position Reclassifications
Disclosure of Grants and Contributions
Disclosure of wrongdoings in the workplace

2015-2016 - 1st Quarter (April to June)

N.B.: The contract date represents the date that the contract is recorded in the departmental financial system.

List of contracts for the trimester, which includes the date, vendor, description and value

Contract Date	Vendor Name	Description of Work	Contract Value
2008-04-22	IGF VIGILANCE INC.	420 - Engineering Services not Elsewhere Specified	$500,695.10
2008-04-22	THE ARCOP GROUP / GERSOVITZ MOSS	423 - Engineering Consultants - Other	$67,145,777.15
2008-04-22	CAPITAL ELEVATOR LTD.	859 - Other Business Services not Elsewhere Specified	$73,651.02
2008-09-04	NORR LIMITED	421 - Architectural Services	$40,100,544.85
2009-02-28	R&R AUTOMATION INC.	859 - Other Business Services not Elsewhere Specified	$1,077,864.27
2009-03-25	CAPITAL ELEVATOR LTD.	859 - Other Business Services not Elsewhere Specified	$108,703.30
2009-04-24	XEROX CANADA LTD.	533 - Renti Machinry, Off Furnitre / Fixtres & Other Eqpt	$34,591.67

If you compare the coding and the rendered page, you can see the various HTML tags and how they translate into the main content displayed on the page. For example, the large headers on the page are easily visible in the HTML inside the <h1> </h1> tag pair. Similarly, you can see the <table> tag that indicates the beginning of the table of data, and some of the data from the table within the two sets of <tr> tags. Within the first row, between the first <tr> and the first </tr> tag, there are four column headers, contained within <th> tags, for the Contract Date, Vendor Name, Description of Work, and Contract Value. Within the second <tr></tr> pair is the first data row of the table, contained within the <td> and </td> tags. It's the same basic structure we saw in the simple HTML file we looked at earlier, but with some added twists.

One of these twists is the use of code such as "class" and "ID" within the HTML page. These tell the browser which CSS style rules to apply to the page when it is rendered onscreen. We'll look at CSS more closely in the next chapter, but for now it suffices to know that CSS stands for **Cascading Style Sheets**. A separate CSS file (or less often, CSS embedded directly within the HTML file) contains the instructions on how to display a page, what colours to use, border widths, font sizes, and much more, written in CSS code. The references to class and ID in the HTML point the browser to the specific style rules contained within the CSS file, allowing for extremely fine-tuned design, so that individual elements on the page can have their own designs. They also allow for ever-more fine-tuned scraping, as CSS classes and IDs can be used by a scraper to pinpoint desired content. As you develop your eye for web scraping, you will learn to examine the HTML markup carefully, which will help guide the design of your scraper.

When we surf the web manually, our web browser does all the heavy lifting of interpreting the HTML and CSS, and any JavaScript code contained in the page—JavaScript is a programming language that allows designers to build in rich interactivity and other advanced features in web pages. When we webscrape (yes, it is a compound verb, or at least will be soon!), we use an off-the-shelf scraping program, or a script that we write in a programming language such as Python, to emulate a web browser. Once the remote server sends back its response, our scraping program reads through the information contained in the HTML of the page, and extracts just the parts we want

You can peek behind the curtain and see the actual source code behind any web page on most browsers. On Chrome, you can select "View Source" to see this raw data. Firefox shows the source code by selecting the Web Developer screen in the Tools menu and then choosing Page Source. In Safari, you'll need to activate the Developer menu in the Preferences settings, and then click on "View Source Code."

(technically, this is called "**parsing**"), usually but not always writing the results to a structured text file that can then be opened in a spreadsheet, database, or mapping application. This is the essence of web scraping. Note that if a page uses JavaScript heavily, more advanced techniques may be required, but the principle is the same.

Options for Scraping

Each scraping project will be in some way unique, as the layouts of HTML pages vary widely. For simpler scrapes, off-the-shelf software may be all you need. Scraping utilities, such as import.io and Outwit will do the job in many instances. Each method works in its own way, and has its strengths and limitations. Some such as Google Sheets and Import.io are free, at least for small jobs, while others such as Outwit are commercial software.

Import.io is a cloud-based application that allows you to paste the URL of a page containing data and quickly get a downloadable extract of the data in the page. It works best for pages that contain straightforward HTML tables, such as the proactive disclosure site pictured earlier in this chapter. When it works, it's almost like magic. Outwit is a program that either runs in a desktop or as a plug-in for Firefox, and allows more sophisticated extraction of data based on the HTML code of the page. These programs and utilities come and go.

You can do simple scrapes using Google Sheets and its IMPORTHTML, QUERY, and IMPORTXML functions. You will find a list of currently available scraping programs and online utilities on the companion website.

The most powerful approach to web scraping is to write your own custom computer scripts. In many cases, these are the only way to extract data from online databases that require user input, such as the searchable databases often found on government sites. You can use programming to scrape almost any kind of site, whether the content is in tables, accessible through a search box, in ordinary web pages, or contained in unstructured text files. You are only limited by your imagination and by your level of technical skill. Fortunately, the skill level required for many basic scraping applications is within grasp for anyone with the time and inclination to learn, and the large libraries of pre-written code available in popular scripting languages mean that most of the heavy lifting of making requests to websites and parsing out the contents of web pages can be taken care of by someone else's code. All you need to learn are some fundamental programming skills, as *Ottawa Citizen* reporter Glen McGregor, one of the contributors to this book, did when he took on a story about the Canadian federal government's "Economic Action Plan," in 2009.[1]

He researched the story in concert with Stephen Maher, then of the *Halifax Chronicle-Herald*, and assisted by journalism students at Ottawa's Algonquin College. In the teeth of the global downturn, the government began spending billions of dollars on infrastructure projects. Across the country, the money flowed for new sewer mains, bridges, road work, university laboratories, hockey rinks, and skateboard parks. The reporters wondered where exactly all the money was going and whether any of it would be the subject to age-old tradition of political pork-barrelling, with elected representatives attempting to steer cash to their constituencies.

Although the government wasn't shy about publicizing the individual projects that it advertised with green-and-blue billboards next to the construction sites, it wouldn't provide a comprehensive list of all the projects or which federal electoral districts, or "ridings," each fell within. To perform their analysis of the spending patterns, the reporters would have to locate every single stimulus project funded, and then assign it to one of the 308 federal ridings (something CBC Manitoba actually did when it researched a similar story in 1995,[2] before the advent of web scraping and GIS).

Plowing through the thousands of press releases issued for every project would take weeks—even months. Looking for a shortcut, they turned to the website the government had created to promote the Economic Action Plan. It conveniently featured an embedded map dotted with more than 6,000 stimulus projects. The two journalists realized that the government had done the hardest part of the work for them by assigning the geographic coordinates to each stimulus project so that it could be placed on the map.

The challenge was to pull the details of the stimulus projects off the government's map and into a database where they could be analyzed. Exploring the structure of the web page, the reporters discovered that the map was pulling data from a single file on the government's server that contained a project number and URL for each point on the map along with its latitude and longitude. They downloaded this file, but found it did not contain any detail about the projects. The name, description and financial details of each project were stored on 6,000 separate web pages, one for each project. Fortunately, the URLs (what you type in your browser's address bar) all followed a consistent pattern, with only the project number varying. The details of projects were also identically structured on each page.

Using the Python programming language, McGregor wrote a simple computer script to take each one of these project numbers and request the associated web page from the government's web server. It took several hours to scrape each of the 6,000 project pages and extract the details, but when the reporters were done, they had a file with a full list of projects with their exact locations saved on their hard drive. By joining this data to the file that had the latitude and longitude coordinates, using the project number that

Projects Map

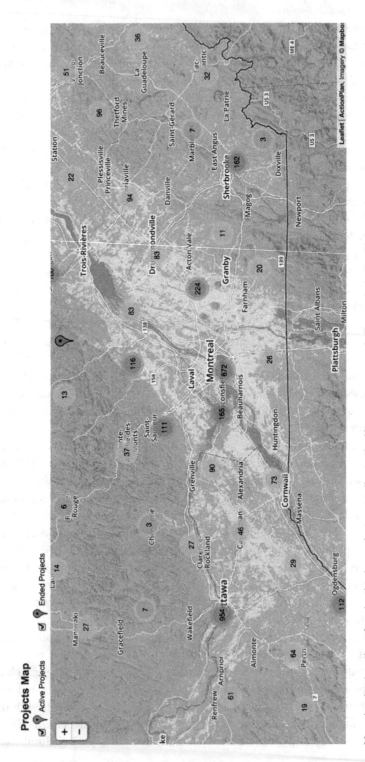

Map showing location of each stimulus project, according to the Harper government's Economic Action Plan website

Source: Economic Action Plan map (http://actionplan.gc.ca/en/projects-map)

was common to both projects, they ended up with a single file that contained both the location and financial details of each project. From there, the journalists turned to ArcGIS, one of the GIS programs we discussed in Chapter 7. The 6,000 projects were overlaid on a map of the 308 ridings, provided by Elections Canada. The software figured out the rest and gave the reporters a list of projects, each placed in a federal riding, along with the name and party affiliation of the member of Parliament responsible for the riding.

The analysis showed that each riding held by government MPs received an average of $32.8 million in infrastructure spending, about $9 million more than in opposition ridings. The stories that resulted from this work—made possible by web scraping—put Stephen Harper's Conservative government on the defensive and led to weeks of questions about the Economic Action Plan in Parliament.

First Steps, Thinking through Your Scrape

The temptation with scraping is often to jump in right away and start writing code, but you can save yourself mistakes and simplify your code by first conceptualizing your scrape. The first thing you should do is go to the target site with a conventional browser, and see how the data you want to scrape is organized. Is it a series of static web pages that you will simply open one after another? How is the information on the pages organized? Are the data elements you want to scrape set off with their own headings, are they embedded in free text, or is the data in a table format? Do you have to follow links to get additional detail? If so, how many layers of linked pages are there? Is there search functionality on the page? If so, what do you need to enter in the search box(es)? Can you enter no characters at all and get all the data back; if not, how many characters have to be entered into a field before a search will work?

Think about how the data you want to scrape would be organized if it were laid out in rows and columns like those in an Excel spreadsheet. Consider what individual elements of data on the web page would be included in each row of the spreadsheet. As you look at the pages, start to think of the steps your scraper would need to take to first get to and then extract each of those data elements. For example, if there is a main page with a list of data items, each of which links to a secondary page, your scraper would probably have to grab each piece of data on the main page, follow the link to grab the related data on the secondary page, then cycle back to get the next piece of data on the main page.

Some people find it helps to draw a flowchart of how a scraper would crawl through the pages. The drawing then becomes a template when it comes time to start writing code. If you take these steps, you will already have a good idea of what you need your script to do.

Once you have conceptualized this, the next step is usually to examine the underlying HTML code of each type of page you need to scrape. In the scenario of the main page with links that lead to detail pages, you will need to examine the structure of the main page and one of the detail pages. What you learn from one should apply to the others.

The leading web browsers all have tools built in that allow you to examine the underlying HTML code. Chrome has its Developer Tools, and Firefox has both its native tools and the Firebug plug-in. All have a tool called an "element inspector" that allows you to hover over any part of a web page and see the underlying HTML and CSS code. You can then see what tags and other text enclose or are near the pieces of data you want to extract. In the following image, you can see the element inspector in Firebug being used to take a close look at the element containing the text "IGF VIGILANCE INC." on the page of public works contracts.

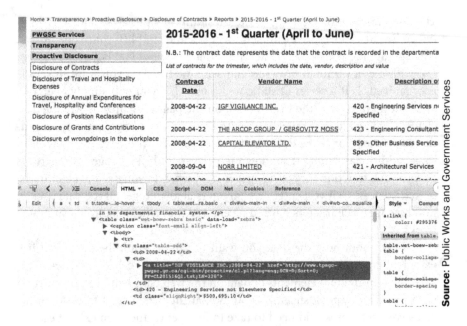

The **developer tools** also allow you to see if more technically sophisticated means are being used to populate the page. For example, a technology called AJAX (short for **Asynchronous JavaScript and** XML) allows part of a web page to be refreshed with new information without the server having to send the entire page again. If AJAX is being used, you can use the network tab in to see the request made by your computer and the data sent back by the server.

The companion website has a tutorial on how to use these tools to examine web pages you want to scrape.

For a more sweeping look at a page, you can also open its source code. By searching for text that is near the elements you want to extract, you can zoom in on the HTML and CSS that is associated with the information you want. You will also be able to see if JavaScript is being used, and how.

Once you have mapped out what your scraper needs to do, and have taken a careful look at the underlying markup of the page, you will be ready to start writing code. Depending on how the pages are set up, designing the scraper could be trivially easy or quite difficult.

Coding Basics

There are various languages that can be used for this task, including Python, Ruby, **Perl**, and PHP. We'll use Python not because it is necessarily better, but because it is reasonably easy to learn the fundamentals, and the large community of fellow users, the "Pythonistas" as they are sometimes called, provides a ready-made support network when you need help. The basic programming concepts are common across all of these languages, so what we will present here is pretty portable if you choose a language other than Python. Python also forces you to write readable code, because of its use of indents rather than curly braces to set off **code blocks**. It's an all-around good first choice.

We already know that the basic process of scraping is one of programmatically accessing network resources (web pages and the like), then parsing the results. What follows is a brief introduction to the basic programming concepts that you will need to learn to build web scraping scripts.

A script is a simple computer program that is written to perform one task. Unlike the sophisticated programs that you use for writing, browsing the web, or playing games, a script lacks any visual bells and whistles. It's just a text file, and you create it in a text or **code editor**. More on those shortly. You usually run a script from the Command window on a Windows PC or from the Terminal on a Mac or Linux computer. Scripts written in the Python language have file names ending with the .py extension, and they require that you have a copy of Python installed on your computer. Macs and some Linux distributions, such as Ubuntu, come with this pre-installed. If you have a Windows PC, you have to download Python from Python.org, then install it. You'll find instructions on the companion website.

A typical scraping script used by journalists needs to access the Internet, parse content returned by web servers, and write the parsed content to a structured text file (e.g. CSV file). This heavy lifting can be done using Python

Python comes in two variants: Python 2.x, which is still widely used and supported (and will be for some time); and Python 3.x, which is intended to be the only version at some point in the future. For now, it would be safe to use either; be aware that there are some differences in syntax between the two versions, though for a beginning user these are not particularly extensive. Examples in this chapter use Python 2.x for consistency, but the example code on the companion site provides versions for Python 2.x and 3.x, where possible.

modules. Some of these modules, such as urllib2 (urllib.request in Python 3.x), used for accessing web resources; RE, for extracting data from web pages and other documents; and CSV, for writing to delimited text files, come preloaded with Python. Others, such as Requests, also for making web page requests; Beautiful Soup, for parsing the content of HTML pages; and unicodecsv, for handling Unicode and writing text files in Python 2.x, must be downloaded and installed separately (complete instructions on how to do this on different platforms are on the companion website).

To change web addresses on the fly, send different search terms to a server, store a retrieved wage page, and so on, a script will use variables. Variables are like virtual containers that can hold text, numbers, or other content for use somewhere else in a script. The most important thing is that what a variable contains can be changed over and over again.

Variables can only hold one value at a time. If you want to hold several values at once, you can use a **list**. A list can hold text, numbers, or even other lists.

Your script will also need to do some tasks over and over again, such as visit a series of web pages, or scan over a series of HTML pages to extract content from each one. For these kinds of repetitive actions, you will use **loops**. Loops do exactly what they sound like they do: they loop around and around, performing the same actions repeatedly, though with some change each time, perhaps in the variable used or the file processed. They usually keep going until some kind of condition is satisfied, such as having looped through all of the HTML pages from which content needs to be extracted. There are different types of loops. "*While* loops" do something over and over again while some condition remains true. "*For* loops" go through and perform the same action on a series of objects that are part of a collection, such as each of the lines in a text file, or each of the items in a Python list of URLs.

If a loop allows your code to do the same thing repeatedly, a **conditional statement** allows your code to make decisions. For example, you may be scraping a site that has a number of different page structures, each requiring slightly different code to extract. For such situations you can use an IF statement.

As you develop your scraping scripts, you will find you have code you need to use more than once in your scripts. By defining functions, you can reuse your code in different places in the script, save a lot of time that might be spent coding the same things repeatedly, and cut down on wrist strain. A good rule of thumb is if you find yourself writing the same code at least twice, put it in a function. Then, if you have to change your code later, you only have to change it in one place. Another advantage of a function is you can reuse it in other scripts, saving you time. There are also pre-made functions that are available automatically as part of Python, and functions that are made available by modules.

By combining variables, loops, conditional statements, functions, and modules you can begin to write powerful scraping scripts that will obtain and parse data from almost any website, and write it to text files.

Getting Ready to Code

As discussed earlier, scraping is really made up of three processes.

First, you make repeated requests to a web server. Second, you parse the HTML that is returned, to extract the data you want. Third, you save the resulting data somewhere, typically in a text file to open later in a spreadsheet or database. To show how each step might be accomplished, we'll walk through an example that scrapes the same "proactive disclosure" page we looked at earlier in the chapter. Because the page might change in time, and will eventually be absorbed into the Canadian government's plan to merge all departmental websites into a single portal, we have created a web page of our own that has the same data as appears on the government's page, available at dataprof.ca/DataJournalist/scraping1a.html. This copy contains only the basic content without the fancy formatting of the original page and will remain available permanently.

To get started, you'll need a plain text editor, either Notepad on a Windows PC or TextEdit on a Mac. As you start to write more complex scripts, you'll likely want to move up to a specialized code editor, such as Sublime Text, Komodo Edit, or Notepad++. These will highlight the syntax of your code as you type it, using different colours for different parts of the code. As well, some code editors, such as Sublime Text, have a built-in function that allows you to run programs that you're writing, from within the editor. This is useful for debugging your programs and for running small snippets as tests. We discuss the advantages of each editor in the tutorial "Choosing a Code Editor" on the companion website.

If we follow the advice to first think out our scrape, we can see that our scraper needs to take the following steps:

1. Retrieve the HTML page;
2. Extract the content from the table of contracts; and
3. Save each line of the table into a text file so we can open it in a database or spreadsheet.

This is about as simple as it gets, but it is always best to start with an easy example, and then move on to more complex scripts. The online companion website has more examples, including more difficult scrapes.

Fetching the Page

The first task is to fetch the page. To do that we are going to need a Python module. If you have not done so, follow the directions on installing Python in the tutorial "Installing and Configuring Python" on the companion website. You may also wish to consult one of the basic Python tutorials for which you'll find links on the companion site.

To grab the text of our target page, we will use the built-in Python 2.x module urllib2. It is a kind of stripped-down browser that takes care of the complexities of making requests on the Internet. The first thing we will do in our script is "import" the module, which is how we make it available for our script to use.

Open an empty text file in your text editor and give it a name such as my-firstscrape.py. The .py extension is important, because this is how the computer knows to have Python run our script.

Write the following two lines at the top of your empty text file. The first line is boilerplate code that should be included at the top of any script. The second line imports our urllib2 Internet module.

```
#!/usr/bin/env python
import urllib2
```

Python is what is known as an **interpreted programming language.** That means that when we write a Python program, it then has to be run through an interpreter to turn the English-like commands we write into something the computer can understand. When you install Python on your computer, one of the things you install is the interpreter.

With that simple line, we now have all of the functionality of the urllib2 module available to us. The nice thing about modules is that we don't have to know how they work inside. All we need to know is how to use them in our code. Modules come with built-in functions that we use to accomplish different tasks.

To start, let's use a variable to store the URL of the web page we're going to scrape. Add the following line directly below the two you have already written:

```
URL = "http://dataprof.ca/DataJournalist/scraping1a.html"
```

Notice the = sign. It is not being used here to mean that URL is the same as the string of text that follows. In Python, and other languages, the = sign is called the "assignment operator." It is used to assign something to a variable. Whatever follows the = sign goes into the variable. This is a bit of a simplification, but it'll serve our purposes here.

In the above line, we are assigning the string of text that is the URL, to a variable called "URL." Any time we use that variable from now on, it will be as if we had written out the URL itself (at least until we assign something else to the variable!).

The text is enclosed in quotation marks (single or double work equally well, as long as you use the same type at both ends) to indicate this is a string. The variable name itself is arbitrary; we could call it "goldenRetriever" and it would work just as well. URL, though, tells us something about what it contains, and code that is easy to understand is better code.

The next thing we have to do is put the urllib2 module to work to request the Internet **resource** that is located at that URL. Here's how we do that:

```
response = urllib2.urlopen(URL)
```

There's a lot going on in this line, so let's tear it apart.

On the right side of the assignment operator (=), we are using urllib2's urlopen function to make a request to the remote server for the resource located at the web address stored in the variable URL. The dot between urllib2 and urlopen indicates that urlopen is a function that is part of the urllib2 module. We are said to be "calling" the function and using the dot is called "dot notation." When urlopen is called, a request is sent to the remote web server, just as if you had manually entered a URL in a web browser.

Assuming the URL is valid and the server is online, it will send back the HTML page, which our line of code assigns to the "response" variable. Technically, the response variable stores what is called a "file-like object," which you could think of loosely as a text file packaged together with a set of predefined functions that can be used to manipulate it. One of these is the .read() **method**. It literally reads the contents of the file object into a long string of text. We'll use the "response" object's .read() method in the next line, to put the text from the web page into the variable "HTML."

```
HTML = response.read()
```

HTML now contains the complete HTML code of the web page.

This is what our script looks like so far (the line numbers are for illustration only, though your text editor may number lines of code automatically):

```
1.  #!/usr/bin/env python
2.  import urllib2
3.  URL = "http://dataprof.ca/DataJournalist/scraping1a.
    html"
4.  response = urllib2.urlopen(URL)
5.  HTML = response.read()
```

With just a few lines of code, we have done the equivalent of pointing our browser at a web page and copying the HTML code from the page source view. To prove this, we can add one more line.

```
print HTML
```

If we run the script now, the HTML content of the retrieved page will "print" to our screen. There's a tutorial on the companion website called "Running your Python Scripts" that will tell you how to run your scripts. You can do so from the Windows Command window or the Mac Terminal. So to run our script in Windows, type this at the prompt in the Command window:

```
python C:/scripts/Myfirstscraper.py
```

On a Mac, type this at prompt in Terminal.

```
python ~/directory/scripts/Myfirstscraper.py
```

You'll need to enter the actual file path to your script, rather than the demo paths we have used here. Creating a folder called "scripts" or something similar, close to the top of your folder hierarchy, lets you write shorter file paths, which is always nice. If all goes well, you'll see a big jumble of HTML print to your screen:

```
<h1 id="wb-cont">2015-2016 - 1<sup>st</sup> Quarter (April to June)</h1><p class="note">N.B.: The contract date represents the
date that the contract is recorded in the departmental financial system.</p><table class="wet-boew-zebra basic">
<caption class="font-small align-left">
<em>List of contracts for the trimester, which includes the date, vendor, description and value</em>
</caption>
    <tr >
        <th>Contract Date</th>
        <th>Vendor Name</th>
        <th>Description of Work</th>
        <th>Contract Value</th>
    </tr>
    <tr>
        <td>2008-04-22</td>
        <td>IGF VIGILANCE INC.</td>
        <td>420 - Engineering Services not Elsewhere Specified</td>
        <td class="alignRight">$500,695.10</td>
    </tr>
    <tr>
        <td>2008-04-22</td>
        <td>THE ARCOP GROUP/GERSOVITZ MOSS</td>
        <td>423 - Engineering Consultants - Other</td>
        <td class="alignRight">$67,145,777.15</td>
    </tr>
    <tr>
        <td>2008-04-22</td>
        <td>CAPITAL ELEVATOR LTD</td>
        <td>859 - Other Business Services not Elsewhere Specified</td>
        <td class="alignRight">$73,651.02</td>
    </tr>
    <tr>
        <td>2008-09-04</td>
        <td>NORR LIMITTED</td>
```

Source: Python Software Foundation

For the illustration, we scrolled down the page to the place where the rows of table data begin.

Since our goal is to end up with data we can analyze in a spreadsheet or database program, just looking at the HTML isn't going to cut it. We need to extract some useful content from the sea of markup code. In this example, we'll use a Python module called Beautiful Soup, which is used to pinpoint precise elements in an HTML page and pull them out to use. A second method preferred by some is to use pattern-matching tools called "regular expressions," which we will use in an example on the companion website.

Beautiful Soup is not one of the modules that is included in the basic Python installation, so you need to add it using an installer called PIP. If you are unfamiliar with PIP, review the tutorial "Getting Python Up and Running." If you have done so and have PIP installed, adding Beautiful Soup is as simple as running this command in your Windows Command shell or Mac Terminal:

```
pip install beautifulsoup4
```

You should see some scrolling text in your terminal window, and an indication that the install was successful. Once you have installed Beautiful Soup, it will be available to you just as the built-in Python modules are. You only have to do this once unless you reinstall Python.

If you make a typing mistake in your code, Python may quit running your script and report an error. The error message will give you clues as to what caused the error, and how to fix the problem. See the tutorial "Dealing with Errors in Python" on the companion website.

You can now add this line to your script, right below the existing "import urllib2":

```
from bs4 import BeautifulSoup
```

Then, at the bottom of your script, delete the "print HTML" statement, if you previously added it in, and replace it with this:

```
soup = BeautifulSoup(HTML)
```

This statement creates a new Beautiful Soup object that contains the HTML of the web page in a special format. The Beautiful Soup object has its own set of methods that can be used to parse the HTML. The variable that contains the Beautiful Soup object is, by convention, called "soup,"

Here's our script:

```
1. #!/usr/bin/env python
2. import urllib2
3. from bs4 import BeautifulSoup
4. URL = "http://dataprof.ca/DataJournalist/scraping1a.html"
5. response = urllib2.urlopen(URL)
6. HTML = response.read()
7. soup = BeautifulSoup(HTML)
```

Let's review what our script does so far. After the modules are imported in lines 2 and 3, line 4 assigns the URL for the proactive disclosure page to the variable "URL." Line 5 passes that variable into the urlopen function of urllib2, and puts the resulting response from the remote server into the variable called "response," in the form of a file-like object. We then use the read method to read out the raw HTML of the web page and put it into a variable called

Beautiful Soup is not technically an HTML parser, but in turn relies on an HTML parsing module to do that work. The advantage of having the parser as a separate module is that different parsers, each with its own strengths and weaknesses, can be used by Beautiful Soup. If no parser is indicated, Beautiful Soup defaults to the HTML parser that comes as part of the basic Python installation, which should work fine for most scrapes as long as you are using the latest versions of Python. The topic of parser choice is beyond the scope of this book, but is explained in the Beautiful Soup documentation. Search online for the latest version.

"HTML." We then pass the variable HTML to Beautiful Soup, creating a version of the page contained in the Beautiful Soup object called "soup."

We can now use Beautiful Soup to extract the data we want. To do this, we are going to use a loop. You'll recall loops are used when we want to repeat the same action over and over again and that there are while loops and for loops. We'll use a for loop, which is a kind of loop that runs a specific number of times, then stops. In this case, the number of times it runs will be determined by the number of rows in the data table within the HTML page. This is probably the most challenging code we have seen yet.

We begin our loop construction by adding this code at the bottom of our script:

```
for eachrow in soup.findAll('tr'):
```

This line initiates our for loop. Translated into English, it says "for each row of data in the HTML file (which is now in our 'soup' object), do something." The "something" will follow in the next couple of lines of the code. Note that the word following "for" can be anything you like. We're using "eachrow" to make it clearer what the code does. We are then using the "findAll" method of the soup object to go through the document and find all of the table rows, contained within <tr> and </tr> tags. The "findAll" method allows you to search through an HTML page stored in the "soup" object and find elements contained within tags, associated with certain text, or matching regular expressions. Because this is a for loop, whatever happens after the colon will be done *for* each row that matches the findAll search expression.

findAll is used so often in Beautiful Soup that you don't actually have to write it in. The code *for eachrow in soup('tr'):* will do the same thing as the version we are using here. We have written the full code for clarity.

What we want to happen, of course, is that we extract the data we want. We'll start by adding two new lines at the bottom of our script. As shown here, indent both of these lines in one tab from the code you have written so far. That ensures that when the for loop runs, the code that is indented will run each time the loop goes around. Indenting is crucial when writing Python loops, if statements, and functions. Fail to indent what follows the colon and you'll get an error when you try to run the script.

```
1. #!/usr/bin/env python
2. import urllib2
3. from bs4 import BeautifulSoup
```

```
4. URL = "http://dataprof.ca/DataJournalist/scraping1a.
html"
5. response = urllib2.urlopen(URL)
6. HTML = response.read()
7. soup = BeautifulSoup(HTML)
8. for eachrow in soup.findAll('tr'):
9.    data =[]
10.   cells = eachrow.findAll('td')
```

Line 9 creates an empty list called "data." Remember that a list is like a variable, except it can hold more than one item. We'll be adding some data to our list soon.

Line 10 creates a second list, this one populated with anything that the findAll method of Beautiful Soup finds within <td> </td> tags, the tags that surround individual data items in a table. So what this line says is, for the current row of the HTML table—remember we are looping through the table so this will happen over and over—find all <td> tags and their contents, and put the result into a list called "cells."

If we were to add the command PRINT CELLS at the bottom of our code and run it, we'd see output like this for each row of the table:

```
[<td>2015-07-08</td>, <td >BRITISH COLUMBIA SAFETY
AUTHORITY</td>, <td>881 - Construction Services</td>, <td
class="alignRight">$138,507.60</td>]
```

Notice the square brackets at either end of the text, and the commas between each of the </td><td> tag pairs. We now have a list of data cells, including all of the HTML for each one, separated by commas. We're almost ready to extract each of the elements of the list into a text file. To do that we need to use one more module. Write this code below the existing import statements at the top of your script:

```
import unicodecsv
```

Like Beautiful Soup, unicodecsv is not one of the standard, built-in modules that come with Python, so you will need to install it using PIP, by typing the following in the Windows Commands window or Mac Terminal:

```
pip install unicodecsv
```

The unicodecsv module allows us to write text to files, which makes it perfect for our purpose. It takes one argument, a Python list, and then writes the elements of the list to a text file, with delimiters such as commas or tabs between each list item. It also writes a line delimiter, which by default is the new line character \n.

Python has a built-in a module called csv that is used for reading and writing delimited text files, but it doesn't play nicely with what is called Unicode, a character encoding scheme that can accommodate any language in the world but which often requires more than one byte to store a character. As a matter of fact, Python 2.x and Unicode don't always play well together, but that's a subject beyond the scope of this book. Python 2.x prefers ASCII-encoded text, which doesn't know how to handle anything but the English alphabet, the numbers 0 to 9, and a variety of special characters such as / ? , etc. Better Unicode handling is one of the main improvements that comes with Python 3.x. Go to Python.org for a more complete explanation of the differences.

Near the top of our script, right below our import statements, we are going to add the following three lines of code:

```
output = open('~ /scripts/ myoutput.txt', 'w')
writer = unicodecsv.writer(output, delimiter='\t',
encoding='utf-8')
writer.writerow(['date','vendor','description','value'])
```

This is the code for a Mac. In Windows we would replace ~/ at the start of the first line with 'C:/ Again, use the path to your actual file, and not the demo path used here. Let's go through each line to see what it does.

The first line creates a new variable called "output" containing a file object. The file object is created by the code on the right side of the assignment operator by Python's open() function. This function opens an existing text file stored on the computer or creates a new one if the file name doesn't exist.

The first argument inside the parentheses of the open() function is the complete path to and file name of the text file, enclosed in quotes. The second argument, the "w", is the mode, in this case "write." This creates a new file. If no mode is indicated, the default is "r", which means to "read" an existing file. Be careful with "w" because if the file name already exists on your computer, it will be overwritten without warning.

The second line uses the "writer" function of the unicodecsv module to create what you might think of as a printer that will print out text into our new file. Inside the brackets are three arguments. The first is the name of the file we will write to, the one we just created, the second determines the delimiter to use between data items in the output text file, in this case tabs, and the third indicates that the character encoding is Unicode utf-8. You should be safe to use these settings whenever you write data parsed by Beautiful Soup.

Line 3 uses the writer we just created to write the header line for our text file, for the four fields of data in the table. The writerow method takes a

Python list as its only argument, which in this instance we have written in manually between the square brackets.

Okay, we're going to add three more lines to finish up our script:

```
1.  #!/usr/bin/env python
2.  import urllib2
3.  from bs4 import BeautifulSoup
4.  import unicodecsv
5.  output = open('/Users/fredvallance-jones/FilingSystem/
    scripts/databook/myoutput.txt', 'w')
6.  writer = unicodecsv.writer(output, delimiter='\t',
    encoding='utf-8')
7.  writer.writerow(['date','vendor','description','value'])
8.  URL = "http://dataprof.ca/DataJournalist/scraping1a.
    html"
9.  response = urllib2.urlopen(URL)
10. HTML = response.read()
11. soup = BeautifulSoup(HTML)
12. for eachrow in soup.findAll('tr'):
13.   data =[]
14.   cells = eachrow.findAll('td')
15.   for eachdataitem in cells:
16.     data.append(eachdataitem.text)
17.     writer.writerow(data)
```

These last three lines will extract the data within the td cells so it can be written to our text file. Notice that the "data.append(eachdataitem. text)" line is indented one tab stop in from the code above it. This is because we are adding a new for loop that will run within the first one. This is called a "nested loop." This new loop loops through the cells list (another way to say this is to say it "iterates" through the list). Inside the loop (in the indented part), it uses the append method to add, or append, each data item to the empty list we created a couple of lines earlier. The last line of the script, which is now indented to be part of the first for loop, not the second, writes the list of data items to the text file. A script runs starting at the first line, and continues until it reaches the end, except for functions that you define, which don't run until they are called. Structures can get more complicated once you learn more advanced Python, but simple scripts run this way.

The result of running this script is a delimited text file that you can open in a text editor or in a spreadsheet program such as Excel:

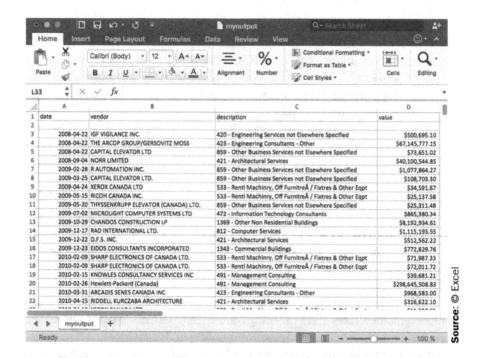

Source: © Excel

Scraping More Than One Page

We're not limited, of course, to scraping a single page. There are actually many pages of contracts for this one department, going back more than 10 years. By adding another loop to the script it is possible to loop through all of the web pages, requesting each one in turn. To do this, you would enclose the code we have already written in another loop that would, each time it runs, populate the URL variable with a new URL. You would first write the script to scrape one page, then write the loop around it. The companion website has all of the code for this example, including code to loop through a series of pages, in Python 2.x and Python 3.x.

More Complicated Scrapes

The example we looked at here was straightforward, but it illustrates the key elements of many scraping projects: requesting web resources, saving the resources in variables, parsing the HTML, and saving the results to a file. We've also introduced you to a few of basic programming concepts. But because each scrape will be unique—indeed every website is unique—there is much we can't cover here. Some of the other scenarios you will face include the following:

- Sites that require you to click through several pages to get all of the information required for one row of data. The proactive disclosure page we looked at initially is actually like that; there is additional information

to be had by clicking the vendor name, since clicking opens a second
page with the information;

- Sites that require you to fill out a search form to get each row of data
  and send the data for the search not as part of the URL but as part of the
  request itself. We've seen web search forms, but so far we haven't had to
  fill them out automatically;
- Sites that use a lot of JavaScript. Some pages use JavaScript to code
  search forms, and others pass data back and forth from your computer
  to the web server and back using AJAX (see page 200). These are some of
  the most challenging scrapes;
- Pages that deliberately make scraping difficult through such tactics as
  saving cookies on your computer containing IDs required to continue
  accessing the site (the Elections Canada site mentioned at the beginning
  of the chapter uses the latter technique). A scraping script will have to
  account for such defensive strategies, or it won't work.

The online companion site has tutorials going through examples of these
more difficult scrapes and explaining some of the technical issues involved, and
exploring further Python programming concepts. We also look at how to use
a special pattern-matching language called regular expressions to extract data
from web pages.

The Ethics of Web Scraping

To the uninitiated, web scraping can look a lot like illegal hacking. It involves the creation of computer programs to obtain data from servers in
ways that the administrators of the sites may not intend. There is a big difference, however: ethical web scraping does not attempt to access data that isn't
already publicly available. It doesn't breach website security or hack through
password protection or access files meant to be hidden from public view.
Even so, if not done carefully, using computer scripts to obtain data can
cause the same kind of havoc to a web server that a malicious hacker might.

An illegal denial-of-service, or DOS, attack, uses software to flood a web server with so many page requests, so quickly, that the site can't handle all the traffic
and bogs down or crashes altogether. Legitimate users of a site under DOS attack
will find it becomes slow, unresponsive, or kicks back "404 page not found" errors.

Hackers who launch these attacks wield some techniques common to
web scraping—specifically, using a custom computer script to quickly make
repeated requests for pages.

An ethical web scraper should never send page requests so quickly that
the web administrator of the site will mistake it for a DOS attack. That could

get the originating Internet Protocol (IP) address blocked and limit future access to the site. You must take precautions to avoid flooding the server you're scraping with page requests.

A computer script can cycle through multiple page requests at enormous speed, sending dozens of requests a second, at a rate that can easily be mistaken for a DOS attack.

When you write a scraping script, it's important to put in a timeout for the program between each page request it sends. In Python, this will likely be a time.sleep(1) command, which uses the Time module to have the script take a one-second (or whatever interval you choose) breather before making another request. A web server maintained by a large government agency shouldn't have any trouble handling a single page request per second, but exercise particular caution when scraping smaller sites with less robust infrastructure behind them. We'll demonstrate the sleep command in the additional scraping scripts you'll find on the companion website.

Before scraping any website, it's good practice to see if it has a policy about using "robots"—any program that automatically explores the web. Many sites will place a small text file in the root directory called robots.txt that tells these 'bots, "spiders," or web crawlers which directories on the site it may access. Some websites use robots.txt to stop search engines such as Yahoo! or Google from indexing their pages. Although adherence to the robots.txt instructions is voluntarily, the search engine giants will typically respect them and skip those directories and subdirectories on sites that are disallowed. So, too, should an ethical web scraper abide by the wishes expressed by the web administrators in robots.txt, though exceptions can be made.

For example, the Canadian government web page we looked at earlier disallows robots from accessing the proactive disclosure pages:

```
User-agent: *
Disallow: /dev/
Disallow: /homepage/
Disallow: /forum/
Disallow: /test/
Disallow: /gos/fpt/
Disallow: /ccsb/e-engage/
Disallow: /site02/
Disallow: /usage/
Disallow: /wlav/
Disallow: /esc/
Disallow: /cae/
Disallow: /fpt/
Disallow: /123test/
# This will prevent robots from entering the dev, homepage and test areas

User-agent:  gsa-crawler
Disallow:  /cgi-bin/proactive/cl.pl

# This will prevent all robots from entering the dev, homepage and test areas
User-agent:  *
Disallow:  /cgi-bin/proactive/cl.pl
```
Source: Public Works and Government Services

The last two lines are they key ones. The asterisk means that all "user agents," and this means all robots, are included in the rule. The second line means that the pages they are unwelcome on are the pages with the proactive disclosure results. This is likely actually intended to prevent the Googlebot and other search engines from crawling the disclosure data. In any case, most journalists would agree that when dealing with public websites that contain information that helps hold governments accountable, that scraping is acceptable even if the government doesn't want it done. Of course, this doesn't apply in any case to the copy of the data we are hosting on our own server: it is intended to be scraped.

It is also wise to check the "terms and conditions" or "terms of use" link on a website. These can shed light on whether the website owners permit scraping. In some cases, they will expressly forbid use of robots, screen scraping, and the like. Especially if the organization is a private one, it can be unwise to ignore such prohibitions and you could become the target of legal action, depending on the jurisdiction. If in doubt, it may be best to consult with a lawyer familiar with the appropriate body of law.

Scraping journalist may also wish to make their intentions known to the custodians of the data. Modules such as urllib2, Mechanize, and Requests can be used to pass on customized HTTP headers along with page requests. The web administrators can see these headers if they look at the traffic logs on the site. These headers are a good way to send a friendly message indicating that you are simply extracting the data—at a limited rate—and provide contact information, such as a phone number or email address, that the web admin can use if your activity on the site is causing server problems.

In a Python script using urllib2, the line might look like this:

```
req.add _ header('User-Agent', 'Mozilla/4.0 (compatible;
MSIE 7.0b; Windows NT 6.0) Hi! I'm journalist Jane
Reporter with the Smallville Times. If my web scrape
causes problems, call me at 555-123-1234')
```

This header first indicates that the page request is coming from the Mozilla Firefox web browser, then goes on to provide the contact information. This step is a courtesy and not all journalists who web scrape will use it. Consult the documentation for the module you are using for detailed instructions on how to add headers. You can't add the line above to the script we created earlier, without modifying other parts of the script.

Some prefer to extract data from their targets stealthily, arguing that their scraper is doing the same thing that someone using a site manually would do, just much more quickly. Others liken the approach to using a hidden camera in investigative television reporting, particularly if the script mimics or spoofs a browser and the contact information is omitted. In that case, the script would appear to the server to be a browser, though other characteristics of the scrape, such as many requests coming at close intervals from the same IP address would probably reveal to an administrator reviewing the server logs that someone was scraping the site. Then again, with appropriate delays between page requests, and therefore no possible overloading of the server, the administrator will probably have no reason to even check the logs. Some journalists scraping sites that actively discourage scraping go so far as to use proxy servers that make each request look to come from a different IP address, or even country. Once again, it may be wise to consult with a lawyer if you have any doubt about the legalities of your planned scrape, according to the laws of your jurisdiction or the jurisdiction where the target web server is located. Arguably, even when a journalist identifies himself through the headers, the scraping technique is a kind of covert reporting. The script, and the journalist behind it, are posing as a real web user with a real user browser.

APIs

Before we leave the subject of scraping, we'd like to talk briefly about APIs.

Sometimes, website administrators anticipate that users might want to access a raw data stream, or make use of site features. To provide this access they create application programming interfaces. If web scraping is a way to get data through the "back door," APIs are a front door provided by the site owner to make it easier for software, including simple computer scripts, to interact with them. There are a great many APIs, including for some of the largest services on the web, such as Facebook and Twitter. APIs allow the scripts you write to send queries and receive data back in a simple format. Many, such as Facebook's Graph API, use a file format called JSON—short for JavaScript Object Notation.

For a 2010 story called "Not Sarah Palin's Friends," the online magazine *Slate* used the Facebook API to download every comment posted on the former vice-presidential candidate's Facebook page. The script, written by journalist/programmer Jeremy Singer-Vine, scraped the comments off Palin's page repeatedly throughout the day, capturing them before they could be deleted by staff members responsible for administering her page. By comparing each snapshot of the page, *Slate* was able to determine which comments had been removed. *Slate* found that negative or critical comments, even those that were respectful and not obscene, were being purged en masse, leaving Palin's page with only supportive and laudatory comments.[3]

To use an API, you will typically have to apply for an access ID and password. Some APIs use a process called Oauth to confirm authorization; it requires teaching your scraping routine to pass on the logon credentials associated with your API account.

To use Facebook's Graph API, you will need to apply through its developer pages for a free Access Token. When you send a page request using the API, it will have to include the Access Token, which looks like a long string of numbers and letters. To follow the *Slate* example, we can access Sarah Palin's Facebook page by sending this HTTP request, with the token information included:

```
https://graph.facebook.com/sarahpalin/posts?access _
token=19192345. . .88d5f0b9083ab02
```

Note that you'll need your own Access Token for this request to work properly. It is actually longer than depicted here; we have removed some of the characters in the token, as represented by the ellipsis.

This URL could be sent through a Python script, or simply pasted into the URL bar in a web browser. The data returned by the API is in JSON format. In that soup of text, you can find numerous Facebook object ID numbers that look like this in the JSON:

```
"id": "24718773587 _ 10153540863978588"
```

Each of these corresponds to a post on Palin's page that may have comments on it. These can be parsed out of the JSON data. Each can then be retrieved by the web scraping script, again using the Facebook Graph API, by sending a page request that looks like this, with your Access Token attached:

```
https://graph.facebook.
com/24718773587 _ 10153540863978588?access _
token=19192345. . .88d5f0b9083ab02
```

The API will respond with a list of the IDs of Facebook users who "Liked" the original post as well as all the comments posted in response to it. By comparing each of these lists of comments with a previous version, you can determine which have been deleted.

Using APIs is not really scraping in the traditional sense, because you are accessing data in a way intended by the site owner, but it opens many possibilities for stories that would otherwise not be possible.

We didn't have the room to go into APIs in detail here. See the companion website for tutorials on using Python to access the APIs of popular services, including Facebook and Twitter.

One note about APIs: Most limit the number of requests each account can send, to ensure they aren't abused. Check the documentation of the API to see how many queries it can handle per hour, per month, and per day, before you begin scraping.

Conclusion

Web scraping is a powerful technique that journalists can use to obtain data from the web when that data is not offered in a convenient, downloadable format. It takes some technical chops, but once you master the basics, you'll be able to apply your knowledge to new scraping challenges that you encounter. You may not follow in Mark Zuckerberg's footsteps and create a worldwide social network, but you'll be able to obtain data to do original stories.

Study Questions and Exercises

1. Find a website that you would like to scrape, but where the data is not available for download. Go through the process described in this chapter to conceptualize a scrape. Make a flow diagram of how the scrape might proceed. Write out the "code" in English.
2. Using the instructions in this chapter and/or on the companion website, write Python code to scrape your website, and do the scrape. Make sure you build in a delay, as described, between requests to the server.
3. You will find another exercise, using live data, on the companion website.

Further Resources

Codeacademy.com. Free self-teaching website for learning programming.
Shaw, Zed A. *Learn Python the Hard Way*. Toronto: Pearson Education, 2013. Available at learnpythonthehardway.org.

Notes

1. Glen McGregor and Maher Stephen, "Tory Ridings the Winners from Stimulus: Analysis Reveals More Than Half of Big-Money Projects Went to Blue Districts," *Ottawa Citizen*, 20 October 2009, A1.
2. Fred Vallance-Jones, CBC *Manitoba*, Infrastructure investigation (untitled), May 1995.
3. John Dickerson, "Not Sarah Palin's Friends," *Slate*, 3 August 2010, http://www.slate.com/articles/news_and_politics/politics/2010/08/not_sarah_palins_friends.htm.

Chapter 10

Web Development

What You Will Learn:

- How news is being changed by the advent of advanced web technologies
- How you can use coding on both the client and server end of the web
- How to use HTML, CSS, and JavaScript to build a simple web page
- How you can use advanced JavaScript libraries

Much of this book has looked at data from the perspective of the information professional who finds, analyzes, and tells stories with it. But there is an emerging breed of data journalist who is as much a programmer as a reporter. He or she brings the strong story sense of the journalist together with the technological prowess of the web developer and is perfectly comfortable in both worlds. These hybrid developer-journalists must have programming skills that go far beyond the kind of simple scripts we looked at in the last chapter. The best can build web applications that lift storytelling to a digital art, such as the joint project done in early 2016 by *Pro Publica* and the *Texas Tribune* on the threat posed to Houston by a large hurricane sweeping in from the Gulf of Mexico.[1]

This book isn't going to teach you to work at that kind of level. Instead, this chapter is an overview designed to show you what's possible next, starting you off with a few simple coding exercises and walking you through the design of a simple web page. From there, the sky really is the limit. We'll recommend some resources for further learning at the end of the chapter.

The revolution that made the programmer-journalist possible swept the planet in the late 1990s and early 2000s, fundamentally changing the way news is disseminated, but also adding new complexities to producing it. In North American and European news organizations, more than half of all web traffic now comes from powerful mobile devices, forcing designers and coders to take into account a wide variety of screen sizes and operating systems when deciding how to present their work.

Tutorials Included with the Companion Website

You will find these tutorials on the OUP Companion Website (www.oupcanada .com/Vallance-Jones):

- A Short Guide to HTML and CSS
- Building a Twitter Bot
- Introduction to JavaScript
- Visualizing with D3.js
- Building Your First News Application

Similarly, the many platforms that can now be used to disseminate content—from social media companies such as Twitter and Facebook to production platforms such as ScribbleLive and Wordpress—force newsroom professionals to decide day-by-day which tools to build on their own and which tools to purchase externally.

Being conversant in the broader structures of the web, and understanding how different applications speak to each other, is an increasingly important skillset for the modern data journalist. By learning the languages and structures of the Internet, journalists can make the web their own playground, make it play by their rules, and regain control of their journalism. On the less complex end of that spectrum, it means understanding embed codes, how all those programs speak to each other, and how you can force them to deviate from their default behaviour. On the more complex end of the spectrum, it can mean writing small apps for web browsers or smartphones that allow readers to explore stories and data on their own terms, in the format that best serves the journalism.

State of Developers in Newsrooms

Which brings us back to our developer journalists.

In the early days of web-based storytelling, journalists would often make their own interactive content and embed it in their stories. That still happens, but as embedded content becomes more prevalent in stories, it has become more common for larger newsrooms to hire developers who are well versed in the ways of the web to produce this kind of content full time. This allows journalists more time to do the hard investigative work and developers to produce more elegant and better-designed products to complement those stories.

In Canada, the CBC, the *Globe and Mail*, and the *National Post* have all hired developers who sit in the newsroom and work directly with editorial staff. These teams are separate from the "product teams" that are responsible for maintaining the overarching website, content management systems, and large-scale infrastructure.

Newsroom developers are responsible for creating a wide variety of interactive content for readers and for supporting other journalists in the newsroom. That can include making quizzes and interactive maps, writing complex web scrapers, and building tools that journalists without any development skills can use on their own to make charts and graphs or quizzes and games.

As with many aspects of journalism, Canadian organizations have been looking at the *New York Times* for inspiration and guidance in this space. In 2000, the *New York Times* first launched a 24-hour news operation that was largely focused on their website. In 2005, the company created a new interactive development team to help journalists navigate the increasingly complex needs of modern journalism. That proved to be enormously forward looking.

By 2010, the team of developers working on newsroom projects was an international leader and example of a high-tech newsroom that many were eyeing with envy. When the *New York Times* opened an account on the popular code-sharing site Github—open-sourcing many of their most popular and important applications responsible for galleries, data parsing, and searching campaign finance databases—it was a sign of the future of web-based reporting.

Only two years later, in 2012, newsroom coders were officially declared to be in short supply. The Knight-Mozilla Foundation had launched programs to tempt developers away from high-paying Silicon Valley jobs to try their hands at the adrenaline-fuelled world of newsrooms and tight deadlines.[2]

"The big problem I want to solve is not 'Journalism needs to care more about the Internet and being native on the web,'" Dan Sinker, one of the leaders of the program, told Nieman Lab in 2012.

> Yes, that's a problem, but journalism's doing a pretty good job on that. The main problem now is that there are way more openings for these kinds of jobs than there are people who know they want to fill them. So we have to bring more people into the fold.[3]

Since then, the intersection of technology and journalism has been defined less by the idea that developers should learn to commit acts of journalism than by the debate over whether journalists should learn to code. Those arguments gained mainstream attention in journalism around 2010, and have continued since then.

The question of whether journalists should learn programming, though, is often a screen for the more prescient question of how technically competent journalists should be, and how technologists are incorporated into newsroom life.

Journalists who know how to code, or who are simply more technologically capable than others, not only open up more advanced tools for their own use but also allow themselves to have meaningful conversations with developers who are working to help present their work. Just as broadcast journalists have to understand the basics of camera work, shot structure, and editing, journalists working in a digital space must be at least conversant in the technologies that affect their work, lest they be left behind in conversations about that work.

That doesn't mean that journalists must suddenly concern themselves with the intricacies of how the Internet is built. Running the website, implementing content management systems, and enabling sharing with social media are usually jobs done by others. Newsroom developers have a narrower focus. They work at the speed of news. They are familiar with the demands of breaking news and the speed with which large-scale features come together. They are fast, understand the requirements of a good story and their responsibility to truth and accuracy, are able to speak the language of journalism, and act as educators when others in the newsroom need help. The newsroom developer has become a hybrid position, as involved with digital advocacy and education as it is with journalists and producing interactive content.

By now, most large news organizations in Canada have built teams that can meet these needs. Of course, those working in smaller newsrooms may still do everything themselves and, as we saw in the introductory chapter when we met Naël Shiab, acquiring development skills can help such a reporter's career take off.

As we promised, though, we'll start at the beginning, with a bit of code so everyday you might not give it much thought, the humble embed code. An embed code is used to "embed" content found somewhere else on the Internet in your own web page or content management system.

Most embed codes you'll come across from services like YouTube, Google Maps, ScribbleLive, and Twitter will look something like this:

```
<iframe width="560" height="315" src="https://www.youtube.
com/embed/C1y8N0ePuF8" frameborder="0" allowfullscreen></
iframe>
```

The above links to a YouTube video. Take a look at how this embed code is constructed; each line below is a segment of the embed code:

```
<iframe
width = "560"
height = "315"
src = "https://www.youtube.com/embed/C1y8N0ePuF8"
frameborder="0"
allowfullscreen>
</iframe>
```

Note how the code begins and ends with the word "iframe." The one at the end has a / in front of it. As you saw in Chapter 9, this is how most HTML is written, with an opening tag and a closing tag.

Note also how the two angle brackets (< >) in the opening tag fall on the outside of all the defining **parameters**. So instead of simply having an opening tag <iframe> following immediately by a closing tag </iframe> you instead have the necessary parameters included within the opening tag. So it looks like <iframe parameters></iframe>.

Width and height are defined in pixels. This iframe will embed a YouTube video that is 560 pixels wide and 315 pixels tall.

The src attribute is the link you're sending your iframe to look at. In this case, it's a link to a YouTube video. This is essentially what iframes do: they open a small window in the middle of your article and, inside it, show a different page, or resource, on the world wide web. That different resource is defined in the src link. See Chapter 9 for a refresher on how the web works.

The three parameters—width, height, and src—are all that's required to make a successful iframe. The rest are options and styling. Frameborder="0" just means that it won't have a black frame around the edge of the iframe, and allowfullscreen is self-explanatory.

Iframes are the most common form of embed code, but they are not the only one. Some companies want more control as to how their content appears in your articles and define more of the parameters themselves. Twitter is one of these companies.

A Twitter embed code looks like this:

```
<blockquote class="twitter-tweet" lang="en"><p lang="en"
dir="ltr">What the <a href="https://twitter.com/
hashtag/Toronto?src=hash">#Toronto</a> airport used
to look like <a href="http://t.co/4qTkNBvnVQ">http://t.
co/4qTkNBvnVQ</a> <a href="https://twitter.com/
hashtag/TBT?src=hash">#TBT</a> <a href="http://t.co/
```

```
ETt22GJAZR">pic.twitter.com/ETt22GJAZR</a></p>&mdash;
blogTO (@blogTO) <a href="https://twitter.com/blogTO/
status/626916478864986112">July 31, 2015</a></blockquote>
<script async src="//platform.twitter.com/widgets.js"
charset="utf-8"></script>
```

This is a combination of HTML and JavaScript (see page 227) and there is nothing in there that you can edit or change. If you see an embed code like this, just use it as presented and back away slowly.

Once you understand the nature of an iframe, and what it's doing in your window, you'll get a clearer understanding of what it means to embed interactive content in your story. Understanding that gives you enormous power, because if you start to create your own content and upload it to a web server, it becomes remarkably simple to incorporate it with your written work.

All embed codes that you've ever encountered, and ever will encounter, are a variation on this theme. Of course, what use is an embed code without content to embed? Let's move to discussing the kinds of programs newsroom developers create.

Core Languages Used by Newsroom Developers: An Introduction to the Work Environment

All development in newsrooms basically falls into two categories: Server-side and client-side.

Server-side refers to programs that exist purely within the newsroom or even on one machine in the newsroom. They are meant to be run in a very precise environment and accomplish very specific tasks. Server-side programs are frequently built using programming languages such as Java, Ruby, Python, or PHP.

Client-side programs refer to anything that is meant to be used in the browser (such as Chrome, Firefox, Safari, or Internet Explorer). They are designed to be used by average people who visit websites. Client-side programs written by developer journalists are frequently built to showcase the data behind a feature story, to allow readers to explore a complex narrative more thoroughly, or to artfully showcase photo, video, and text elements of a long-form feature.

Client-side programming often means developer journalists need to be aware of cross-browser compatibility issues the problems that result when someone on the latest version of Chrome sees a perfectly functional website, but the experience breaks for people on Firefox or older versions of Internet Explorer, to give one example. Solving those problems to provide a uniform experience for all visitors to the site can be challenging.

The other big difference is the number of languages involved. On the server, you can write an entire application using only on language, such as Python or PHP. On the client, though, you often need to include three different files, each with their own syntax and language requirements. Creating a web app for a browser most often requires an HTML file, a CSS file, and a JavaScript (or JS) file. But we'll get into that later.

One thing to keep in mind before we progress: You will fail. Your programs will break. That will be frustrating, at times. But this does not mean that you are not meant to do this kind of work. It does not mean that you are a bad programmer.

As writers and editors, we are accustomed to taking the pieces of a project and slowly assembling them into a finished masterpiece. Development is not like that. Developers start out with an idea, and build a project that they think will address their idea, but knowing that it will break. The rest of their job is making it stop breaking. Try not to get discouraged at this new approach to work.

Regardless of what kind of work you're doing, there are some tools that you'll need on your system.

First, you'll need a code editor. You were introduced to these editors in Chapter 9 and there's a tutorial on the companion website to help you choose one.

An important thing to know is that these editors are not like Microsoft Word or other word-processing applications. This is one of the first conceptual leaps that you'll have to make when getting into writing code in the newsroom. Word-processing applications like Microsoft Word apply a mountain of formatting to your document. They define things like bold, italics, fonts, sizes, layouts, line breaks, embedded tables, images, and a thousand other details that are not the text of what you're writing. It's one of the reasons why the word-processor files you've saved on your computer are so big.

Code editors only handle the raw text in a document. The files they save don't include anything about formatting or version history, or any other extra information—just the text.

The Server Side: Writing for Your Own Machine

There are some operations that you can't do in a web browser. Handling large amounts of data, creating or deleting files on your machine: these are all things that browser-based applications, written using JavaScript, HTML, and CSS, are incapable of handling.

In journalism, two of the most common reasons to write server-side apps are to make a Twitter bot, or to scrape the web of data as discussed in Chapter 9. A Twitter bot is an automated Twitter account. You can write a program that sits on your computer and, at intervals you define, it will post tweets to any Twitter account for which you have the credentials. This can be used to raise awareness about certain issues, like the @wearethedead account created by Glen McGregor and the *Ottawa Citizen* to tweet the name of a fallen member of the Canadian Forces every hour. It can also be used to promote your work when you're not around, by reading an RSS feed of recent content and posting Tweets at set times while you're asleep. It can even be just for fun, as with @PEICompare, which tweets daily on how large places in the world are compared to Prince Edward Island. Full disclosure: @PEICompare was created by this book's lead author, Fred Vallance-Jones. See the tutorial "Building a Twitter Bot" on the companion website for a detailed rundown on how to make your own bot using Python.

Writing server-side programs essentially allows you to automate the most repetitive aspects of data collection, research, and promotion. If you get good at writing code, and wrapping your head around the logical leaps it makes, there is really no limit to how powerful your apps can be.

The Client Side: Writing for Everyone Else's Machines

Working for the web is an inherently complicated game to play. Everyone who uses your program will have slightly different web browsers, running on slightly different computers with vastly different capabilities.

For this reason, in a newsroom environment, writing simpler code is often more advantageous than writing more complex programs. The simpler the program, the more likely every user who visits your website will be able to run it, no matter the device they're using.

Modern newsrooms use the term "mobile-first" to describe much of their newsroom development work. This reflects not only the idea that websites should easily adjust their size for mobile devices—like smartphones and tablets—but that even the most complex interactives should be fully functional on mobile devices. That automatically discounts tools such as Adobe Flash and Microsoft Silverlight, which few newsrooms use anymore.

Instead, most newsroom development teams use JavaScript and libraries that are built around it. JavaScript is a programming language that is built for the web. It runs inside your web browser to make the web interactive. Most buttons you see on the Internet, every animation, every interactive component, it all comes down to JavaScript.

That brings us to the three component languages of every web page.

HTML

HTML is an initialsim: HyperText Markup Language. We had a look at simple HTML in the last chapter, and as we noted then it builds the bare bones of a web page. It is the scaffolding upon which everything else hangs. It determines the order of elements on a page (what is closest to the top of the page; what is further down the page) and determines the rough content of the page.

HTML is the code that says, "This headline is here!"

CSS

CSS is also an initialsim: Cascading Style Sheets. This defines all the styles of a web page. It determines how big text is, what colour it is, how wide images are, whether the borders on them are sharp or curved and to what degree, how elements are positioned on the page, and even how you might transition between two states (like clicking a button turns its colour from blue to green over the course of 1.3 seconds, for example).

CSS is the code that says, "This headline is black text, Times New Roman, 18 points tall, and centred between the photo and the article."

For more detail on how HTML and CSS work, see the tutorial "A Short Guide to HTML and CSS" on the companion website.

JavaScript

JavaScript is the magic sauce. JavaScript can make changes to both HTML and CSS depending on what the user decides to do. JavaScript can change the layout of a page, or it can control how it behaves as a user scrolls down. JavaScript is what makes the web so deeply customizable.

But the HTML document is what ties it all together. In the end, everything is happening to the HTML document. The CSS file and the JavaScript file are just manipulating it.

So here's how we get started. First, we have to create a new folder on our computer and give it a name. We'll call this one "FirstWebSite." There are no spaces in the name because web URLs have a habit of reacting poorly to spaces, so when we build applications for the web, we tend to do so without spaces in the file names.

Now open your code editor. Create a new file and save it as index.html. Then create another new file and call it styles.css. Then create another new file and call it scripts.js. Those are your three files. Save them all in the new folder that you just created. They will work in harmony with one another. They will be friends. They will complement each other to the end. Together, they will make magic happen.

But first, we need to tell them how to talk to each other. So open your HTML file. Your HTML file is the heart of everything. It's where they all come together. There are two parts to an HTML file: a head and a body. The body is where the content goes (everything you see when you open the page), but the head is where you link all your files together. It's where you tell your HTML where it can find all the JavaScript and CSS that it needs to do its job properly.

Enter this in your HTML document:

```
1.  <!DOCTYPE html>
2.  <html lang="en">
3.  <head>
4.  <title>SiteTitle</title>
5.  <link rel="stylesheet" href="styles.css">
6.  </head>
7.  <body>
8.  <script src="scripts.js"></script>
9.  </body>
10. </html>
```

These lines are numbered, as they would be in a code editor, so you can easily reference bits of code when you need to. You don't need to write in the line numbers yourself. One of the core ideas behind HTML that you're going to have to get used to is the idea of opening and closing tags. Every time you open a tag, you have to close it. Look at the example above. You can see <head> (line 3) and </head> (line 6). You can also see <body> (line 7) and </body> (line 9). Similarly, you can see <title> (line 4) and </title> (also line 4).

When you open a tag, you're going to put something inside it, and then you're going to close the tag. Closing tags is very important, otherwise they go on forever.

Let's review the example above line by line to see what it's doing.

The first line declares the document type. It tells the web browser that this is an HTML file. Plain and simple, nothing more.

The second line declares that the language of this file is English, and begins the HTML content.

The third line begins the head of the document. You can see that there is a <head> tag and, four lines further down, a </head> tag. These are the opening and closing tags of the head portion of the HTML document. So everything we need to go in the head of the document needs to go between these two tags.

The first thing we do here is define the title of the page. This is what will show up at the top of your browser window when people load the page, and it's what webcrawlers such as Google will pick up on about your page first. The title is very important.

Next you'll see a <link> tag and then, further down the page toward the bottom, a <script> tag.

```
<link rel="stylesheet" href="styles.css">
. . .
<script src="scripts.js"></script>
```

This is where your HTML discovers its partners in crime, CSS and JavaScript.

The <script> tag begins the call and tells your HTML document that JavaScript is en route. Then, the src="scripts.js" in the middle specifies where the file is, and what the file is called. The src stands for "source," so it's looking for the source of the script. You'll notice the <script> tag is near the bottom of the page. This is done because the browser loads the HTML file from top to bottom. If the JavaScript is encountered first, the elements on the page it is intended to modify may not have loaded yet. If we put it at the end, we know everything will be there before the JavaScript springs into action.

Now your HTML file has access to all of the JavaScript commands that are to come in your .js file.

Next, the <link> tag specifies where to find your CSS and what that file is called. The <link> tag also specifies that this is a style sheet through the rel= attribute. We have to specify that the rel="stylesheet" because a link tag can also be used to specify bookmarks, icons, authors, and other details of an HTML page. This <link> tag, as written, tells the browser to look for a file called styles.css and treat it like a style sheet.

So now let's make it all do something. Update your file so it looks like this:

```
1.  <!DOCTYPE html>
2.  <html lang="en">
3.  <head>
4.  <title>My First Website</title>
5.  <link rel="stylesheet" href="styles.css">
6.  </head>
7.  <body>
8.  <p>My first website body text.</p>
9.  <script src="scripts.js"></script>
10. </body>
11. </html>
```

We only changed two things in this version of the HTML file. We added a site title, which reads My First Website. This is a great title for your first project. Then, right after the opening <body> tag, we added something new: a <p> tag with some text in it. The <p> tag is a paragraph tag, and it's the natural way that we divide up blocks of text in a web page.

If you open this file up in your web browser (by double-clicking on it from the folder) you will see the new title at the top of the browser window and the text in the top left corner of your screen.

Welcome to your first website. Now let's make it look good.

You already know how HTML works. Tags open and close, and there's content in between the opening and closing tags.

CSS is just about as easy. There are selectors, and rules associated with those selectors. What's a selector? Selectors are how the CSS knows what's happening in the HTML document. What's a rule? It's the style that applies to the selector.

Here's an example:

```
p {
color: black;
}
```

The p is the selector. Right now, that p is selecting all the p tags in the HTML document. The rules are contained inside the { } brackets. There can be as many rules for each selector as you wish. This snippet is going to make all the <p> tags in the HTML document black.

Now if we were to add a few more rules, it would look like this:

```
p {
color: black;
text-align: center;
text-decoration: underline;
}
```

There are three rules attached to that selector. Now every <p> tag in the HTML document will be black, centred on the page, and underlined.

Simple, right? That's how all styling in web pages happens. Select the element you want to style and then write rules for it to follow.

But, hold up, what if you want some <p> tags on your HTML page to behave differently than other <p> tags? For instance, you may want a pull quote in the middle of an article, or you might want headlines to look different from your body text. That's where the idea of classes comes in. Classes are essentially ways to subclassify your HTML elements. Instead of simply selecting a <p> tag, you can select a <p class="headline"> tag. We can add class attributes to your tags and make them easily identifiable by the CSS file.

That means you can take your practice HTML file and modify it like so:

```
1.   <!DOCTYPE html>
2.   <html lang="en">
3.   <head>
```

```
4.  <title>My First Website</title>
5.  <link rel="stylesheet" href="styles.css">
6.  </head>
7.  <body>
8.  <p class="headline">My first website body text.</p>
9.  <p class="bodyText">This is a bit of body text below
    my first website headline.</p>
10. <script src="scripts.js"></script>
11. </body>
12. </html>
```

Then, in your CSS file, you can write rules that will target each of those lines individually, like so:

```
.headline {
font-size: 24px;
color: black;
text-align: center;
}
.bodyText {
font-size: 13px;
color: grey;
text-align: left;
}
```

Make sure you delete the previous style that affected all <p> tags.

There are a few things to notice about these lines of CSS:

- The period at the start of the selector. That's short form for "class." Instead of writing class=headline, we just write .headline. It's just faster that way.
- The semicolon in the rule. Each rule ends with one or else it all breaks. That's one of the nitty-gritty things about CSS.
- Color. Note that the American spelling of "color" is used rather than the Canadian/British "colour."

That's HTML and CSS working together. But now let's add a little bit of JavaScript to the mix.

JavaScript is a bit of a different beast in that it's not really setting out rules for how the document looks, as HTML and CSS do. Instead, it's setting out rules for how the document behaves. This is about how it moves, how it responds to user input, and how interactive it is.

Write this code into your scripts.js file.

```
document.addEventListener("click", function(){
  document.body.style.backgroundColor = "blue";
});
```

This looks much different than the code we were writing earlier. There are no tags to speak of, and it's not looking much like English. In fact, this has some distant resemblance to the Python code we saw in Chapter 9. This is because both are true programming languages, though each has its own particular syntax, structure, and purpose. To learn even more about JavaScript, see the tutorial "Introduction to JavaScript" on the companion website.

The periods in the JavaScript seen above are the key part to pay attention to in this snippet of code. The periods are what divide commands and allow us to string together our train of thought. Just as in Python, this is called dot notation. "Document" tells us what the program is looking at. It's looking at the document. "addEventListener" is a command that tells the preceding part to listen for something to happen. So together, these two commands tell the document to listen for something. That something is a click. The click is defined in the next part.

Of course, when you click on something, you expect it to do something. That's where everything after the "click" comes into play. Where you see function(){ that's the beginning of the code that is triggered after you click. The }); is the end of that code.

Between those two portions, you can see one line of code:

```
document.body.style.backgroundColor = "blue";
```

It follows a similar structure to the first structure we looked at. "Document" identifies the part that we're about to modify—we're about to modify the document. Then "body" identifies the part within the document. Then "style" identifies the attribute of the body that we're going to modify. Once we've identified that attribute, we're going to identify the style rule that we're going to change, which is the background colour. We're going to change it to blue.

Save your JavaScript file. Refresh the HTML page in your browser. Then click on the document. The background changes colour instantly. Try changing the colour indicated in the code and see how that affects what happens.

Welcome to interactivity on the web. Most of the interactivity you see online is JavaScript. Almost everything that moves, everything that you can click on, everything that animates, it's all JavaScript. When you get good at JavaScript, the entirety of the Internet falls under your control.

It feels good. But we can do more.

Case Study: Using freeDive

Sometimes, you'll want to share all or some of your raw data with your readers. Here's a tool to do that.

The project: "837 Law Enforcement Officers Have Given Canada Their Lives."[4]

Following the murder of three RCMP officers in Moncton, NB, in 2014, Canada.com endeavoured to tell the story of all those officers who had given their lives in the line of duty throughout Canadian history.

The result was an interactive database that allowed readers to search and sort the entire history of law enforcement officers who had died in the line of duty. Here's how it came together.

The Officer Down Memorial Page (www.odmp.org) is a not-for-profit project that endeavours to maintain a running archive of every police officer throughout Canada and the United States who has been killed in service. By using that data and isolating Canadian officers, Canada.com was able to create a list of every Canadian officer who had died on the job. They stored that list in a Google Spreadsheet. Then, using a free tool developed at the Berkeley School of Journalism called freeDive, they were able to convert that spreadsheet into an interactive database for readers to use. You can download the tool at https://github.com/ldegroot/freedive.

Download this file by clicking the "Download ZIP" button on the Github page. Unzip the file and open Wizard.html to start working with the freeDive wizard.

FreeDive works by taking all the data stored within a Google Spreadsheet and organizing into an application that users can interact with. But the tool requires you to supply the ID, rather than simply the link, of the spreadsheet you're using.

Google documents and folders all come with unique identifiers. Every unique identifier is unique in the entire Google universe and can be used to reference specific documents and folders across the Google network.

This is the full URL of the spreadsheet that contains the Canada.com data:

```
https://docs.google.com/spreadsheet/ccc?key=0ArinWIqzWofqdHBDe
EhiYVdpZll3QVItb0J0X2treFE&usp=drive _ web#gid=0
https://docs.google.com/spreadsheet/ccc?key=0ArinWIqzWofqd
HBDeEhiYVdpZll3QVItb0J0X2treFE&usp=drive _ web - gid=0
```

Break it down. The portion of that URL that says key=######## is the unique spreadsheet identifier. This tells Google exactly which spreadsheet you're looking for. Paste it into the freeDive wizard. Now go through the rest of the steps, which are self-explanatory.

At the end of the wizard, you'll see a text window that gives you a large file of JavaScript. It's compressed into a small window, so looks less intimidating than it is, but copy and paste it into your code editor and you'll get a feel for just how big it is.

Once you have the large JavaScript file in your code editor, add basic HTML tags, making sure you put the JavaScript inside the HTML body. Save the file with the name index.html. Open it in your browser to see what it looks like.

If you want to share your interactive with the world, you can add the same JavaScript code to a page on your website. Unfortunately, many content management systems, such as WordPress, will reject code that contains a lot of JavaScript because of the possibility it could be malicious. To get around this, you can upload the HTML file you created directly to the web, then embed that page in an iframe.

To get your file onto the web, upload it to your web server either using an FTP program such as FileZilla or as directed by your server's administrator. If you don't have access to a web server, you'll need a hosting account from a company providing web hosting services. Once you have uploaded the file, put the URL to the uploaded file into an iframe.

```
<iframe src="URL of your interactive" scrolling="no"
frameborder="0" marginheight="0px" marginwidth="0px"
height="60px" width="468px"></iframe>
```

You can now add the iframe to your story in your web page or content management system, and it's ready for prime time.

Working with JavaScript Libraries Such as jQuery and D3

Once you master JavaScript and learn how it can interact with HTML and CSS to manipulate your web pages, it's time to take advantage of how smart other people are with their programming skills.

One of the great things about getting involved in this community is that it's a very open space. People trade ideas, successes, and techniques with each other very openly. Because of that, it means you don't have to solve most problems that others have already solved, problems such as how to get a browser to react to a click or how to select the second item from a list while bypassing the first.

More complex problems, such as how to make your browser recognize what a latitude and longitude means in terms of pixels, or how to make your app compatible with older versions of Internet Explorer, are also problems modern interactive developers don't have to worry about.

This is the world of libraries and frameworks.

JavaScript is an extensible programming language, which means you can import JavaScript written by other people and use its functionality in your own work. This allows you to take advantage of the skills other people have developed and solve your problems with their work. It's part of what makes working in software so collaborative.

jQuery is the most popular JavaScript library in the world. It's designed to make writing normal JavaScript like on-click events and handling data easier than it would be with normal commands in JavaScript.

Other libraries are developed to accomplish other specific tasks. D3, for example, is designed to handle huge amounts of data and animate them online. It cleanly creates visualizations and handles complex calculations related to geography, time, and other ways of measuring the world around us. Data visualizations made with D3 are quickly becoming the standard for news interactives in media organizations around the world.

To use these libraries and take advantage of their functions, we actually use the same techniques as our previous JavaScript file: we have to tell our HTML where to find it. To do that, we use a <script> tag, just as we did in the original document. It looks something like this:

```
<script src="https://ajax.googleapis.com/ajax/libs/
jquery/2.1.4/jquery.min.js"></script>
```

Instead of pointing to a local file, we can point to a web link. That means we don't even have to download any code, we just have to tell our file where it can find the code it needs. When it's all put together with our HTML, it looks something like this:

```
1.   <!DOCTYPE html>
2.   <html lang="en">
3.   <head>
4.   <title>My First Website</title>
5.   <link rel="stylesheet" href="styles.css">
6.   </head>
7.   <body>
8.   <p class="headline">My first website body text.</p>
9.   <p class="bodyText">This is a bit of body text below
     my first website headline.</p>
10.  <script src="https://ajax.googleapis.com/ajax/libs/
     jquery/2.1.4/jquery.min.js"></script>
```

```
11. <script src="scripts.js"></script>
12. </body>
13. </html>
```

And if you wanted to use D3, taking advantage of all the functions that it offers, you simply have to link to its file. Add the following code as a new line 11, shifting the remaining three lines down.

```
<script src="https://cdnjs.cloudflare.com/ajax/libs/d3/3.5.5/
d3.min.js"></script>
```

Once the libraries are loaded, you are free to use them to your heart's content in your JavaScript file. But how? It's all about prefixes.

Think back to when we were writing JavaScript and remember how we used periods to link together ideas and commands. Periods are a way of drilling down into an object and pulling out what you need from deep within it. Just as we used "document" at the top of our JavaScript commands, to dive into the document and identify the parts that we wanted to work with, in other JavaScript libraries we can use other prefixes to control those libraries.

jQuery uses a dollar sign, for example. All jQuery commands start with $. So instead of writing the comparatively complex code from the previous section:

```
document.addEventListener("click", function(){
  document.body.style.backgroundColor = "blue";
});
```

We can write the same thing in jQuery like this:

```
$(this).click(function() {
  $('body').css('background-color','blue');
});
```

You may have noticed the ".min" that is part of the src strings in the code used to import jQuery and D3. This stands for "minified," and means you are downloading special versions of the libraries that have all of the extra spaces and anything else unnecessary removed. Using the minified versions speeds up page loading, as the files are smaller. If you want to see the code in a human-readable versions of the libraries, you can always download the non-minified versions and open them in a text or code editor.

There are fewer commands because jQuery knows what we're trying to do and handles the rest. Let's explore what's actually happening in this section. The $ indicates that we're going to use jQuery. The (this) is selecting what jQuery is going to act on, in this case the entire HTML document. Then there's that familiar period, to link together what we've selected with the command that comes next. The "click" keyword kicks off a function for what will happen when that item is clicked. Instead of going through the process of adding an event listener, we can use a single word to summarize that process.

The next part:

```
function(){
});
```

This is the code that will be triggered once someone clicks on the document. Once again, $ indicates that we're using jQuery and ('body') indicates that we're about to act on the body of the document. The .css indicates that we're going to modify the CSS of the body, which means we're going to change its styles. Which styles? That's what we define in the parentheses. The first item in the parentheses is the style parameter that we're going to change. In this case, it's the background colour. Then, the second item in the parentheses is the value that we're going to assign to the style parameter—in this case, blue.

Collectively, these three lines will allow the user to change the background colour of the body of their HTML file to blue.

D3 operates similarly, but instead of starting each command with a $, each command begins with D3. D3 has a number of important functions, and you can explore the entire suite of operations at d3js.org, but the basic format of the code in JavaScript is as in the next bit of code. Paste this in at the bottom of your scripts.js file if you like. Then save the file.

```
d3.select("body").append("p").text("I'm a new paragraph!");
```

This is a simple line of JavaScript that uses D3 to add a <p> tag to your HTML document and place text in it that reads "I'm a new paragraph!"

The first bit of that code is simply D3. This means we're going to use the D3 library for the following operations. The select command identifies where in the HTML document the operation is going to take place. In this case, we're about to modify the body of the HTML document. The append command means we're going to add a new element to the HTML document, with the element defined in the parentheses. It's going to be a <p> tag. Once it's added the <p> tag, it's going to modify the text in the <p> tag with the text command.

What appears in the parentheses of the text command is what will actually appear in your document.

So you see how this works: It's a command, followed by parentheses that define how that command will behave. Then another command followed by parentheses that will define how it will behave. These are strung together with periods. This is called "method chaining."

If you added the D3 code at the bottom of the scripts.js file, the new paragraph appears as soon as the page loads. You could also add the line of D3 code to the function you defined inside your jQuery code, so it would look like this:

```
$(this).click(function() {
d3.select("body").append("p").text("This a new paragraph!");
});
```

That's a good starter example, but D3's real magic for journalists is its ability to visualize data without the need for proprietary tools such as Google Fusion Tables. And with some additional code you can make your dataviz interactive.

Let's start with a series of numbers: 150, 300, 450, 600, 750. We'll call these the daily salaries of journalists depending on their knowledge of data journalism. Now let's say we wanted to display the salaries on a horizontal bar chart; we can, in a few lines of D3 code.

First, we'll put our data into an array, the JavaScript equivalent of the Python lists we saw in Chapter 9 (for more on arrays, see the tutorial "Introduction to JavaScript" on the companion website). To begin coding our example, clear out the previous jQuery and D3 code in your scripts.js file, and write this statement in at the top of the file.

```
var salaries = [150,300,450,600,750]
```

This creates an array and assigns it to the variable "salaries."

Next, we'll add some D3 code for the bar chart. Since writing the chain of methods all together, the way we did before, would be pretty hard to read, we'll put each D3 method (a fancy word for a function) on its own line. When you type in the code, don't include our line numbers; they're here for reference.

```
1.  d3.select("body")
2.      .append("svg")
3.      .attr("width",800)
4.      .attr("height",400)
```

```
5.          .selectAll("rect")
6.              .data(salaries)
7.              .enter()
8.              .append("rect")
9.              .attr("x",0)
10.             .attr("y",function(d,i){return i * 40;})
11.             .attr("height",39)
12.             .attr("width",function(d,i){return d;})
13.             .attr("fill","blue")
```

An important thing to understand about chaining together methods with periods is that each one inherits the output of those before it. It's like an automotive production line on which each worker does something to a car. That worker depends on the work of those who came before and passes the partially completed car to the next worker. By the end, you have a complete vehicle.

So, in line 1 above we are once again selecting the body of the HTML page, as we did in our first D3 example. We then pass that selection along to the next method in the chain, .append(), which appends an SVG element to the web page body. SVG stands for Scalable Vector Graphics, a way of adding graphics to a web page. Think of this SVG element as a container for our bar chart.

Lines 3 and 4 apply attributes to the SVG container to make it 800 pixels wide and 400 pixels tall.

In line 5 we use D3's selectAll method to select all SVG "rect" elements in the body of the web page. Since there aren't actually any "rect" elements yet, selectAll returns what is called an "empty selection" and passes it along.

In line 6 we meet D3's ultra-cool .data() method. We'll talk in detail about how it works in the tutorial "Visualizing with D3.js" on the companion website, but for now it suffices to say that lines 6 and 7 work together to join or "bind" our data to our soon-to-exist "rect" elements. Each element now has a piece of data attached to it that can be visualized.

The result is then passed to the .append() method on line 8, which finally adds the "rect" elements to the page body, complete with the bound data.

In line 9, we set the "x" attribute of our new "rect" elements to 0. That means each rectangle will start at the far left side of the containing SVG element, where "x" equals 0. If we set "x" to a higher value, the rectangle shifts to the right by however many pixels we indicate.

From here, things get a bit more complicated.

The "y" attribute controls the up and down placement of the rectangles. It has to be different for each rectangle or the bars would be drawn one atop the other. So we'll make use of the special D3 variables "d" and "i".

Whenever the .data() method is called, two values are made available for use later in the code, for each web page element that has data bound to it. The first value, by convention called "d", is the data value now bound to that element. The second, by convention called "i", is the index number of the HTML element in the selection of elements.

So in our array of daily salaries, [150,300,450,600,750], now bound to "rect" elements, the "d" value for the first "rect" element is 150 and the "i" or index value is 0. The second value has "d" and "i" values of 300 and 1, the third 450 and 2, and so on.

We'll now use these special variables in functions.

In line 10, to set the "y" attribute of the rectangles, we'll multiply the index number of each data element by 40, inside an unnamed, or anonymous, function. It's crucial to include both "d" and "i" in the parentheses of the function; D3 expects them to be in this order and when "i" is used, both have to be there. With this code, the first bar ends up starting at "y" position 0 (0 times 40), which is at the top of the SVG container. The next bar starts 40 pixels down (1 x 40), the next 80 down (2 x 40), and so on.

On line 11 we set the height of each bar to 39 pixels, which means each bar will end one pixel above the next one, with a bit of whitespace between them.

In line 12, we use another anonymous function to set the horizontal width of each bar to the value of each data element ("d") in the original array.

Finally, we use the "fill" attribute to set the colour of the bars to blue.

To see your code in action, re-save your scripts.js file, then open or refresh your index.html file in your web browser. Since scripts.js is within index.html, the new code is again automatically included in index.html.

If nothing appears when you open index.html in your browser, it likely means you made an error copying the code. If you'd rather just cut and paste, the complete code is in the D3 tutorial on the companion website. The tutorial also explains how to root out errors in your code, and takes you deeper into the world of D3 visualizations with more functions and examples.

Beyond jQuery and D3, there are dozens of other JavaScript libraries, each built to solve a different problem that programmers face in their daily lives. As a new developer, you need to remember that these other developers are not competitors, but resources. The news developer community is tightly knit, and always eager to welcome more people into the fold. Mentors are surprisingly easy to come by, and questions are always answered enthusiastically.

For basic questions, when you're not sure why your script isn't working when all your instincts tell you it should be (a surprisingly frequent problem that you'll run into), Stack Overflow is a web community where developers meet to help each other out. It's a question-and-answer site where the best answers to everyday programming questions are up-voted by the membership.

It's very active and is a relatively new, but incredibly powerful, resource that many professional developers rely on daily.

Conclusion

This chapter has been quick introduction to the burgeoning world of the news developer and the tools they use. Most software developers work on a much slower scale than news developers do. Developers are the hackers of the newsroom, the people who solve problems on the fly, working at the speed of breaking news and providing assistance to other journalists. It's a world in which developers commit acts of journalism with code instead of with paragraphs, adding new dimensions and possibilities, and accomplishing things journalists a generation ago couldn't even dream of.

It's a stark shift from what most journalists are accustomed to, and a very different workflow. A one-time freelance journalist in Edmonton, Justin Bell, described reporting as building something that slowly comes into shape, moulding itself to the author's vision. Coding, however, is different. "I find it really interesting that web development (and programming in general) involves making something you know won't function properly, then start fixing it," he said.[5]

He's right. But that makes the final victory sweeter. Once the bugs are solved, the logic works, the program behaves as expected, and your skills are making complex news stories more relevant, more easily understood, and more accessible to a broad audience, there are few feelings of accomplishment more complete.

Study Questions and Exercises

1. Come up with your own idea for a web application. When starting to learn how to develop a project, it helps to have a clear idea of your finished product in your head before you start. Learning the theory without a clear idea of how you might apply it can be frustrating. Take the time now to come up with a simple idea for a server-side application and a simple idea for a website (client-side application) that you could build. Here are some ideas to get you started:
   - On the server side, you might try writing a program that connects to a website and checks to see if a keyword exists on the page. Or you might try writing a program that downloads a site's HTML to your computer.

- On the client side, you might try making a simple static page like amidumb.com. Or you might try writing a program that allows a user to click a button that opens a new email to the person of your choosing.

  Having an idea to start from gives your learning a sense of purpose and direction, and provides a comforting sense of accomplishment when you achieve your goals.

2. Please see the companion website for additional exercises using live data.

Further Reading

Duckett, Jon. *HTML & CSS: Design and Build Websites*. Indianapolis: John Wiley and Sons, 2011.

——*JavaScript and jQuery: Interactive Front-End Web Development*. Indianapolis: John Wiley and Sons, 2014.

Murray, Scott. *Interactive Data Visualization for the Web*. Sebastapol, CA: O'Reilly, 2013.

Notes

1. Neena Satija, Kiah Collier, Al Shaw, and Jeff Larson, "Hell and High Water," *Pro Publica* and *Texas Tribune*, 3 March 2016, https://projects.propublica.org/houston/.
2. Joshua Benton, "Luring Developers into the Newsroom," *Nieman*, 8 November 2012, http://www.niemanlab.org/2012/11/luring-developers-into-the-newsroom-a-new-class-of-knight-mozilla-fellows-tries-to-bridge-a-cultural-divide/.
3. Ibid.
4. William Wolfe-Wylie, "837 Law Enforcement Officers Have Given Canada Their Lives," *Canada.com*, 4 June 2014, http://o.canada.com/news/national/837-law-enforcement-officers-have-given-canada-their-lives.
5. Justin Bell with the author, 1 April 2015.

Part IV
Telling Stories with Data

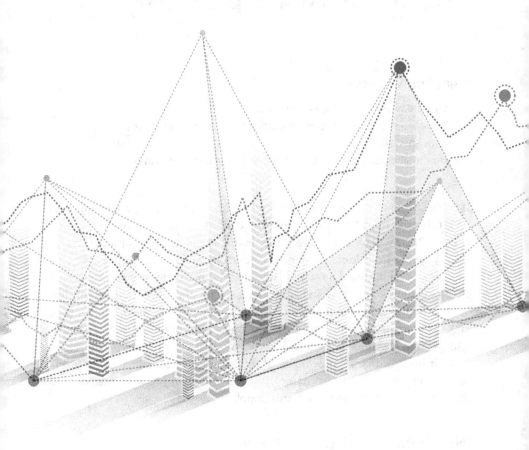

Chapter 11

Incorporating Data Journalism into Traditional Reporting

What You Will Learn:

- Why data analysis alone is rarely enough
- The essential "shoe-leather" reporting techniques that must accompany data analysis
- How to find compelling human tales to accompany the numbers

If you've come this far with us, you know a lot about getting, analyzing, and presenting data. And indeed, on many occasions the result of your data journalism efforts will be a visualization or map. But on others, your analysis will lead to a more traditional written, broadcast, or multimedia online story.

When combining data with traditional methods, the story is king. This chapter explores how to write data-driven stories and connect your findings in data with traditional reporting methods that provide meaning, context, and—perhaps most importantly—the people behind the numbers. In short, telling a simple story driven by data means determining which numbers make it into your story, how many of the numbers to use, what other information may be needed to provide crucial context, and how to connect the data-driven information to human examples.

Why Data Is Just the Beginning

Sometimes, the temptation is to proclaim "mission accomplished" once you have acquired what you think—or hope—is a killer dataset. But this is a mistake.

There is a lot of work that goes into showing the impact of your story, which begins with the need for traditional legwork; shoe leather, as the old saying goes.[1] Showing the impact also means explaining how your data affects people. Are filthy restaurants making more people sick? Do the increasing numbers of problematic restaurants in your city mean that the municipality needs beefed-up inspection bylaws? When it comes to crime, what do the increases in break-ins say about particular neighbourhoods, the police force's ability to monitor them, and the city politicians' ability to keep tabs on the problem? Or, conversely, what do the decreasing instances of certain crimes mean in light of political claims that stoke fears about the increased need for law and order, or the police force's lobbying for more money and more boots on the ground?

Datasets can contain blockbuster stories in and of themselves, especially as a follow-up to common and potentially catastrophic events such as food poisonings, horrific crimes, or motor vehicle accidents. For instance, when Toyota recalled vehicles in 2008 due to problems with so-called sticky peddles and unintended accelerations, CBC and National Public Radio(NPR), in separate and unrelated stories, used datasets from Transport Canada and the US National Highway Transportation Safety Administration, respectively, to show that these problems had been around a lot longer than most people—including politicians responsible for monitoring road safety—realized.

The CBC's story used Transport Canada's vehicle-recall database to illustrate that Transport Canada began posting similar recall notices as far back as 2003.[2] Using the department's online database, the CBC searched for Toyota models with problems concerning floor mats, and turned up a 2003 example that cited "the driver's floor mat may slide along the interior floor carpet when pressure is applied to the mat by getting in or out of the vehicle."[3]

Using a similar technique of mining an online database for clues as a follow-up to a major vehicle-recall story, NPR searched the National Highway Transportation Safety Administration complaints database to locate concerns about unintended accelerations, another problem that caused Toyota to issue a recall notice in 2010. "We have a surge or skip on de-acceleration [sic]. This will happen from 40 to 60 MPH," read one complaint.

NPR analyzed more than 15,000 complaints in the administration's database. "Toyota's problems seemed go back to 2002," said NPR data journalist Robert Benincasa.

> That's a few years before these recalls we've been hearing about with the floor mats and the sticky gas pedals. So back in 2002, they had about 10 percent of the U.S. auto market and they had about 19 percent of the complaints on acceleration.[4]

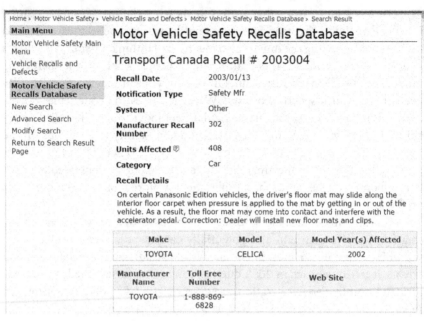

Main Menu

Motor Vehicle Safety Main Menu

Vehicle Recalls and Defects

Motor Vehicle Safety Recalls Database

New Search

Advanced Search

Modify Search

Return to Search Result Page

Motor Vehicle Safety Recalls Database

Transport Canada Recall # 2003004

Recall Date	2003/01/13
Notification Type	Safety Mfr
System	Other
Manufacturer Recall Number	302
Units Affected ⓘ	408
Category	Car

Recall Details

On certain Panasonic Edition vehicles, the driver's floor mat may slide along the interior floor carpet when pressure is applied to the mat by getting in or out of the vehicle. As a result, the floor mat may come into contact with and interfere with the accelerator pedal. Correction: Dealer will install new floor mats and clips.

Make	Model	Model Year(s) Affected
TOYOTA	CELICA	2002

Manufacturer Name	Toll Free Number	Web Site
TOYOTA	1-888-869-6828	

Source: Transport Canada

Screen capture from Transport Canada's online recall database

Because recalls tend to be regular occurrences, these types of stories should also be followed up with further analysis with an expanded focus, something that the CBC and NPR did in addition to their original coverage.[5] However, there is no need to stop there.

Given the importance of cars, especially in large North American and European cities, it is worth pushing the analysis further to find out, for instance, why similar types of recalls recur? Who is to blame? Should vehicle manufacturers take more responsibility? Or are carmakers the mere beneficiaries of weak regulations that depend too heavily on ill-equipped governments to take tougher action? So when dealing with problems that affect many people—be they drivers, patients taking prescription medicine, patients in hospitals, students in schools—hunt for data, and then look for instances where the problem making the news may have occurred before becoming headline material. As was the case with the vehicle-recall stories, such discoveries can be an excellent starting point for meaningful stories that inform and challenge all the major players involved.

Once the starting point has been marked, the traditional reporting takes over, which means tracking down victims who may be suing a carmaker for compensation, former regulators who may have tried to sound the alarm, or lawmakers who may have been lobbied by automakers to push for weaker regulations. Indeed, the data is just the beginning. In other words, the data tells you what, and people tell you why.

Finding Outliers That Lead to Human Stories

As strange as it might sound, many of the stories we tell are outliers. That is, they chronicle unusual, unique, or rare occurrences. In statistical terms, outliers are those occurrences that stand on the margins of a dataset, far from the mean. In the case of a dataset that tracks the length of time it takes paramedics to respond to emergencies in certain parts of a city, many of the response times may be similar, except for one number that jumps out. Initially, you may think it is an error—and you should definitely rule that out—but upon closer inspection and a conversation with the municipal official responsible for the data, you discover that the number is solid. The question becomes, why is it so different from all the others? The answer to that question could be your story. It could be that construction is making it more difficult for the first responders to reach their destination, that the neighbourhood in question is simply too far from the nearest station, or as we encountered with the example of fire calls in Chapter 7, it could have something to do with the first responders themselves.

Salaries are another good example of outliers leading to interesting questions. In the spirit of open-data policies, an increasing number of provinces, such as Alberta and Ontario, are releasing downloadable datasets of public sector salaries of more than a set amount, typically $100,000.[6] On the margins are those salaries over the $1-million mark. They are the outliers because they stand apart from the norm. Inevitably the stories that emerge from those datasets are about the highest-paid public sector executives.

For instance, in 2014, Ontario Power Generation CEO Thomas Mitchell earned the highest salary at $1.5 million, about 12 times higher than the average salary of $127,178. His salary led to inevitable stories about the highest income earners on Ontario's so-called sunshine list.[7]

Crime is another example for which the coverage is disproportionate to the number of instances cited in police statistics, especially for homicides. Your chances of being murdered are statistically remote, especially in a Canadian city. And yet, stories about murders, murder investigations, and the ability or inability of police departments to solve homicides are common. There are many reasons for this. Perhaps one of the simplest explanations is that incidents of the most violent crimes are relatively easy to cover: police usually issue news releases, or hold a news conference if they want the public's help to solve the crime. The victim's family may hold a tearful and heart-felt news conference pleading for information about a missing loved one police suspect may have been the victim of foul play.

Homicides are human stories complete with a cast of compelling characters: the retired judge and his wife who were inexplicably murdered in their condo; the innocent young woman slain by a bullet just because she was in the wrong place at the wrong time after failing to hail a cab after a night of clubbing downtown; the child who accidentally kills his or her parent, because the parent let the child try out a weapon. These stories are unfolding human dramas that can be more compelling than a Hollywood movie. The stories contain characters with whom we can identify: perpetrators, victims, a frightened community, determined community leaders, police, Crown prosecutors, lawyers, and judges.

There is nothing wrong with outliers. As natural storytellers, we regale family, friends, acquaintances, and co-workers with tales of the unusual. We see movies about the unusual. We tend to remember unusual events with far more clarity than the routine. Of course, as we have explained in this book so far, working with data also takes us beyond the unusual or the anecdote, allowing us to dig deeper for explanatory trends.

Testing Your Data in the Real World

Data on murders, which stand out from the norm, is easy to verify in the real world. There is a victim. There is a perpetrator. The event is recorded. Dealing with data related to a vehicle recall, on the other hand, may be more of a challenge. In both instances, it is crucial to link the data to the real world.

For example, if an individual has filed a lawsuit and wants to publicize a near miss after her car inexplicably accelerated, you are in luck. You have been able to find a compelling story with a central character and you've found a real example of the problem suggested by the database. But more often than not you must hunt harder for people who exemplify the patterns and trends seen in data, if only because if you can't find the problem in the real world, you have to question if it exists.

People may be difficult to identify if the database has been carefully vetted to remove identifying information, before release. That is common, particularly in countries such as Canada that have strict privacy laws.[8]

Other datasets pose different challenges that are typical when conducting tests in the field. The data may represent but a fraction of those who have experienced problems. Indeed, with most datasets that record complaints, the ones that make it into the database are usually just the tip of the proverbial iceberg. The simple fact is that many people do not complain or communicate with authorities when their car does something unexpected, or when they get food poisoning at a restaurant, or when they have an unexpected side effect after taking a prescription drug they thought was safe.

So, for instance, if someone reports to Health Canada or the US Food and Drug Administration (FDA) an unexpected side effect that she has experienced after taking a prescribed pill, that complaint would form part of the "5% of all adverse drug reactions. . . reported to appropriate agencies."[9] There are many reasons for the under-reporting of side effects from drugs, but perhaps the most significant one has to do with physicians, who are not obliged by law to file a report. For pharmaceutical companies, filing such reports is mandatory. Consumers can report, too, but their participation is also voluntary.

The lack of true representation represents a weakness of the adverse drug reactions datasets that Health Canada and the FDA concede, in part to shield themselves from lawsuits, and in part to come clean with the people using the datasets.

Developing a robust understanding of what the data can and cannot tell you, even before using any of the information, represents the due diligence that we discussed in Chapter 2. Knowing the weaknesses of the dataset in question even allows for the proper framing of your story. For instance, you could frame the story in terms of the limited number of adverse events that are reported to the regulatory authority in question, be it Health Canada or the FDA. You might want to know what the regulatory authority is doing to encourage more physicians and patients to report adverse reactions. The data might prompt you to ask if there are any measures in place to increase the number of reports. After having established a frame, you can then find real people and tell their stories. Or you could find doctors who refuse to file reports and then ask them why. Remember, the dataset is only the starting point.

Chances are that the individuals we find may have experienced the side effects at the heart of an investigation, but a report of their reaction never made it into Health Canada's database. This was the case when CBC News told the story of Wilma Johanessma, a British Columbia senior who became addicted to a benzodiazepine called Ativan. Johanessma's case was never reported to Health Canada, but her symptoms mirrored those found in the data: the Parkinson's-like tremors, the irritation, the craving for more pills. For Johanessma, it was worse than being addicted to crack cocaine.[10] Her trembling voice lent an urgent credibility to the seriousness of the cases being reported to Health Canada.

Connecting Data Patterns with Real-Life Patterns

Using datasets that record an entire activity removes a lot of the guesswork. A perfect example is the dataset that Human Resources and Skills Development Canada uses to keep track of employers who want to use temporary foreign workers, a controversial subset of employees that ballooned before the former Conservative government was forced to apply the brakes.

For each worker hired from overseas, an employer must fill out a Labour Market Opinion Application, explaining why the business needs to recruit a foreign worker.[11] CBC News obtained the PDF that contained the data compiled from these forms from 1 January 2009 to 30 April 2012, and then converted the information into an Excel file. The dataset represented the exact number of employers seeking foreign workers for that time period. The data extract that the CBC obtained had two key columns: the employer and the province.

The dataset represents all the employers who were on the hunt for the given time period, which means that summaries by province created in a pivot table represents a real picture that is easy enough to test in the real world. It is simply a matter of contacting the employers listed in column B.

A1	▼ (⁸	ƒₓ Province/Territory	

	A	B
1	**Province/Territoryof Organization Location**	**Organization Name**
2	Newfoundland and Labrador	589731 Newfoundland Labrador Corp
3	Newfoundland and Labrador	Abba Inn Gower House B B
4	Newfoundland and Labrador	Abg Investments Ltd Tim Hortons
5	Newfoundland and Labrador	Aborignal Cleaners
6	Newfoundland and Labrador	Acergy Canada Inc
7	Newfoundland and Labrador	Acquaint Contracting Services Inc
8	Newfoundland and Labrador	Adg Holdings
9	Newfoundland and Labrador	Akcs Offshore Partner
10	Newfoundland and Labrador	Aker Marine Contractors
11	Newfoundland and Labrador	Aker Offshore Partner
12	Newfoundland and Labrador	Altamar Atlantic Ltd
13	Newfoundland and Labrador	Angeliclean Services Inc
14	Newfoundland and Labrador	Asco Canada Ltd
15	Newfoundland and Labrador	Atlantic Diversified Transportation Systems Inc
16	Newfoundland and Labrador	Atlantic Orthotics Limited Fit For Work
17	Newfoundland and Labrador	Avalon Animal Hospital Limited
18	Newfoundland and Labrador	Bae Newplan Group Limited
19	Newfoundland and Labrador	Ball Holdings Inc
20	Newfoundland and Labrador	Bamboo Garden Inc

Newfoundland and Labrador's temporary foreign worker wish list

Building Powerful Interviews and Writing the Story

Once you have located a real person represented in the dataset, there is an opportunity for some powerful storytelling. As discussed in Chapter 5, the *Edmonton Journal* and the *Calgary Herald* teamed up for a six-part series called *Fatal Care*, which revealed that 145 children had died in Alberta's foster care system between 1999 and 2013, nearly triple the number publicly reported by the government.[12] In her *Media* magazine write-up about the series, which won the 2014 National Newspaper Award for investigations and was a finalist for the Michener Award, former *Journal* political reporter Karen Kleiss explained the investigative process, which included filing freedom-of-information requests, poring through public records related to child deaths in Alberta's foster-care system, reviewing legislation and lawsuits, and then assembling all the information in Excel.

Kleiss, who also had experience with data journalism from her stories about restaurant inspections,[13] noted that once all the information was in Excel, she

> cross-referenced all the material. . . on each individual child: news reports, fatality inquiry reports, annual reports and lawsuits. When the province finally released the internal death records for the children, I added this information to the database. This was a painstaking process, mainly because the children's names were protected by privacy laws and a publication ban, so I was working with initials or nothing at all. Still, our database remains the only comprehensive list of children who had died in provincial care.[14]

The reporting team concluded that the province's "child death investigation system was an unmitigated disaster, and that the government had no system in place for following up on recommendations to improve the system."[15]

The information allowed them to tell powerful stories such as that of the 15-year-old Aboriginal girl who was found frozen in a ditch. She was murdered, but no one was ever charged. They also interviewed grieving mothers such as Jamie Sullivan whose daughter Delonna, was only four months old when she was found dead after just six days in foster care.[16] Shortly after having her daughter taken from her, Sullivan went to court where she learned she would have an hour-long visit. After holding her daughter, she knew something was wrong. Delonna was lethargic, had severe diarrhea and "an angry diaper rash. She had a scratch on her ear and red marks on her head."[17]

Sullivan and her mother asked the foster mother to take Delonna to see a doctor. She never did. Three days later, paramedics arrived at the foster mother's house, finding her attempting to perform CPR on Delonna. An hour later, the four-month-old was pronounced dead at the hospital. Medical examiner Graeme Dowling ruled the cause to be sudden and unexpected death in infancy. He noted Delonna had been left to sleep in an infant carrier with a loose blanket on top of her. It was covering the lower half of the infant's face when she was found. Sullivan was the last to find out.[18]

Sullivan won a court application to lift the publication ban on her daughter's name. In excruciating detail, she and her mother, Marilyn Koren, explain how the tragic events unfolded for them. The two also appear in a video that accompanies the story. Delonna Doren and her family were just some of the faces behind the key number: 145.

Conclusion

Frequently, finding and examining a dataset is just the starting point. The numbers represent a tip sheet that allows us to keep digging. *Fatal Care* is a perfect illustration. Without the verification, the cross-referencing with other databases and documents, and most importantly, conducting the interviews, the data are just numbers without context.

In developing the story idea, the key is to stress substance over process, especially when dealing with bureaucracies such as Alberta's child-welfare system. "The good stories stress the impact of government action or inaction on real people in real life," advises journalism professor Carl Sessions Stepp. "Often, government's impact is formidable. The challenge: Show the impact of your story."[19]

Study Questions and Exercises

1. Starting with the results of analysis you did for one of the earlier chapters, think about what other reporting would be needed to complete the story. Consider non-data documentary sources, possible interviews, and techniques such as observation. Write a memo to your editor or producer pitching your story.
2. Find a data story that was published online or in a newspaper. Consider the story, and write a memo explaining whether the reporter completed all of the reporting that was needed.
3. Read a story that references a key number from a database, then locate the dataset and see if you can find a better number.

Notes

1. Fred Vallance-Jones and David McKie, *Computer Assisted Reporting: A Comprehensive Primer* (Toronto: Oxford University Press, 2008), 264.
2. David McKie, "Toyota Floor-Mat Problems Arose in 2003," CBC *News*, 23 March 2010, http://www.cbc.ca/news/toyota-floor-mat-problems-arose-in-2003-1.974720.
3. Transport Canada recall #2003004, 13 January 2003, http://wwwapps.tc.gc.ca/Saf-Sec-Sur/7/VRDB-BDRV/search-recherche/detail.aspx?lang=eng&mk=2734!2474&md=CELICA&fy=2002&ty=2002&ft=&ls=0&sy=0&rn=2003004&cf=SearchResult&pg=0. Retrieved 25 July 2016.
4. NPR News Investigations, "Unintended Acceleration Not Limited to Toyotas," NPR, 3 March 2010, http://www.npr.org/templates/story/story.php?storyId=124276771.
5. David McKie, "Gas-Pedal Problems Plagued Several Carmakers," CBC, 30 March 2010, http://www.cbc.ca/news/gas-pedal-problems-plagued-several-carmakers-1.941619; "Unintended Acceleration Not Limited to Toyotas."
6. The Alberta database is available at http://data.alberta.ca/data/public-disclosure-salary-and-severance-0, while the Ontario one can be found at https://www.ontario.ca/page/public-sector-salary-disclosure.
7. Keith Leslie and Allison Jones, "111,438 Public Sector Workers on Ontario's 2014 'Sunshine List'," *Canadian Press*, 27 March 2015.
8. Jim Bronskill and David McKie, *Your Right to Privacy: Minimize Your Digital Footprint* (Vancouver: Self-Counsel Press, 2016), 97.
9. Bruce C. Carleton, "Drug Safety: Side Effects and Mistakes or Adverse Reactions and Deadly Errors?" *British Columbia Medical Journal* 48.7 (2006): 329–33, http://www.bcmj.org/article/drug-safety-side-effects-and-mistakes-or-adverse-reactions-and-deadly-errors.
10. Vallance-Jones and David McKie, *Computer Assisted Reporting*, 260.
11. See the "Labour Market Opinion Application Higher-Skilled Occupations" form from Human Resources and Skills Development Canada, http://www.hr.ubc.ca/faculty-relations/files/hrsdc-emp55172013-07-008e.pdf.
12. See the *Fatal Care* series home page, http://www.edmontonjournal.com/news/children-in-care/index.html.
13. Vallance-Jones and David McKie, *Computer Assisted Reporting*, 259.
14. "Karen Kleiss, Tragedies Cloaked in Secrecy," *Media Magazine*, 2014 Awards Edition, 37, http://issuu.com/canassocjourn/docs/47131-media_magazines_summer_2014_f/37?e=0/11257214; Robert Cribb, Dean Jobb, David McKie, and Fred Vallance-Jones, *Digging Deeper*, 3rd ed. (Toronto: Oxford, 2014), 271–2.
15. Ibid.; Karen Kleiss, "'I Died that Day': Mother Engulfed in Grief over Baby's Death," *Edmonton Journal*, 3 January 2015, http://www.edmontonjournal.com/life/died+that+Mother+engulfed++grief+over+baby+death+Four/9202964/story.html.
16. Ibid.
17. Ibid.
18. Ibid.
19. Vallance-Jones and David McKie, *Computer Assisted Reporting*, 264.

Glossary

alias An alternative name given to a column or table in a SQL query statement.

AND principle An acronym that describes the process the journalist should follow when trying to obtain data from public and quasi-public institutions: Ask, Negotiate, Demand.

application programming interface (API) A set of programming rules and protocols that permit a computer program to interact with another program, often to request a service or data.

arguments The values required to be passed into a function for it to perform a task. See also *parameters*.

Asynchronous JavaScript and XML (AJAX) A technology that allows part of a web page to be refreshed without the need to request a completely new page from the server. Data is transmitted from the server as JSON or, less frequently, in XML, then integrated into the existing web page by JavaScript running on the client machine.

attribute table In a GIS, a database table that contains information associated with the features in a map layer.

azimuthal (planar) projection A class of map projections that projects the ellipsoid-shaped Earth onto a flat surface by projecting the Earth directly onto an already flat surface.

big data Data that is so large in volume or velocity (the speed with which it is collected and transmitted) that traditional desktop analytical techniques are not sufficient to analyze it.

binary file A computer file that can be read only by a computer.

buffer A feature created in a GIS through the process of buffering.

buffering In a GIS program, the operation by which a circle of specified diameter is drawn around a point, line, or polygon that can then be used for further analysis.

Boolean logic A form of logic in which statements evaluate to either True or False. It is used in computer programming, spreadsheets, and SQL queries.

CartoDB A web-based mapping service.

calculated field In SQL, an output field that results from an operation done "on the fly" at query runtime, such as a calculation or concatenation, rather than consisting of the native content of an existing field.

Cartesian join In a relational database program, a join between tables in which a join condition has not been specified and which will therefore attempt to join every record in one table with every record in the other.

Cascading Style Sheets (CSS) The code that defines the look of web pages, allowing manipulation of fonts, colours, borders, and other design elements. It is used in conjunction with HTML.

categorical map A map that colours different regions based on categories of data. Example: congressional districts coloured red for Republican members and blue for Democratic members.

cell The smallest unit of data organization in a spreadsheet worksheet, formed by the intersection of a row and a column and designated by the column letter and the row number. Example: cell C6 is at the intersection of column C and row 6. A cell can contain a literal value or a formula.

central processing unit (CPU) The electronic "brains" of a computer. The CPU processes instructions contained in computer programs, and in concert with the operating system, controls the other components of a computer to produce desired outcomes.

choropleth map A map that displays statistical data for different regions by colouring the areas differently depending on the values. Example: median income by county.

client A computer program that can request, receive, and manipulate files and data located on a server. Examples are MySQL front-end programs and web browsers. Also: the computer hardware on which a client program runs.

code A common shorthand for instructions written in a programming or markup language, for example HTML code, Python code.

code block In a programming language, a section of code executed within a function, conditional statement, loop, or other similar construct. In Python, blocks are set off by indentation, while JavaScript and Perl use curly braces.

code editor A specialized text editor used for programming. Code editors usually number lines of code, highlight different code structures in different colours, highlight syntax errors, and automatically indent lines within code blocks (Python). Some editors can also run code from within the editor.

coding The act of writing code.

column A vertical column in a spreadsheet worksheet.

comma separated values file (CSV) A delimited text file that uses commas as field separators or delimiters. Individual text fields may be enclosed in quotation marks so commas contained within the fields are not misinterpreted as delimiters when the file is imported into a data analysis program.

computer-assisted reporting (CAR) The first generation of data journalism, starting in the 1960s in the United States and the 1980s in Canada, using data analysis to identify stories that were then reported on further using traditional journalistic methods.

computer program A collection of instructions for a computer, written in a programming language. Programs range from simple scripts that perform single tasks to complex applications such as Microsoft Excel.

concatenation The process of combining two or more strings of text in a programming language, a spreadsheet, or a database program.

conditional statement In a programming language, a code structure that allows the program to choose from two or more possible courses of action based on the test of a condition that evaluates to either True or False.

conical projection A class of map projections that projects the ellipsoid-shaped Earth onto a flat surface by first projecting the Earth onto a virtual cone, placed as if on top of the Earth, then rolling out the cone.

coordinate system In digital mapping and GIS, a system of numeric coordinates used to define the location and/or projection of points on the surface of the Earth. See also *geographic coordinate system, projected coordinate system.*

cylindrical projection A class of map projections that projects the ellipsoid-shaped Earth onto a flat surface by first projecting the Earth onto a virtual cylinder, with the Earth in the centre, then rolling the cylinder flat.

data A Latin term, which in English means something given in an argument or taken for granted. For the purposes of this book, the reference is to structured data, information organized into categories and arrayed in rows and columns to facilitate analysis.

data analysis program A spreadsheet, database, or GIS program.

data cleaning Preparation of a dataset for analysis by removing duplicate entries, correcting spelling errors, ensuring all data is in the correct columns, accounting for missing data, and restoring it when necessary.

data frame In a GIS program, the working area in which map layers are displayed and manipulated.

data journalism A branch of journalism in which data and data-manipulation skills are an integral part of the reporting or presentation process.

Data Pilot Equivalent of the pivot table in the OpenOffice Calc spreadsheet program.

data type In a programming language, or spreadsheet or database program, a classification that defines the underlying characteristics of an element of data. Common types include text types, numeric types, and the Boolean type. In a database or GIS program, the data type must be specified for each field in a table. Programming languages vary in their handling of data types.

data visualization The graphical display of data for analysis and/or presentation.

database An organized collection of data. In some database programs, the name of the file(s) containing the data tables and related objects.

database manager A computer program used to organize and manipulate data.

datum A mathematical model of the Earth that allows for the location of any point at a specified latitude and longitude. Based on an *ellipsoid.*

datum shift The phenomenon by which two points with the same latitude and longitude coordinates are located at slightly different points on the Earth when different datums are used.

datum transformation In a GIS program, a mathematical calculation that changes the underlying datum of a map layer to a different datum, to ensure features in different layers align correctly.

delimited text file A plain text format for exchanging data between users. Fields of data are separated by a character such as a comma or tab and, depending on the operating system, the end of a line is represented by a carriage return and/or newline character.

developer tools A suite of tools that is part of all modern web browsers that allows for the inspection of HTML, CSS, JavaScript code, the observation of requests to web servers and the responses, and other tasks.

dirty data Data that contains errors, has duplicates, or is incomplete. See also *data cleaning.*

domain name A name, usually purchased from a domain name registrar, that is used to identify a website, for example "oup.com."

ellipsoid In GIS and digital mapping, a mathematical model of the shape of the Earth. See also *datum.*

empty string A string with a length of zero; different from *null.* Also called a zero-length string.

Extensible Markup Language (XML) A markup language for encoding data that is interchanged between computer systems in which individual elements of data and field names are enclosed in tags. It is sometimes used for release of data to the public. Hence, XML file.

feature In a digital map, a point, line, or polygon.

feature class In ArcGIS Desktop, a file containing a collection of features of one type, such as points, lines, or polygons.

field In a database program, a column in a table, with a fixed column name and data type.

filtering A process in spreadsheets, database managers, and mapping software that allows users to select certain data elements for viewing.

foreign key In a relational database table, a field that is the primary key in another table.

front-end program A client program that facilitates the querying, manipulation, and alteration of data stored in a server database, and the administration of the server itself.

function A piece of computer code that takes one or more inputs and returns a value or performs an action. Spreadsheet, database, and GIS programs, as well as scripting languages, come with collections of predefined functions for performing specific tasks (e.g. SUM() in a spreadsheet). Functions can also be user-defined when writing code in a programming language.

Fusion Tables An online mapping and visualization service provided by Google.

geocoding A process through which an address or other location data is assigned latitude and longitude coordinates so it can be displayed on a digital map.

geodatabase In ArcGIS, an alternative to shapefiles for storing geographic data. A geodatabase allows for larger file sizes. Individual layers are stored in feature classes within the geodatabase.

geographic coordinate system (GCS) In digital maps and GIS, a coordinate system that uses latitudes and longitudes to place points on the surface of the Earth, and decimal degrees as the unit of measurement. A GCS incorporates a datum.

geographic information system (GIS) A computer program used to organize and analyze geographical data.

GeoJSON Text-based file format based on JSON and used to store geographical information.

heat map A map that converts clusters of points to areas of colour, with areas with greater concentrations of points or greater total value of an attribute associated with the points typically shown in "warmer" colours such as orange or red, and areas of lower concentration or lower total value shown in "cooler" colours such as blue.

host name The plain-language name of a computer connected to the Internet, for example www.oup.com. Converted to an IP address by a domain name server (DNS) when a request for a resource is made.

HyperText Markup Language (HTML) The code that defines the basic structure of web pages. Content within a page is delineated by tags contained within angle brackets.

image file A type of binary computer file that encodes an image. Common image formats are tiff, jpeg, and png.

infinite loop In a computer program, a loop that never stops running either because there are no instructions that cause it to stop, or because the condition that would stop the loop is never triggered.

inner join In a SQL query, a join between two tables that produces as output only those records for which there is a match. See also *joining, outer join*.

Internet Protocol (IP) address The numeric designation of a specific computer connected to the Internet, for example 195.289.33.16 (in the IPv4 protocol).

interpreted programming language A programming language in which instructions are written in an English-like syntax and, at runtime, translated to code the computer's CPU can execute.

JavaScript An interpreted programming language used by web developers to create interactivity in web pages. JavaScript code is embedded in the HTML of a web page or in a separate file called from within the HTML code.

JavaScript Object Notation (JSON) Text-based format used to store data and designed to be machine-read. Data elements are contained in key:value pairs. Based on the data structure of JavaScript objects.

joining In a relational database or GIS program, the means by which two tables or related information are linked together to provide combined output. Hence, "a join."

Keyhole Markup Language (KML) A markup language that is a subset of the XML standard and used to store geographic data.

KML file A map file in which geographic data is encoded using KML. It is the standard map format for Google Maps.

Lambert Conformic conic projection A projection that minimizes east-west distortion in mid-latitude regions. Often used for continental-scale maps in Canada and the United States.

latitude A map coordinate derived by measuring the angle formed by the meeting of a line from a point on the Earth to the centre of the Earth with a line from the equator to the centre of the Earth. Going north from the equator, latitudes are measured from 0 degrees to 90 degrees and going south from 0 degrees to -90 degrees.

layer In a GIS application or web map, a single layer of geographic information, containing a set of points, lines, or polygons, or raster images. Layers are arrayed one atop the other to create a map. See also *raster layer, vector layer*.

line On a map, a feature formed by drawing a line between two or more points. One of the three main classes of features used in digital maps.

line of latitude On maps, a circle drawn parallel to the equator, joining all points of the same latitude. Also called a parallel.

line of longitude On maps, a semicircle running from the North Pole to the South Pole, joining all points of the same longitude. Also called a meridian.

list An array in Python.

logical error In programming, an error that is not caused by errors in syntax, but which produces incorrect or illogical output.

longitude A map coordinate derived by measuring the angle formed by the meeting of a line from a point on the Earth to the centre of the Earth with a line from the Prime Meridian to the centre of the Earth. Going east from the Prime Meridian, longitudes are measured from 0 to 180 degrees and going west from 0 to -180 degrees.

loop In a programing language, a control structure that causes an instruction to be performed repeatedly.

machine-readable format A class of data file format that can be opened by a spreadsheet, database, mapping or other data application. Examples of machine-readable formats are Excel, delimited text, and JSON.

Mercator projection A map projection that preserves directions and is therefore valued for use in navigation charts. The projection distorts areas in northern and southern latitudes, making them appear much larger than they really are.

metadata Data about other data. In a GIS program, a map layer's metadata includes information about the layer, including its coordinate system(s).

method In a programming language, a function that is attached to an object such as a file or a string.

Microsoft Access A proprietary desktop-based relational database management system from Microsoft.

Microsoft Excel A proprietary spreadsheet from Microsoft.

module In a programming language, pre-written code that can be incorporated into a program/script to provide functionality to accomplish common tasks such as networking and text manipulation. Modules provide functions that can be used within a program, removing the need for extensive, often complex code.

MySQL An open-source, server-based relational database management system.

normalization In a relational database, the process by which duplication is eliminated from tables by separating information that would otherwise have to be entered repeatedly, into separate tables.

null In a database program, a null value is one that has no value.

numeric data type A data type that can hold numbers and which permits mathematical operations. Integers are whole numbers, negative or positive. Floating point numbers use decimal places but are not quite as accurate as decimal data types. Dates are a specialized numeric data type.

on-the-fly projection In a GIS, the ability of the program to automatically change the projection of a new layer added to the data frame to the existing projection of previously added layers.

one-to-many join In a relational database, a join between two tables in which there is only one matching record in one table but one or more matching records in the second table.

one-to-one join A join between two tables in which there is only one matching record on both sides of the join.

Open Data Charter An umbrella principle developed by leading G8 countries, including Canada and the United Kingdom. It establishes five principles that dictate how data should be made public. The first principle is the requirement that data should be "open by default."

Open Database Connectivity (ODBC) A protocol that allows database and GIS programs from different vendors to connect to one another or with external applications to share data.

OpenOffice Calc An open-source spreadsheet program.

open-data website A website, usually one belonging to a government, that proactively posts datasets that can be freely downloaded in machine-readable formats to be analyzed in a spreadsheet, database, or mapping software.

open-records law Legislation that gives individuals or corporations a legal right to obtain records held by government bodies. Access is limited by exemptions or exclusions to protect such things as privacy, solicitor-client privilege, and cabinet secrecy. In different jurisdictions, these may be referred to as freedom-of-information, access-to-information, or right-to-information laws.

open-source software Software that is not proprietary software and for which the source code is freely available. The development process is open and cooperative and the software can generally be used at no cost.

OpenStreetMap An open-source, crowdsourcing project that provides street layer maps from around the world, with the data contributed by volunteers.

optical character recognition (OCR) A process used by a computer program to convert images of text to machine-readable text.

outer (left/right) join In a SQL query, a join between two tables that produces as output the records that match between the two tables as well as the unmatched records from one of the tables.

outlier A statistical value that stands apart from the others in the sample or on the margins of a dataset.

parameters The names listed within the parentheses in the definition of a function in a programming language. They are replaced by passed-in arguments when the function is called in a program. See also *arguments*.

parsing In web scraping, the process of programmatically examining a HTML or other text file so as to extract desired data elements.

paste special A menu option in a spreadsheet program that allows users to paste data previously copied to the clipboard, while simultaneously altering formats, performing simple mathematics, switching rows and columns, etc.

PDF image file A PDF file that contains an embedded image rather than embedded text. For extracting text for analysis in a spreadsheet, database, or mapping application, the image must first be converted to plain text using optical character recognition software (OCR).

Perl An interpreted programming language.

PHP An interpreted programming language used to manipulate the content of web pages. PHP code is contained within HTML code, and is executed by the web server before a web page is served to a browser.

PIP In Python, a small applet that allows for installation of modules that are not contained within the Python Standard Library.

pivot table A tool in spreadsheet programs used to summarize raw data. Used by journalists to search for newsworthy patterns.

plain text file A computer file containing only plain, human-readable text.

point On a map, a feature that indicates a specific location, according to the coordinate system of the map. It occupies no space and only indicates the location. One of the three main classes of features used in digital maps.

polygon On a map, an enclosed many-sided shape, such as an electoral district or city boundary. One of the three main classes of features used in digital maps.

portable document format (PDF) A file format designed to reproduce the design and layout of a physical document. Even when containing data, these files cannot be opened directly in data analysis software such as a spreadsheet, database, or mapping program, but must first be converted to a data format.

primary key In a relational database table, a field containing a value that is unique for every record in the table; the field is used to join, or connect, the table to related records in other tables in the database.

projected coordinate system (PCS) In digital maps and GIS, a coordinate system that uses numeric values to place geographic points on a plane. A PCS also incorporates a projection.

projection The means by which shapes on the roughly spherical Earth are depicted on a flat surface. A projection introduces distortion, the extent and type of which varies with the projection chosen.

proprietary software Software that is owned by an individual or company. It is subject to restrictive licensing conditions and cannot be freely shared. The source code is not freely available and the vendor usually charges for each usage license.

Python An interpreted programming language that can be used in application development, or in scripts. When used by journalists, Python is often used for web scraping, accessing APIs, and other utility tasks.

Quantum GIS (QGIS) An open-source GIS program.

query A command issued to a database program to organize, summarize, or manipulate data.

raster layer In a GIS, a map layer made up of raster images. A raster image consists of pixels, and the quality of the image will degrade as the image is enlarged because the pixels themselves are enlarged. Raster images may be used for base layers depicting satellite or other imagery.

rate A comparison of two statistical variables in which the frequency of the occurrence of one is measured in relationship to the other. Often used to measure the occurrence of a variable in a population. For example, a crime rate is the number of incidents in specified jurisdictions for a specified number of people, typically 100,000. Rates allow valid comparisons between entities that differ in size, such as comparing crime rates in different cities, provinces, states, or countries.

ReadMe file A file that contains information about a computer program or dataset.

record In a database program, one row of information in a table.

relational database A database program that can store and query data in multiple tables joined by key fields.

request In Internet terms, a request made by one computer connected to the Internet for a resource located on another computer.

resource In Internet terms, a computer file that can be obtained from a remote server and transmitted to the computer requesting it.

row A horizontal row in a spreadsheet worksheet.

script A computer program that executes one or more tasks, is interpreted at runtime, and is not compiled.

select by attributes In a GIS, a SQL-like query operation that allows features in a layer to be selected by querying the associated attributes in an attribute table.

select by location In a GIS, a SQL-like query operation that allows features in a layer to be selected by means of their proximity to features in another layer.

server A computer program that provides access to centralized resources or processes to one or more clients. Also, the computer hardware on which server software runs.

shapefile A commonly used file format for the exchange of geographical data. It consists of several text and binary files that work in unison.

simplification In a GIS, the process of reducing the size of a polygon layer file by removing some of the vertices that define the polygon features.

sort A process in spreadsheets, database managers and mapping programs that allows users to organize values in columns in descending or ascending order.

spatial join In a GIS program, a join that is accomplished not by matching two identical data fields, but by comparing the location of features in two map layers.

spreadsheet A computer program such as Microsoft Excel, OpenOffice, LibreOffice, or Google Sheets that can be used to open, sort, filter, organize, and summarize numeric and textual data.

standard library In Python, a collection of modules that comes prepackaged with a standard installation of Python.

statement A line of code in a programming language that contains one complete instruction to the CPU. In JavaScript, a statement ends with a semicolon unless it ends with a new line.

string In databases, spreadsheets, and programming languages, zero or more alphanumeric characters of any type. Numbers on their own can be contained in strings, but mathematical operations cannot be performed on them.

string (or text) data type A data type that can hold strings.

Structured Query Language (SQL) A specialized command language used to write database queries.

subquery In SQL, a query nested within another query.

summary statistics Statistics derived from the analysis of raw data and which summarize the data in some way.

syntax The form of a programming or markup language and a set of rules that dictate how the code must be written.

syntax error An error in the syntax of a programming or markup language. Also sometimes refers to the report made by the interpreter or other software of the presence of an error.

table In a database program, a collection of information stored in a systematic structure of rows and columns.

text import wizard A tool in some spreadsheet and database applications that is used to import a text file.

tile In a web-based mapping service, the individual, square-shaped image segments that combine to form the base layer for the map.

union query In SQL, a query that combines the output of two or more queries with identical column structures and eliminates any duplicate rows in the combined output.

union all query In SQL, a query that combines the output of two or more queries with identical column structures and retains any duplicate rows in the combined output.

Universal Resource Locator (URL) The string of characters entered in the address bar of a web browser that represents the address on the Internet of a web resource.

variable In a programming language, a virtual container that can hold a string, number, or other object, for use later in the program. In statistics, a data element that can be counted or measured.

vector layer In a GIS, a map layer in which features are composed of geometric shapes that can be scaled larger or smaller though mathematical calculations performed by the application, rather than through the enlargement or shrinking of pixels. This maintains image quality as scales change. Shapefiles, KML files, and GeoJSON are vector formats.

vertices (sing. **vertex**) In a line or polygon feature, the points that, when joined by lines, define the line feature or the outlines of the polygon.

web browser The web browser, or simply "browser," is a software application used to gain access to, and view websites. The most popular web browsers are Mozilla Firefox, Google Chrome, Microsoft Internet Explorer/Edge, and Apple Safari.

web scraping The process of programmatically accessing Internet resources to gather data.

workbook In a spreadsheet program, a file containing one or more worksheets.

worksheet A single working area within a spreadsheet program, organized in a grid of columns labelled with letters and rows labelled with numbers.

Universal Transverse Mercator (UTM) A projected coordinate system that divides the world into 60 north-south zones. Often used to depict areas with a large north-south extent.

web mapping service An online service that provides a platform for the creation of digital maps combining user-provided geographic data with data provided by the service. Example: Google Maps.

Web Mercator projection A modified form of the Mercator projection that is used as the base map projection by online mapping services such as Google Maps and ArcGIS Online.

xls or xlsx The extensions for the older and newer versions of Excel spreadsheets, respectively.

zip file A text or binary file that has been compressed using the zip protocol.

Index